NATURAL HAZARD

MAINSTREAM SPORT

# NATURAL HAZARD

## THE DIARY OF AN ACCIDENT-PRONE GOLF WRITER

## NORMAN DABELL

MAINSTREAM
PUBLISHING

EDINBURGH AND LONDON

First published in Great Britain in 2002 by
MAINSTREAM PUBLISHING (EDINBURGH) LTD
7 Albany Street
Edinburgh EH1 3UG

ISBN 1 84018 842 1

Updated 2004

A catalogue record for this book is available from the British Library

Typeset in Ehrhardt and Kartoon

Printed in Great Britain by
Cox & Wyman Ltd

This book is dedicated to Doddy, Michael, Frank, Oakers, Billy, Alister and Peter, sadly no longer around to hear my tales of woe.

# CONTENTS

# ACKNOWLEDGEMENTS

MY THANKS GO to all my comrades in the media, especially the Association of Golf Writers, the players, and the officials of the European Tour. It's been a hoot so far. Thanks also to Mainstream, especially Bill, for giving me the chance to revive fraught, but fond, memories. And thanks to my family and my wife Sharon for your courage in living so close to the edge.

# ONE

# IT WAS NEVER GOING
# TO BE PLAIN SAILING

ACCIDENTS HAVE ALWAYS come easily to me. So many calamities
have befallen me during a lifetime that I wonder if I might have
been dropped when I was born. My mother, Sheila, insists I
wasn't. I bet it was raining in Nottingham, though, on 9
November 1944. I wasn't named after Norman Wisdom, but
certain of his traits have attached themselves to me uninvited.
I grudgingly concede that my middle name could be apt,
however: Alfred, a man who could burn a cake with the best of
them.

While life has often been trial and tribulation there have
been instances that make me wonder if, alternatively, I was
actually born under a lucky star. Even though I toppled 30 or
40ft down a gypsum pit on my tricycle three years after setting
foot on this mortal coil, I didn't break my neck. I just received
an enormous bump, which a passing pit train driver was able
to reduce with a huge blob of butter from his lunchbox before
Mum had a chance to pass out on seeing the spare head I'd
grown. Even then, the phrase 'good job it was his head or he
might have been badly injured' was, I'm afraid, crossing
people's minds. But, while I spilt my share of milk, got
separated from my parents frequently during trips or holidays,
and even got attacked by Grandad's cockerels, there were great
escapes, too, so perhaps I wasn't born all unlucky. For instance,
somehow, every car and lorry roaring through Quorn – I'd
gone to stay with my grandparents in Leicestershire when

11

brother John was imminent – managed to miss me as I toddled over the road to post a crayoned 'letter' to my pregnant mum. In a huge stroke of fate and fortune, my dad Neville probably saved my life. He was returning from a driving assignment and, thunderstruck, came through Quorn in his lorry just as I made the middle of the road, seeing nothing but the pillar-box on the other side of it.

Thus the Dabell 'happenings' had begun at an early age. Dad didn't escape unscathed. A few years later he and I were on our way to market with the usual load of beast in the back of his lorry. Sitting in the cab alongside him, I idly pressed the button on his electric cattle-prod – and watched aghast as Dad suddenly yelped and sat bolt upright. The electrically charged prongs of the prodder had made contact with the metal strip on his cab window, which he was leaning on, bare-armed. As we were heading downhill and coming to quite a dangerous bend at the time, only Pater's superb driving skill prevented substantial calamity. The old behind got a good dusting, I can tell you.

Talking of behinds, around that time I sat on a broken bottle while at play and needed several stitches in a very tender spot indeed. It was a woman doctor who performed the surgery. I was mortified with embarrassment.

Just to show I was avoiding the really serious stuff, though, when I was six I fell on my sword. This was a wooden one with a sharp end. I tripped over and the point missed my eye by less than a centimetre. It buried itself under the eyebrow, stopped by my eye-socket bone from piercing me. Mum saw it happen from our nearby bedroom window. I couldn't prevent her passing out this time.

My accidents were not all life threatening, or even harmful. I possessed a fairly sweet treble voice when I was a kid and sang in the church choir. Despite being a bundle of nerves before my renditions, I also pursued a short solo career and for a time my voice was trained. One Sunday I was down to sing in a concert and turned up at the Methodist Chapel in Kegworth, Leicestershire, where I grew up, full of butterflies but determined to do well. Mum and I were expecting to meet up with my choirmaster but there was no sign of him at the chapel. The concert was in full swing and I was asked who I was and what I would be performing. Despite a few blank looks I duly took to the stage halfway through the concert and did my piece, did it reasonably well according to a fair round of applause, even with a strange pianist who took a little while to bond with me. Afterwards, the concert organiser came over and congratulated me but confessed my appearance was all a bit of a mystery. Were we sure we were at the right place and did we know there was also a concert being held that afternoon at the Baptist Chapel just up the road? That awful feeling in the pit of my stomach, which I would experience time after time in years to come, visited me. As I had been the one trusted with going to the right venue, Mum had to do some gentle interrogating. I'd got my instructions hopelessly wrong. We should have been at the other chapel, where my choirmaster had had a lot of explaining to do.

Mother never did learn her lesson and, not long after, came with me to a nearby village, Castle Donington, for another concert, this time a prestigious local schools' event with my singing teacher, an octogenarian who was pretty hard of hearing even with his hearing-aid in place, as my accomplice. We called him 'Fiddler Brown', an enthusiastic soul despite his years, who often accompanied me on the violin during my lessons. Personally, I couldn't stand the racket he made and dreaded singing practice at his home, when I'd much sooner be pretending to be Sam Bartram or Bert Williams on the nearby playing field. Fiddler was to accompany me on the violin at this particular concert. I'm sure he forgot to turn his hearing-aid on. The performance was a fiasco. Soon I was well in front of Fiddler's hideous screeching and scraping and tried to slow down to meet him. Seeing the panic in my eyes, he must have guessed he was lagging and speeded up, easily overtaking me. I then hit the accelerator to go gamely after him but failed miserably, and the second quatrain of our piece ended in some disarray. I looked out at my mother and our next-door neighbour for sympathy and rescue, but none was forthcoming, mainly because the pair were doubled up, helpless in their seats. No time to feel betrayed. Fiddler was off again. His bow produced an even more terrifying noise on its way to our crescendo, this time some seconds after me. It was a noise that I would be reminded of again many years later in Devonport

13

Dockyard, when listening to rusting barges dragging their chains in a gale. It was sheer humiliation and ended my singing career right there and then.

Scars, some of them dating back to the '50s, litter my body. Many of my bones have been broken, a lot of them broken during sport. As a goalkeeper, a pretty fearless (foolhardy) one at that, I found that where there was a boot there was my spare frame ready to cushion it. I passed the 'eleven-plus' and won a scholarship to Loughborough Grammar School, where rugby was mandatory. Rugby produced its share of injuries and escapades. I turned up for a match with one rugby boot – and one of Mum's black high-heeled shoes. I'd packed my bag in the dark in the morning, before setting off for my newspaper round and, packing it by feel, had accidentally put in the rogue footwear. It was bad enough having to use said bag, a satchel with the proud monogram 'Sheila Dabell, Corset Fitter' left over from Mum's days with the Spencer Corset Company. 'We're not buying you a new satchel when this one is perfectly adequate. And it's leather.' Those chilling words used to haunt me on the school bus as I tried to smuggle the embarrassing bag away. Getting changed for my rugby match, I wondered what on earth I was going to do. Our rugby master, one Tom Docherty, was a bit of a Tartar. I was fearful he'd make me play with one boot and one high-heeled shoe. Luckily for me, he never discovered my mishap. After my team-mates had been unmerciful in their ragging, we united against the common enemy. Somebody produced a spare boot, lost for years in the dust under the lockers. While it hurt like hell because it was a size too small and also had several nails coming through, it was better than having to suffer the Doc's treatment.

Entry into the world of commerce brought more spills. I took a holiday job as a general help and delivery boy for Kegworth Co-op. A bike with a heavily loaded grocery pannier above a small front wheel needed a muscular young god to keep it on the road. Stick insects like me had to suffer frequent crashes that squashed butter, broke eggs and smashed pickled-onion jars.

After my dad tragically died in a road accident, I spent time with various relatives during school holidays. At one point, I was sent to an aunt and uncle who lived on a farm in

Northamptonshire. While I was there, I managed to fall off the very top of a hay barn but survived with only a sprained wrist. While I got sympathy then, a few days later there was none when my aunt and uncle woke up to find their orchard and some of the barns under flood. I had diligently (single-handedly, indeed) dammed the stream behind the farmyard. With a little overnight rain, it had neatly diverted itself.

Eventually, I had to think about a serious career, and chose the Royal Navy. Training at HMS *Ganges* was for Spartans, but gave me a grounding that has stood me in great stead all my life. As I made the transition from boy to man at a still tender age in 1960, my most formative 30 months gave warning that life was never going to be all plain sailing.

We were up early (no problem; my paper round had ensured I could rise alert before sparrows had even considered an opening fart). Then it was school or communications training, with interludes of sporting afternoons, of which I could not get enough. One sport which I'd thought I ought to take up to help protect a puny body was boxing. Having been encouraged by a couple of modest successes in the 'character-building' boxing bouts in the pre-training annexe, I toyed with the idea of trying to join the boxing training group. Then one of the lads warned me about one major pitfall: the early morning sparring. It would be bad enough getting up at dawn before the rest of the lads in the mess had received the usual 'hands off cocks and on socks' scream from the duty Petty Officer. But then you were supposed to go out and have your nose punched before breakfast. I volunteered for the bugle band instead (I'd attended a couple of band practices with my cornet-playing cousin in Nottingham) and was snapped up. However, when I insisted on trying to emulate Gene Kruper on my drum, I was given my marching orders.

While HMS *Ganges* was run with strict discipline, we learned skills that would prove vital when I became a journalist some 15 years later – touch-typing, telecommunications and radio voice training. I enjoyed learning the morse code and could even tolerate school, as we studied for our GCEs. But I loved the afternoons of sport, and that included dabbling about on the rivers, the Stour and Orwell, although I wasn't too keen on sailing when your hands froze to the gunwales. I was deemed a proficient enough sailor to be made bowman of our cutter when we went on 'expeditions', where boys were given tasks to carry out, many miles away from HMS *Ganges*. Once, our target achieved, we were heading back triumphantly down river when, as the man in charge of direction, I stranded us on a mudbank. We spent the whole night marooned, shivering, with just one loaf of bread and a tin of salmon between eight of us. I was not popular with my messmates. They got their own back eventually. One night after lights out, I accepted a bet of a bar of chocolate that I couldn't get over the mess roof and back naked, without the duty officer and guard spotting me. I was left stranded, shivering, on the roof. My vengeful messmates had locked all the windows. I was caught and ordered to do 'Faith, Hope and Charity'. This evil punishment involved having to double up and down the three towering flights of steps to the foreshore at Shotley, wearing an oilskin – buttoned on back-to-front.

Entering the fleet, I was then able to foist my accident-prone body on to the seven seas and the wide world. Dabellisms, as they are now known on the European golf tour, happened with frequent regularity. I plunged into a canal in Venice (smelt awful), fell out of various hammocks, dropped like a stone into the tank deck of a landing-craft and broke my nose for the second of five times, got my jaw dislocated by a burly Scots centre-forward's football boot and nearly got fried while working on a ship's aerial. I only needed to look at a radio dial, too, and it would go off frequency. I was given the sobriquet 'Snags' and nearly always lived up to this nickname. When I served on HMS *Rampart*, a landing craft, we lost a whole cadre of Royal Marines up a mountain in Norway. Their disappearance and subsequent rescue even made the news back in Britain. My captain, Neil Durden-Smith, got it in the neck for the episode, but I felt pretty guilty about losing contact with the group on my radio. Some years later I met up with Neil, by now a famous sports commentator, and his wife, Judith Chalmers, at a charity cricket match at Stowe School. I watched him go a funny shade of grey when the penny dropped and he realised who I was.

The Dabell jinx proved costly when representing a Navy side in goal against a Beirut team in Lebanon in the days before that once glorious place was racked by strife. It was a really tight match and half-time arrived with no score. I'd had a night on the local food and it was getting to me all through the first half, so while the team was enjoying the half-time oranges I slipped away to the loo. When I tried to get out, the changing room door was locked. Try as I might, I couldn't force the door. I resorted to banging loudly on it and shouting. This went on for a few minutes, when suddenly the door was flung open by our team manager. 'What the sodding hell happened to you, Dabell? We're a goal down now.' The match had restarted without me, my dunderhead colleagues not even noticing Dabell was not in his rightful place between the sticks. A Beirut forward, hardly able to believe his luck, lobbed our defence straight after the kick-off, and found an empty net. We lost the match by that single goal, which the local referee refused to disallow. If the crazy British didn't know where their goalkeeper was, it wasn't his fault.

Once again there were great escapes, though. Days after leaving HMS *Battleaxe* it was in collision with another ship and the whole of the front of the destroyer destroyed – including the bit where I used to sling my hammock. And in Aden, a terrorist threw a grenade out of a car into the bazaar next to the one where my shipmates and I were shopping.

On leaving the 30th Escort Squadron I eventually ended up in Gibraltar. News of Dabell's presence there travelled fast. The Spanish were no mugs. Not long after I arrived, the Rock's land border closed to traffic. That didn't keep me in. I didn't drive anyway, so a few months later the border was closed to pedestrians as well. I still found a way, travelling to Spain by ferry. So that mode of escape was cut off, too. Spain was at last safe, although I did manage to beat the blockade by entering the country via Tangiers, where I was to meet my first wife, Dianne. I decided to rent a garret in Gibraltar with two shipmates, for a little privacy. When I found myself locked out of the flat, I opted to scale the building to try to make it to an open window. I became hopelessly stuck, with no hope of either gaining the window or shinning back down to safety. Some bright spark of a neighbour had a great idea. My fiancée Dianne, a Wren, arrived from her HMS *Rooke* barracks to find the fire brigade hauling me down on an extended ladder.

That was the first of two experiences with the brigade lads for me. Many years later, by now remarried to my second wife Jennie and living in Kent, another enthusiastic neighbour phoned the brigade when he saw flames belching out of our chimney. All I'd done was fire a rook's nest that was blocking it. Maybe it had got rather out of hand, though. The firemen insisted on evacuation, while they damped down the chimney breasts upstairs.

When first wife Dianne and I returned to the UK from Gibraltar in 1968, it was her parents' turn to be persecuted. In a rush to catch a train, I dashed from my in-laws' home, where we were staying while our first house was being built, leaving a tap, under which I had washed my contact lens, running and the plug in place in the sink. When mother-in-law came home and switched on the lobby light there was a huge flash. She was incredibly lucky to escape electrocution. The overflowing sink had sent water to all parts of the upstairs and into the light fitments.

I finally realised that I could not look forward to any serious high rank in the Navy when, as a Leading Radio Operator, I was given charge of a group of men protecting an airstrip during an exercise with the RAF. It became boring. On one of the nights of guard duty I couldn't sleep, and so mooched idly around our patch. I spotted a Cherry Blossom Boot Polish tin on the ground and, giving vent to my ire at wasting my life away on a 'bloody pointless exercise', kicked it. Immediately flares went up and thunderflashes went off. It was part of a booby-trapped tripwire.

With future commodore status undermined, I decided to retire from the Senior Service and, after a fruitless 18 months in the Foreign Office (finding out I was not going to be the next James Bond), got myself a job on a weekly newspaper covering the little market towns of Buckingham, Towcester and Brackley. The trials (and I attended many as a court reporter) continued. For instance, little market town things happened to me all the time, like all the ducks in a duck race I had previewed at length being slaughtered by a fox the night before the race.

I finally found my niche as a sports writer, around about the time I married Jennie. It was a romantic wedding, for the most part, at Gretna Green. It would have been far more romantic if my best man's new Jag hadn't suffered a puncture. He was also giving Jennie away and the tyre blew as they were on the way to meet her blushing bridegroom. With a wheel locked solid on the wedding car, immobilising it, and time ticking away, Jennie arrived at the registry office in a pick-up truck. She had not only gained a husband but a jinx, too.

My sports writing included covering plenty of golf. I was given the responsibility (not if they'd known the chance they were taking) of driving Henry Cotton in a buggy during the 1979 Dunlop Masters. At Woburn I was also introduced to some of the doyens of golf writing, including the man who played a large part in starting, then helping nurture, my full-time career in golf, Renton Laidlaw. About that time I also met Seve Ballesteros. He had a cold and couldn't speak much English. The interview I did with him was a real test, but I managed to get what I thought were really good quotes – if a little fragmented because of my shaky Spanish and his shaky English. A pity, then, that someone broke into my car that night and stole my bag, not only with my wallet in it but my notebook, too. I don't think Seve read the *Milton Keynes Gazette* the following week. If he did he never complained at being misquoted.

We had two Dunlop Masters events while I was at the *Gazette*, and I got the bug for golf writing, so a post on the *Echo* at Bournemouth as golf correspondent was right up my street. The two Hennessy Cognac Cup events at Ferndown, near my home, also brought their share of highs and lows. In 1982, in the company of golf writing peers, I was enjoying post-prandials in the clubhouse when there was an almighty racket outside. A car full of caddies had gone straight over a roundabout, turned over and caught fire. Thankfully, the caddies were totally unharmed. I had a scoop because it was past deadline for my national daily newspaper colleagues.

Even though golf was not really her bag, Jennie made a valiant attempt at sharing my enthusiasm for the game. We attended the second of the Hennessy Cognac Cup tournaments in 1984 at Ferndown together. I rather wish, however, that she'd stayed away. I'd carted my huge cast-iron Imperial typewriter with me to the tournament and, at the end of the first round, not wanting to lug it and my bags any further than necessary, asked Jennie if she could fetch the car. It was parked under the trees by a chipping practice area near the 18th green. I stood around for ages wondering why she was taking so long. Then I heard this screaming revving of a car engine. Something told me Dabell, née Rhodes, was involved. I left bags and typewriter and hared off to locate the anguished car engine. When I got down to the temporary car park I saw the problem. Our car was pointing skyward, arse-end down in the practice bunker – with Jennie desperately trying to gain sanctuary, somehow unaware her front wheels weren't even grounded. This was one sand-save that was not going to be made. We needed a tow. The bunker was shredded and needed a good going-over by, I have to say, very understanding assistant greenkeepers, who, nonetheless, could not hide their amusement at Jennie's plight. I discovered she had tried out a few of the sponsor's golden beverages while waiting for me to finish work, not expecting to have to do any driving. The tricky negotiation of a Capri around trees and a bunker had proved just a little too much. I'm sure being married to me had a little to do with it, too.

Eventually, I realised a dream and in 1987 landed the job as deputy editor of the oldest golf magazine in the world, *Golf Illustrated*. We had a super little office in Sevenoaks in Kent. I had plenty of interesting features to plan and write and had ample chance to meet the sort of people I had only either read about or met fleetingly as a golf correspondent at the *Evening Echo*. One interview sticks in my memory. I was given the assignment of asking Nick Faldo what he thought of a particular testing hole at Valderrama, while doing a feature on the Irish Open at Portmarnock at the same time. When I arrived at the legendary Irish links on pro-am day, as luck would have it, I saw Faldo walking from the 18th green. I scampered after him, caught up with him in the locker-room and, pulling out my notebook, blurted out my all-important question. To his eternal credit, Faldo took a breath, realised I must be a new kid on the block, and gave me his answer; short, but sweet for me. I thanked him profusely. Faldo then said, 'Now do you mind if I have a pee? I've still got nine holes to go.' Having only been to tournaments where everyone started at the first tee, such as Open Championships, I was unfamiliar with the two-tee start system. Faldo had begun his round at the 10th and did, indeed, still have nine holes left. For some mystifying reason, he treated me sympathetically. He should have bitten my head off.

I should have known that magazine life was all going to end in tears, however. About the time when the gales that struck Britain in the late '80s suddenly reduced our beloved Sevenoaks to Oneoak, *Golf Illustrated* was taken over by the *New York Times* group and the office was disbanded. I was moved to *Golf World*'s headquarters at the Isle of Dogs and relegated from deputy editor to dogsbody. It proved a purgatory of insular colleagues and endless journeys to and from work. Soon after covering Greg Norman's fantastic finale in the 1989 Open (won by Mark Calcavecchia) and seeing not a word of it make the magazine, in sheer frustration I resigned to set up in business on my own. I went on the road with commissions and contracts from Rapid Golf Line (the call-in golf service which eventually gave me the experience to be a broadcaster), United Press International (the worldwide news gathering agency) and *The Independent*, working as second reporter to Tim Glover.

That, as they used to say on *The Goon Show*, is where the story really starts.

# TWO

# BLINKING IN THE DAYLIGHT

WITH OVER TEN years' experience in golf behind me, in August 1989 I lit out for the European Tour. I'd covered tour events before, and several Open Championships, but had no experience of writing quickly, as you need to do for often crippling deadlines. As a freelance, you also needed several customers to ensure some kind of profit, after forking out for flights, hotels and meals. I was rather jumping into the deep end when I set off initially for Malmo, my first event, the PLM Open. As I travelled by train from our home in Smarden (the one well known to the fire brigade) I wondered what scoops lay around the corner in the next three weeks which would be spent in Sweden, Germany and Switzerland. With little capital to begin my freelancing career, I began my journey to Europe at Victoria Coach Station, heading for Malmo via a cross-Channel ferry on a ContinentBus that would take me through the Low Countries to Hamburg, then I would take another ferry to Malmo. It took over two days of torture, cramped up on the top deck of the bus or sitting for hours on a bench-seat on two ferries. The second ferry, to Sweden, sank a few years later. Looking back, knowing what I know now about Dabell and the European Tour, I'm surprised it waited.

When we got to Hamburg, we picked up a large group of students. By the time we arrived at dockside in Malmo I was indistinguishable from the rest of the group, unshaven and unkempt, decidedly crumpled and bleary-eyed. Whether it was my appearance or a typical Swedish 'no one is excused' attitude, I was herded in with the students into a large customs shed to be body-searched. I suppose they were looking for drugs. They were certainly thorough. Every orifice got the once-over. It was a very undignified way to start my freelance golf-writing career. Of course my host, Thorbjorn Falk (a Malmo journalist I had met on holiday in Spain a few years before), thought this was a great hoot as he waited for me to come out of the shed.

In case the bus broke down or something, I'd already prepared a preview for *The Independent* on Mark Roe's bid to make the 1989 Ryder Cup team. As it turned out, I was able to speak to Mark on the Wednesday morning – the event began the next day – in unexpected circumstances. Having no idea of the Bokskogens course layout, I got thoroughly lost while out trying to find play, and made a detour through a spinney. Lost again, I had to force my way through the undergrowth. Bursting through, I found myself next to the 12th green, on which a startled Roe, playing in the pro-am, had stopped in mid-putt. After gathering his composure, he chatted to me on the way to the next tee and gave me an even better story. When I went to file my stories, though, as if to show me that I wasn't going to get any easy ride, we had a power cut and the Telex machine was inoperable. I had to read out several hundred words to copy takers over the phone by the light of a security guard's torch. Australia's Mike Harwood won. Mark didn't quite live up to his preview and took 27th place. I felt a bit miserable for him. Oh, and Renton Laidlaw broke the record for the number of Cornettos consumed in one week, polishing off a remarkable 28.

So this was life on tour. Next stop, Frankfurt for the German Open and Ryder Cup selection. First I met up with my wife Jennie, who had flown over on a freebie courtesy of her sister Wendy, a check-in operator for British Airways at Cologne Airport. After a short break at Wendy and her husband Dieter's apartment in the beautiful surrounds of the Koenigforst just outside Cologne, I hit the trail for Frankfurt. There I stayed in a modest little pension downtown. It wasn't far from the hotel where the players were staying, so I set the alarm clock to get me there on time for the first bus to the course (a ploy I have used myriad times to avoid taxi fares to the tournament). I found myself alone with Colin Montgomerie. This was before Monty had really made his mark, although we press men were well aware of him because of his feats in the amateur ranks and his 'Rookie of the Year' award the previous year. He was in only his second full year on tour and obviously keen to know everyone. Mine was a face with which he was not familiar, so he was very chatty and wanted to know all the publications for which I worked. I told him I was a new kid on the block and he felt he was pretty much the same. As he disembarked from the bus Monty said: 'Well, nice meeting you. As we're both just starting off in our careers we should keep an eye on each other and see how successful we become. It'll be interesting.' Bless him. Monty and I have stayed pretty friendly over the years. He's earned a few bob more than me and he's reached peaks in his career while I've made the foothills. But I've taken great pleasure in writing about him and watching him – warts and all.

The German Open became almost secondary because, on the Sunday, Tony Jacklin announced his European Ryder Cup team, made up of nine players who had claimed their places for The Belfry in the points table and three wild cards. Jacklin's announcement caused a real stir when he was forced to admit that Sandy Lyle had refused to be one of his 'picks' and he'd therefore chosen Christy O'Connor Junior. This news, coming late Sunday night, with deadlines tight, meant my second event provided a fraught finale. I took too long to get everything done. The caddies' bus on which I'd booked a seat to Crans-sur-Sierre in Switzerland left without me. I had to take the train to Sierre. I'm sure it would have been staggeringly picturesque, but it was an overnight journey – and it cost me nearly all my profit.

Any feelings of gloom, though, dispersed when I got to Crans. It was the most amazing sight, it still is for me. The Alps in all their glory, and I was right in the thick of it for the week, brushing shoulders with the pros every way you turned. My greatest thrill at Crans was getting a round of golf on the Tuesday with a couple of the writers and the tournament chief John Paramor. Paramor, intrigued at this callow newcomer, made me his partner. Our opponents, Bill Elliott and Mitchell Platts, were in a spot of bother on one hole but Elliott appeared to play his ball from an impossible position under some trees. Seve Ballesteros then appeared from around the spinney and agreed what a great shot it was. The fact that the great man himself had played the ball for Bill hardly mattered.

It was in Crans that I found that perhaps I really was amongst friends in the golf-writing ranks. Having splashed all my ready capital on the train journey, I was pretty skint. For dinner one night I'd smuggled out a couple of the cheese and ham rolls provided for journalist working lunches and I was making my way to the hotel, late as usual, when tapping on a restaurant window arrested me. Inside were all the gang, Elliott of *The Star*, Platts from *The Times*, *The Sun*'s rough diamond Frank Clough, Michael Williams of *The Daily Telegraph*, Michael McDonnell from *The Daily Mail*, *Today*'s Bill Blighton, doyens all. 'Where are you going, Dabell?' I was asked. 'Oh, just to the hotel for an early night,' I replied. 'Come in and have a drink with us,' invited the gang. 'Better not,' said I nervously. However, the lads insisted. They wouldn't let me pay for a thing. I drank at least one bottle of wine and ate my fill, after they had a whip-round for me.

The subsequent mild hangover, thin air and altitude which played havoc with my ears and eyes (I am a martyr to sinusitis) left me pretty groggy on the Wednesday morning. My left eye looked like an AA Road Map. It was so sore I decided to leave out my contact lens and went to work with one lens in and one out. It left me a little unbalanced (so what else was new?), but I managed. When I got back to my hotel room, though, I couldn't find my other contact lens anywhere. It was supposed to be in the little emergency receptacle I'd left it in, having taken the usual case with saline solution in it with me in the event of the other eye becoming sore. After much searching and a heated discussion with the landlady, a tearful chambermaid admitted she may have thrown it away when cleaning my bathroom. That left me running around the next day looking like some demented Long John Silver. The landlady was very good, though. The next morning she took me to an optician friend who found me a lens very close in power to my own.

Because the Telex lady in the press room refused to let me

use her machine, I had to dictate all my copy to her and then she punched it in. It could take an age. Consequently, on the Sunday night after Seve Ballesteros had won and provided us with oodles of copy, I missed the caddie bus again, this one going to Geneva Airport. I managed to cadge a lift with local reporter Phillipe Hermann, who by chance had given me my first first-hand experience of a hole in one when he had one playing with me in our little press tournament on the Saturday morning. Phillipe was an ace car driver, too, but even his hair-raising dash down the mountain could not quite get me there in time to catch the last plane to England. To my dismay, a ticket for a plane the next day was going to cost £75 more than the one the caddies had booked on, the one I'd missed. It was crushing having to fork out £175 for the fare, a good chunk of profit gone again, so I decided not to seek digs. And anyway, my flight was at 0715. The airport seats looked fairly comfortable, so, with two caddying brothers who had also missed the flight, I settled down for the night. Within half an hour we were moved out of the comfortable area into something much more austere, with only hard benches that weren't long enough to take a man's frame. At about this time, whether it was the onset of IBS (irritable bowel syndrome) I don't know, the old tum started to play up. For the whole night I was either flat out on a hard floor with my luggage for a pillow – or running for a toilet, which, thankfully, was available.

Andrew Murray won my next event, the European Open. Andrew rather slipped from the limelight after that but he and I became good friends when he joined the Radio Five Live broadcasting team. After shaking his head at my feeble chipping one day, he gave me the sand-iron with which he won at Walton Heath. I responded by snapping the shaft the first time I used it when I struck a tree. I had to get a new shaft, of course, and then a couple of years later I had to get a new head put on the shaft after a stone dug a huge dent in it. I still tell people proudly, though, that my sand-iron was given to me by Andrew Murray – and that he won the European Open with it.

The Lancôme Trophy in Versailles is always a very elite affair. So I was worried. It was sure to be expensive. Most of the press, on expense accounts, and the top players, were staying at the Trianon Palace Hotel, virtually in the grounds of Versailles Palace. It provided headquarters for the Nazis during the war and had a grandeur I could not hope to afford. But could I? Encouraged by some of the lads, I dared to ask for a discount, explaining, in my Edward Heath French, that I was paying for myself and could they help with a cheaper rate?

'Non, monsieur,' was the reply. 'But we do 'ave ze basement room going sheap. Zere is no en-suite but it does 'ave a sink. Normally it 'as been for ze staff. We can let you 'ave it for two 'undred francs the night.' I jumped at it. It was comfortable enough, and quite spacious. The only trouble was the bathroom was a couple of floors up.

The next morning, rising early as usual to make sure I caught the first courtesy bus to the course, I ruminated on how to tackle my ablutions. I needed a shower before embarking on a hard day's Rapid Golf Line, which began as soon as the first few holes' scores came in. With the shower and loo two floors up, though, it could have meant a real rigmarole. I didn't want to dress, undress, shower, and dress again, too much of a fag, that. So I opted to swathe myself in the large bath towel supplied – and go for it in the lift. I had only made one floor when, to my chagrin, the lift stopped. A little old lady clutching a Pekinese to her bosom embarked. There am I, looking very awkward indeed in my towel, clutching my shirt and trousers to my bosom. She merely smiled and in a perfect English accent said sweetly: 'Good morning.' As I scuttled out at the next floor, I heard her talking to pooch in French. From what I could pick up, she was assuring the doggie that he would get his walkies now. They were safe after all.

The tournament was won by a cat, though. Eduardo Romero, whose nickname is The Cat (I had no idea why at that stage in my career, except that he did sport a superb set of whiskers in the shape of a luxuriant Viva Zapata moustache). Star attraction Curtis Strange didn't really live up to his hype and finished well down the field. Perhaps that was why he was in crotchety mood on Monday morning when we both checked out of the Trianon Palace. I'd very kindly been granted a courtesy car by the sponsors to get me to the airport first thing, a luxury for me (I think Lancôme just assumed I was a top scribe because I was staying at the five-star hotel). When I came down to check out, Mr Strange was at reception (unlike me he had no bill to pay, of course) looking just a tad agitated. As I signed my credit card I spotted my car pulling up outside. Before I could respond, the Silver Fox confronted my driver, who was quietened into submission after a weak protest. The upshot was that the US Open champion pinched my car to transport his luggage which, I understand, he said would have made the journey to the airport uncomfortable for him and his wife. My horror at the thought of having to pay a French cab fare all the way to Charles de Gaulle, possibly an hour away via either the Seine or the congested peripherique, must have been a sight to behold. It was beheld by two very nice English gentlemen from Sheffield who, when they heard the story, offered to share their chauffeur-driven Mercedes with me. They had been there for a leather-tanning conference and would be glad to help out. Three years later Strange returned to the tournament and put his ball into the pond to run up a humiliating score. I didn't gloat – honest.

The year's top event was then upon us, the Ryder Cup. I found it all so exhilarating, being positioned by the 18th to watch all the triumphs and disasters of the last day's singles before Europe retained the Cup. It was a gripping few hours, O'Connor proving he was worth the pick by setting up the victory chance with that famous two-iron shot, Rafferty winning against the odds, Europe on the brink. Then somehow we managed to let it go and, even though the tie ensured the Cup stayed in Europe, it was a bit of an anticlimax. But what copy it provided. It was arguably the most exciting Ryder Cup of all time.

Triumph and disaster seemed to be all around me. At my next event, the Portuguese Open, I was privy to Colin Montgomerie's career kick-starting. I thought back to our conversation on the bus at Frankfurt. Monty was on the way. I was making progress as well, if not in as glorious style as Monty's wonderful 11-shot victory at Quinta do Lago. It was quite a week watching Montgomerie let the world know he'd arrived. Certainly it was a luxurious one. We were put up in an opulent apartment by the sponsors, which I shared with the esteemed Frank Clough. It even had an esteamed Jacuzzi.

Frank didn't know whether to laugh or growl when I sneaked in on him using said Jacuzzi and emptied a bottle of bath foam over him. He bubbled up big-time and soon looked like Doris Day. There were cocktail parties and dinners. You could spend all your time lurching around drunk and with permanent flatulance if you were to accept all the largesse on offer at tournaments like that. I'd learned very quickly not to drink during the day. Slurring your words on radio or Rapid Golf Line was not acceptable.

After the luxury of Quinta do Lago, though, it was to the austere surrounds of the Hotel Patricia in Sotogrande, lino floors, no television and a bathroom clogged with mould. Bombay Runners, sort of Sellafield cockroaches, abounded in the room. The hotel was so bad I feared they might pinch *my* towels. Breakfast consisted of a cheese roll that had the texture and smell of an aging trainer. Dinner, because I had no transport, was, terrifyingly, only available across the infamous Costa del Sol 'Road of Death', which demanded a nightly duel with drivers exceeding 100 mph. But after Ronan Rafferty carried off the Volvo Masters and won the order of merit at Valderrama, it was a delightful surprise in my first year freelancing that I was invited to do a turn at the annual party to celebrate the European Tour year finishing. All the journalists were asked to do a party piece. Blighton and Clough, for instance, were excellent as Flanagan and Allen. But when I walked on stage with five plates in my hand, threatening to do a juggling act, my colleagues scattered, my reputation already gathering apace. I then handed out the plates to the perplexed and still cowering audience, remarking that any contribution, no matter how small, would be appreciated by an impoverished freelance. Then I sang in a quiet little falsetto voice: 'Why don't they make pickled onions square, instead of making them round? Every time I stick my fork in the jar – all I ever get is vine-garr.' I've no idea why I chose this ditty.

The year wasn't quite over and neither were the excursions in Spain. There was still the Benson and Hedges Mixed Team Trophy, for men and women tour players, and then the 1989 World Cup to come. Both events were on courses alongside each other in Marbella, so we stayed at the Andalucia Palace and Casino. Here Dabell's money problems could have been over, but in the end he was grateful to escape with his life.

Mitchell 'Plato' Platts, soon to become a European Tour director, was (and still is, by all accounts) an inveterate gambler, very experienced. I latched on to him in the casino and was doing quite well. Eventually we both had about the same winnings, £100 or so. We decided to combine at the roulette table and it grew even more. Soon, around £400 was stacked up. Plato, with me whimpering alongside, decided most of it should go on four numbers. He had a system, you see. One of them came up. We stood to pick up about £1,000 each, a small fortune, at least to me, which could have kept the wolf from the door. Up to this point the usual cry of 'no more bets now', as the wheel slowed down, had been bellowed out by the croupier, but, also as usual, no one took any notice and no one had had their bets refused. Until, that is, our number came up. The croupier insisted we had placed our bet too late, even though the wheel had not stopped and the ball not come to rest by any means. We cajoled, then protested. Mine was a desperate protest. Platts was much better off than me but was not prepared to be cheated out of his stake money for his next race meeting. In the end we were 'invited' to leave. And I didn't even have a chance to cash in my chips.

A few days later I nearly did cash in my chips. Floods had ravaged the Costa del Sol, swamping homes on *barrancos* and flooding the holiday spots on the coast so badly that six people were drowned. On the way to the airport with Jennie, who had come out for a free stay at the Andalucia Palace for a few days courtesy of the sponsors, we had a torrid time as our car was forced to take several detours to avoid the floods. But the rain kept on teeming down and when we got near to the airport the floods collapsed a bridge we had just driven over, sending a wall of water at us that threatened to engulf us. I am indebted today to the young courtesy car driver, Felicia, who somehow steered our car to safety and, I'm sure, saved our lives.

Having safely sent Jennie on her way it was back to the World Cup at Las Brisas. The rain continued, we walked around with plastic bags over our shoes. In the end, just two waterlogged rounds were possible before the tournament gave in to the elements. I drove back on the Sunday afternoon to Malaga Airport with one of the New Zealand Cup team members, Simon Owen. I couldn't hold back a body-wracking shudder when we came to the swollen river that had nearly snuffed out a budding freelance career.

## THREE

## HEADING FOR TROUBLE

I WAS REALLY looking forward to 1990 on tour, not least because I'd been offered the job of press officer for the Safari Tour. This was a three-tournament affair starting in Zimbabwe, going on to Zambia and finishing in Kenya. I had never been to this part of Africa and had no idea what adventures lay before me. If I had known what was coming, I'd have stayed at home.

The first thing that went wrong was actually flying out to Harare. Following my instructions to the letter, I arrived for a mid-morning flight from Heathrow, for which I had to collect my ticket at the Air Zimbabwe desk. Unfortunately, I discovered that I was supposed to be at Gatwick. The secretary who had typed up the letter for my travel arrangements had got in a muddle. I missed the plane and flew the next day.

My first experience of Harare was frustrating and worrying. Was I even going to be allowed to stay in the country? I had to register with the Zimbabwean equivalent of our Home Office. This entailed a six-hour wait at an office in Harare before I was allowed to go any further. As I had 'journalist' as my occupation on my immigration form, I was treated with utmost suspicion and spent at least an hour persuading officials I was merely covering a golf tournament. Eventually, with reluctance, they let me loose. Then I met up with the rest of the pros, with whom I'd caught up after being taken to Chapman Golf Club where a sort of a cattle market went on. We were given the once-over by a jockeying bunch of expats. They were scrutinising us because we were all to be housed by families for the duration of the Zimbabwe Open. I was chosen by a man who, at first, seemed to be a little gruff, a dour-looking Scot called Abe Stewart. As a rather introvert fellow (well at this time, I was) I was dreading staying with a family and would much rather be in an impersonal hotel. In the event, though, the very friendly Abe and his lovely wife Margaret afforded me a wonderful stay on the outskirts of Harare, close enough to the bush to be potentially invaded by all sorts of wild animals but inside a comforting compound that kept them out. I was given first-class treatment, my own apartment within the Stewarts' ginormous house, and transport back and forth to the tournament.

Conditions in the laughably labelled 'press-room' at Chapman Golf Club were not as impressive, however. It was just a bamboo hut with no light (they brought me some candles when, well after the rounds had finished, I was still working on my portable typewriter) and no communications. I went out to watch plenty of golf, but was never quite sure who was leading until the scores had been rounded up at the end of the day. Mercifully, I wasn't doing my Rapid Golf Line beat and it was before I'd really got into live radio. The telephone in the clubhouse didn't seem to want to get me through to any of the newspapers for whom I was reporting and, nearly every night, I had to resort to a frantic dash into Harare to send my stuff on Abe's office fax machine.

You had to be careful out on the Chapman course. There were crocodiles in every one of the ponds and lakes. I thought it brought a new meaning to the expression 'snap-hook'. As the tournament unravelled, it seemed Gordon J. Brand was going to provide us with a top-name winner. Brian Barnes mounted a challenge, too. Barnes was an incredible player. He could booze all night, have a couple of liveners before playing (and several during the course of his round) and still perform at top drawer. Either of these two players would be a good story, I thought, but it was Grant Turner, a former 'Rookie of the Year', who prevailed.

I got quite close to several of the players during the three-week run and heard some great tales, such as when a monkey was supposed to have tried to pinch Gordon Brand's ball. He chased the monkey off and up a tree and finished off the hole.

The next day, though, when he came to the same green, just as he was about to putt a whole bombardment of debris came from out of the tree above him. Brand's monkey friend of the day before had a good memory and had lain in wait to take revenge.

After the tournament finished I decided to head for Victoria Falls. After filing my story to a golf magazine on the Telex machine at the Victoria Falls Hotel, I spent a few memorable hours with tournament players Paul Carrigill and Glenn Ralph marvelling at the sights of the falls. I got thoroughly soaked as I took photographs amid the spray. The trip from Harare and back on a rickety old single-engined plane, that was about flying doctor size, added to the buzz.

Our next port of call was Lusaka for the Zambian Open. How the country could afford a street party, let alone a golf tournament, was beyond my comprehension. I was amazed to see dirt roads in downtown Lusaka for a start. It proved a miserable week. I was housed with a former copper mining executive on hardish times, who had a real shrew of a wife. They were supposed to feed me and take me back and forth to the tournament, but I ended up paying through the nose for everything. And I wasn't exactly well off. It rained a lot as well, something I hadn't allowed for when I packed my suitcase. The course was soaked and nobody turned up to watch much. They were keen to get me involved in the tournament, so they gave me a place in the pro-am on the Wednesday. My caddie informed me proudly: 'My name is Matthew, Mark, Luke, John Mutumbah. I normally caddie for Mr Sandy Lyle, but this week I am proud to caddie for you, Mr Norman.' He stole my Swatch, half-a-dozen golf balls, two sweat-soaked golf gloves and even my pen. He was an artful lad who melted away as soon as he'd pocketed his 'kwacha'. And nobody had heard of the name Mutumbah, although there were plenty of Matthew, Mark, Luke, Johns about. Luckily I'd kept my wallet in my pocket.

President Kaunda played in the pro-am. I watched from a distance as his bodyguards disposed of a brown snake in the rough, where Mr Kaunda had hit his ball. The President was, of course, the moving force behind the Zambian Open. He was a real golf nut. I'm not sure his impoverished people were completely all for it. But the tournament itself, barring the stoppages for lightning and downpours, was well run and there were plenty of good stories before Brand pulled this one off. The trouble was, hardly any of my pieces could get through. None of the telephone lines would connect internationally. I kept being told that the lines would be available in a few minutes. But they just never worked. Had Kenneth paid his telephone bills? I was close to being apoplectic all week, swiftly moving from slamming handsets down in disgust to hurling one into a wastepaper basket – full of unfulfilled Dabell copy. Expats shook their heads in sympathy but this time no one offered an office or a home phone line. If they had them working, they were keeping quiet about it.

Therefore it was a great relief to get away and go for the trip on the Zambezi which I'd been told would be a real eye-opener. True, the sight of hippopotami in their natural state next to our little cruiser was a real experience. But I made the mistake of eating lots of the salad on the cruise. It was obviously washed in something iffy because the trip deteriorated into more than just an eye-opener. Still not recovered fully from Zambezi falls, I moved on to Nairobi for the Kenyan Open.

Great joy. In Kenya I was to stay at the Hotel Utali. It was a pleasant looking place on the outskirts of Nairobi, even if the room was a little small. There was a fine looking restaurant and a swimming pool which was surrounded by palm trees and lots of pretty air stewardesses in bikinis. I was soon amongst them (the palms, I mean). My little paradise was not all it was cracked up to be, however. At the restaurant I found out the hotel was for chefs and waiters just learning the catering and waiting business. The food was unrecognisable as anything an Englishman would have as part of his diet. Even famished, I didn't feel adventurous enough to go for anything more than the soup, which was red but didn't taste of tomato. I didn't have to worry about tummy troubles this time. Prickly heat, from sudden exposure to the Kenyan sun, provided me with a tortuous night. Swathed in damp towels, I didn't get a wink of sleep.

I had to find the Karen club the next day, not the Muthaiga course where the tournament was being played, but a sister Nairobi club that was hosting the pro-am to save the tournament course getting chewed up by amateurs. I was there looking for stories – in fact I got a nice scoop from Nick Price's brother Tim – but got inveigled into playing in the pro-am. With borrowed clubs, as usual, I wasn't really enjoying myself, but then came an incident I've dined out on quite a few times. Our group was nearing the par three that had been designated as the one for a hole-in-one prize. In the distance you could see a car was on a little platform behind the green, signifying the prize for the ace. As we progressed at our hole, there was sudden action from the par three up ahead. We picked out two men who seemed to have come hurtling out of the trees. They dived into the car and must have hot-wired it because no one in their right mind would have left the keys in. They screamed off the platform in a plume of dust and made to escape. They misjudged the gap in the trees badly though, and the car became stuck fast. As it was a two-door job, they were imprisoned. Security men arrived and the pair were apprehended. Not enough hole for a car in one.

When I arrived at the tournament course I was amazed to find it looking just like a European Tour event, with all the trappings, including a tented village. It had everything but a press room. No matter, there was a small telephone exchange just down the road. It took a hundred attempts to get through to England (conservative estimate). By the time I had filed my stories to three newspapers, I was totally drained. The rest of the week would be the same – endless attempts at getting through before hearing the wonderful voice of an Englishman or woman. Then the line would get lost or they couldn't hear you, even if you could hear them. Or you got lost being put through to copy. It was sheer agony all week. And only one phone was available. The local Kenyan reporter never seemed to be off it. He could always get through, of course. We ended up squaring up to each other on a daily basis.

It proved a great tournament, though. Christy O'Connor Junior, the hero of The Belfry the previous year, won and provided superb copy. The photographs I took during the week, this being the final event of three, were available to the magazines within days, and were therefore used extensively. I made enough money from a memorable week's stories to keep the wolf from the door. But I never wanted to see an African telephone again in my life.

Oporto and the Estela links for the Atlantic Open in Portugal launched my European Tour year of 1990. As befits a seaside course, it blew a hooligan on the final day and the winner was the one who could stand up in the end, with the rest reeling like punch-drunk prize-fighters. It turned out to be a six-ball lottery. The question often crops up, 'What was the biggest play-off in European Tour history and who were the six players involved?' The answer is, 'The Atlantic Open at Estela in 1990, and the players were Richard Boxall, Ronan Rafferty, David Williams, Stephen Hamill, Anders Sorensen and (the winner) Stephen McAllister.' Not a lot of people know that. Fortunately for me, McAllister won pretty quickly for such a cluttered play-off that was more like a cavalry charge, because I had arranged to play golf over the tour course the next day with the man from *Exchange Telegraph*, Brian Cutress. Had the play-off gone on much longer with the light going fast in the wind and rain, it would have spilled over to the next day – and no golf for yours truly. As it was, the tournament organisers might have just wished it had gone on to a fifth day. With the wind continuing to howl on the Monday, tee-shots became as big a lottery as the previous day's play-off. I think I'd lost about six balls by the time we came to the final par three. Here a gleaming car was proudly on display still, the hole-in-one prize for the pros during the Atlantic Open. As soon as I followed through, so awkwardly I nearly ruptured myself, I knew my three-wood and the capricious wind had betrayed me yet again. With my partner wincing and turning his head away in fear, my ball described a perfect arc and slammed into the car's door at a great rate of knots on the full. We felt duty-bound to abandon the game there and then, as Cutress was already the winner, three holes up, to inspect the damage. A dent you could fit much of your fist into had appeared in the door. There was no hiding place either. Some of the members who were enjoying lunch also turned out to inspect. It was their second lunch interruption. Two holes before, from the other side of the clubhouse, I'd fairly rattled the plate-glass entrance door with another errant drive. I left my name and address in case it was needed for insurance purposes and Cutress and I beat a hasty exit to the airport.

Nearly everything was done on the run for many years as I perhaps took on too many clients than was healthy for peace of mind. At the Mediterranean Open at Las Brisas in Spain, I hurtled out of the press tent with course card, notepad and pen, intent on collaring players in the clubhouse. As I ran down a corridor I spotted one of the men I wanted in the restaurant ahead. My progress, which was of about 100 metres county second team standard, was halted very abruptly as I came extremely forcibly in contact with a full-length plate-glass window. I slid down the window in similar fashion to Tom when he has been suddenly, and violently, thwarted by Jerry. As I got to my knees in a daze, I looked through the window, which had been naïvely highly polished. I saw Roger Chapman and Carl Mason standing gape-mouthed and with spreading tea stains on their trousers, evidence of how they had sprung to their feet in fright as I hit the window running.

Ian Woosnam's magnificent win in his first event of the year showed just how well the pocket-battleship Welshman can master stormy conditions. The wind was so bad that Gibraltar airport, from where we were due to fly, was closed because of debris on the runway from an already fairly dangerous take-off. I knew all about Gib because I'd spent over two years there in the Royal Navy Communications Centre in the bowels of the Rock. The runway was eventually cleared by engineers from the Gibraltar Garrison but nobody seemed to want to risk taking off in the high winds. Many of the players went off to the Rock Hotel for the night but a few of us bribed, cajoled and threatened staff to get us on a plane. Even though we had been told that places on the first plane away were at a premium, and that the flight was full, when we got on board there were only about 50 of us for a 150-seater!

My freelancing career had moved on apace. I now had a large portfolio. Having so many customers was good for the bank balance, bad for the nerves. UPI had supplied me with a Tandy laptop to make transferring files and scores a lot easier than resorting to copy-takers and Telex. But would I cope at the Tenerife Open if I extended my clientele? Fellow freelance Micky Britten and I were the only British press at the tournament. There was going to be a lot of running around after players when they came in to get their stories because there weren't going to be any official press conferences. I knew all about 'doorstepping' by now (waiting for a player to sign for his score and then pouncing on him for a story as soon as diplomatically possible). We prayed for an easy tournament.

With Tenerife being in the same time zone as Britain and the tournament not finishing until twilight, beating deadlines was a real scramble. But Micky and I somehow made them all for the first round. Then came the nightmare of the second round. It had seemed a tidy enough story – José Maria Olazábal locked in battle with Miguel Angel Jiménez (that had the Spanish press puffing out their chests). Ollie was easily the most famous player in the field, so it was a good yarn. I was just mentally patting myself on the back after filing my last story . . . when into the press room walked Olazábal, shoulders at the droop, with the tournament director. Ollie had been disqualified, he told us with a despairing shrug. It was all to do with Ollie misinterpreting the rules regarding balls ending up in lava outcrops. He'd nearly not come to Tenerife because of damaging his irons in the lava the previous year and so this time, when he had found himself in it, he made sure he moved the chunks of rock before carefully playing his shot. The rules about balls in lava outcrops at Golf del Sur the year before, though, were not quite the same at this year's course, the adjacent Amarilla. Unbeknown to Ollie, his ball had landed in lava outcrop curiously designated a 'water hazard', where you couldn't move loose bits or ground your club. A casual conversation later that evening had set off an alarm bell. And after the tournament director, armed with a flashlight, had been summoned and gone out with him to the scene of crime, there was no way back. As he had already signed his card long before, and thus signed for a wrong score because he had not penalised himself, it was no way, José. Ollie was out of the tournament.

You can imagine the panic that set in for two reporters who had filed myriad stories talking about Olazábal being on course to win again. As his disqualification came at about 8.30 p.m., it meant near-hysterical calls to sports desks to try to halt copy going to bed. Everything had to be changed to read how Olazábal had been dumped out of the tournament by a lava outcrop deemed a water hazard. If we'd had even a hint there was going to be trouble for Ollie it would have made things a little easier, but it all happened completely out of the blue just as we were packing up to leave the course. Some of the newspapers had already gone to press at that time of night, so first editions carried one story and later editions the other. The Spanish press were beside themselves with indignation and wailed long and loudly. It was utter chaos. Nothing the Tenerife Open could throw at me after that could worry me, although the tournament did its best to try us once again over deadlines. It took a three-hole play-off on the Sunday night before the veteran Vicente Fernandez disposed of Mark Mouland.

It was a fortnight which produced an Argentine double, because the following week Eduardo Romero won the Florence Open. Monty did well, too, finishing second. I was plotting his progress, as he'd suggested. Don't suppose he was mine, though. While the hosting Ugolino course location was wonderful, in the rolling Tuscany farmland, and the food delicious, Florence was a mixed experience. Strolling along by the Arno and taking in the hive of activity that is the Ponte Vecchio, was unforgettable. So was staying at our city centre hotel. It had been invaded by students of all nationalities, all keen to enhance their skills in speaking English. The telephone went at all times of the night as the young insomniacs called to chat to someone with an English voice. Word seemed to spread that in room 232 was an Englishman and some hitherto unknown juicy swear words were to be had. I needed to keep the phone on for my morning alarm call, so I rarely escaped the purgatory. Harangued, I was. And the plumbing was hopeless. Every time someone went to the loo the pipes would clank and scream all around the building. And not only did we have students. There were also about a hundred Italian OAPs at the hotel, a mean percentage of whom were obviously suffering prostate problems. Once again on tour, I hardly slept a wink all week.

In direct contrast to the buzzing Florence, alive with bright young things, as well as the chic and cheerful, the French holiday resort of Montpellier was, well – closed. It was a curious experience wandering around a sort of upmarket

Butlins where we were all based for the week, seeing only pros, caddies, tour staff and golfing press. Not a local showed his or her head above the parapets. Just three or four restaurants were open out of hundreds, where you might wait an hour for a table if you were determined enough. However, the AGF Open provided the colour and the memories for what could have been quite a dreary week. On the first day no less than six players unaccountably moved out-of-bounds marker posts in order to play their balls. All, according to golf's pedantry, were disqualified, among them the cream of the tournament. On the Saturday morning things were quietish, as they can be before the leaders go off in early afternoon. Not for long. There was a terrific commotion outside the press room, which was inside the clubhouse. As I nipped outside to investigate I saw the eponymous 'Wild Colonial Boy', Wayne Riley, on the first tee, appearing to achieve the impossible by tieing up his shoelaces while completing his downswing. Riley, looking rather dishevelled, marched off down the fairway, muttering loudly and berating a hapless caddie. News soon reached the press room that 'Radar' had again homed into trouble. He had been late on the tee and incurred a penalty for his tardiness. Reports soon started to come in from bemused and amused colleagues staying at Riley's hotel. He had been spotted running down the stairs in his underpants, managing to pull on his trousers in mid-flight as he tore out of the foyer screaming for a taxi. I had the perfect vehicle for such a yarn. The *News of the World* would just love this one. And when Radar then went from the ridiculous to the sublime and incredibly had a hole in one on the 16th, I couldn't wait for him to give his version of the affair. He reckoned he had not received his alarm call and awoke to realise he had only 15 minutes to his tee-off. It was a wonderful effort to make it to the course and only get penalised for being late on the tee instead of being thrown out of the tournament. Somehow Riley and his cab driver (Alain Prost?) had salvaged his third round – at the expense of terrifying the hotel staff with the hideous sight of the even wilder colonial boy charging past them half dressed.

Incidents like that seemed to occur periodically to 'Radar' Riley. He was always in trouble. For instance, tour officials looked on aghast when a girlfriend waddled on to a green during one of his rounds, wearing a tight skirt and stilettos and brandishing an ice-cream for the perspiring Australian. Some years later he was charged with 'air rage' and he's shown plenty of golf club rage over many years. Riley once missed the start of the season after falling off a settee at a Sam Torrance party. With that, I can empathise.

It's a pity we don't go back to El Bosque, near Valencia, any more. It is a course that I can never forget. I only have to run my fingers across my scalp to bring the memories flooding back. I'll bet Vijay Singh will never forget the course either. The double-Major champion's career really sparked into life at El Bosque. And in my own way, I guess, I set him on the road to success. I have in my collection of memorabilia a ball and score-card which remind me of a crazy week, if the old grey matter ever fails me.

Singh had established an early lead in the tournament and by the time we began the third round on the Saturday the big Fijian seemed well set. His first 10 holes, though, saw him going backwards as he dropped a whole load of shots. By the time he stood on the 11th tee, Singh was no longer in control. I'd managed to take a break from duties to go out on the course to see where things were going wrong. I needed early stories because, apart from my normal customers, I was covering for a glut of newspapers not in my normal portfolio because their staff reporters were all at the US Masters. All would want their pieces at the same time, so I had nerve-wracking deadlines. By this time, too, I was broadcasting live for Century Radio in Dublin, with a brief to talk about the Irish players in particular. It was a frantic schedule, so I needed some colour. I took up station about 180-200 yards down from the highly elevated tee, outside the ropes, standing and chatting to Singh's charming wife Ardena, who was six months' pregnant. Understandably, she was worried about hubby dropping shots but, typically, found time to ask how things were going for me. (We'd first met when I played with Vijay in a pro-am a little earlier.) Vijay's caddie, Dave 'Moggy' Morgan, came down the hill to join us. He was doing point duty to try to spot his master's ball. Moggy was none too happy. He could see his percentage being whittled away with every dropped shot. It was the caddie's sudden turn of the head after the distant familiar 'whang' of metal on Balata golf ball cover that caused me to look teewards. This movement probably saved me from very serious injury and left me with only injury. The next noise I heard was the very adjacent, unfamiliar 'bonk' of Balata on head. It was accompanied by a searing pain and a look of horror on Ardena's face as her legs wobbled and she fought to avoid swooning on the spot. That was because my face was covered in blood, which I had to shake out of my eyes. My hands were bloodied as they felt an instant bump which competed adequately with the one I'd once suffered through hurtling down a pit on a trike. My knees wobbled, too, but I refused to go down, sucking in breath to fight the pain and doing a pretty good impression of Frank Bruno after he'd stayed on his feet following a thump from Mike Tyson. As I reeled, I heard the voice of Singh's playing-partner Paul Carrigill, my Victoria Falls companion, barking into a walkie-talkie: 'Get a buggy over quickly to the 11th fairway. Norman Dabell's been hit on the head by Vijay's ball and he's in a bit of a bad way.' Out came the buggy, with a large golf towel to soak up the gore. I was whisked into the tournament office and the tournament doctor summoned. Within five minutes or so, he was inserting six stitches into the torn scalp which now rested on top of an Easter egg. Halfway through the surgery, one of my press colleagues, Jon Bramley from *Exchange Telegraph*, interrupted, saying: 'Irish Radio are on the phone. They say you're due on live in a couple of minutes. What shall I tell them?' Spotting a phone on the desk I was leaning on for comfort during surgery, I told Bramley to get the call transferred to me in the tournament office and tell me how the Irish players were faring on the scoreboard. I then did my radio broadcast just as the last stitch was sewn in. Stitching complete and head bandaged, it was to the press room to ensure early stories were prepared for imminent tight deadlines. I got a call from the *Mail on Sunday*. They were just making doubly sure I would be able to file for them. They had seen an agency report that I had been hit by Singh's ball. They'd contacted their regular man Peter Higgs, one of the staffers in Augusta, worried about his chosen understudy. Higgsy had asked them, 'Where has he been hit?' On being told 'on the head', he then observed: 'Oh, he should be all right then.' Singh went on to win the tournament. His ball had bounced off my cranium back into the middle of the fairway, when it was heading out of bounds. His slide was arrested, he regrouped and never again looked back. When Vijay came in for the winner's press conference, Bramley, perhaps feeling a little contrite at causing me embarrassment by giving his agency the story the day before, asked Singh if Dabell might receive a percentage of the first prize. I settled for a signed ball and the third-round card. I was more than happy that I had turned my head towards the tee at the fateful 11th. Otherwise the Singh ball would have struck my temple. My golf writing days could have been history.

I was soon back in Spain for two tournaments, both in Madrid. This meant a two-week run away from home as, financially if not emotionally, it was logical not to return to Blighty in between the tournaments. The meagre pensions I booked into offered little in the way of comfort, and I lived on tapas for a fortnight. Some of my customers were a bit tardy in their payments, so I was skint and I'd just decided to splash out on a new Tandy laptop (monthly payments, of course) to avoid having to keep returning UPI's decrepit machine, which was always breaking down. But there were luxurious diversions to brighten up the two-week stint. The opening tournament was at Puerta de Hierro, an elite club that offered cuisine and wines that would have graced the best restaurants in the world. While I turned down the array of top Riojas, each lunchtime I ate until I nearly burst to allow me to make savings on food later on. There were functions to go to as well. On the Friday night we were invited by the Spanish Federation to a dinner which turned out to be quite a sporting headline-maker. As often happens in these kinds of events in Spain, talk soon turned to football. As usual in the capital, Real Madrid was all anybody Spanish wanted to talk about (mostly about how much better than Barcelona they were – unless Seve Ballesteros was in the chair, that is). On this night, the topic was 'Which new striker will John Toshack bring in to increase Real Madrid's fire-power?' The obvious man to ask was the reporter right alongside me, Frank Clough, former football writer for *The Sun*, and now the tabloid's golf correspondent. Frank was far more interested in juggling his cerveza with his cigarette than tossing football questions around in his head but gave the matter a few moments' thought and replied: 'Well, without a doubt John Barnes would be the man. Toshack's been threatening to go back to Liverpool for players and Barnes would fill the bill nicely at Real Madrid.' With that Frank went back to trying to set the record for cervezas consumed and cigarettes smoked in one hour and thought no more about it. The next day in the press room, Cloughie got an urgent phone call telling him to drop the golf immediately and get on to a story that had come from Spain. John Barnes (still lauded for his magical goal against Brazil) was on his way to Real Madrid. Frank protested that it was probably just a rumour – which he knew, as it was started by him. But his office wouldn't take no for an answer and, bizarrely, Frank was sent off to cover a non-existent story he'd unwittingly instigated the night before. Cloughie had been talking to a Real Madrid director who read rather more into his words than proved comfortable.

The Dabellisms continued. While playing the early Saturday morning press tournament with the Davies duo, Dai from *The Guardian* and his wife Patricia, the *Times*' freelance, I was startled by a sprinkler. Because we were out so early, the watering of the course hadn't been completed. The fairway sprinkler went off under my right foot before I had completed a downswing, leaving me playing one of the more comical looking hanging lies. It wasn't the only good watering I got. The rain in Spain stayed mainly on Dabell the following week. We were invited north to play in a tournament at Pedrena, Seve's course at Santander. It never stopped raining. A more bedraggled bunch I've rarely seen. Dai, Patricia and I were the only ones daft enough to squelch around all 18 holes, so we scooped the prizes. I was third, of course.

When we returned from Santander to Madrid for the Spanish Open it was to a high-powered press conference with Nick Faldo, who was back in Europe after clinching his second US Masters. Faldo finished second. Frank Clough concentrated on golf and stayed quiet when football cropped up in the conversation at a Club de Campo cocktail party.

Waterloo was one of our stops during the year, not the station but where Wellington marked a few cards near Brussels. The Belgian Open proved a tempestuous week. One of the

45

tournament stars, Howard Clark, provided the early story by walking in off the course during the second round. Howard was always good for a yarn. The caddies and television cameramen called him the 'Pinless Grenade'. He was fined for demolishing tee markers with his driver once, and he'd been in trouble for berating a talkative spectator in the Volvo Masters. The spectator was the Valderrama course designer Robert Trent Jones. Anything could drive Howard scatty and he frequently flipped his lid at spectators fidgeting or moving on his line while he was putting. Richard Boxall, a contemporary of Howard, tells a story of how he visited Clarky in hospital after he had had an operation on the right elbow injury that plagued his career. 'He was just coming round after his op as I stood over his bed,' says Boxy. 'He slowly opened one eye and snarled "You can't stand there."' I maintain I once heard Howard shout at the 'sodding frogs' at the National course in Paris. He wasn't being xenophobic, just annoyed at croaking amphibians on the 18th.

I'm afraid to admit that hot temper nearly landed me in a great deal of trouble during the tournament in Belgium. Suffering a heavy cold, I'd politely asked a waiter in a downtown Brussels restaurant for a non-smoking table when I went in to eat on the Saturday night. Now whether the waiter's ancestor had been on the losing side against Wellington or not, I don't know, but he seemed to take great exception to his table plan being disturbed by an Englishman craving fresh air. He seated me, but with a theatrical flourish flung open the fire exit door right next to me. It was very parky indeed and so when my starter arrived I got up and closed the door. Within seconds he was back, wrenching the door open, freezing my meatballs off. Well, a sort of Laurel and Hardy scenario developed over a good few minutes until, after I had once more slammed the door shut, the manager arrived with the waiter. To my disbelief, I was told to leave the restaurant. Having had a glass of wine and a plate of cold meatballs, I was fairly replete so I informed them that, of course, I would not be paying. To the accompaniment of growls from the manager about me being (perplexingly) a 'stupid Yank', I collected my waterproof jacket and went into the toilet on my way out. When I came out it was to see my friendly waiter walking past with both arms wrapped around a crate of mineral water. I'm ashamed to say that my annoyance at being asked to leave hadn't evaporated. I tripped him up and he measured his length, scattering bottles all over the passageway. Understandably, pandemonium broke out, with waiter wailing and manager returning to scene. Standing at the narrow doorway I knew they could only come at me one at a time, though, and none appeared brave enough to make the first move. I turned and hightailed it, flicking the Yale lock up on the door. My hotel was just around the corner and I nipped smartly into the lift. As the doors closed, I just got the chance to see the restaurant manager and his crew go hurtling past the hotel, ready to do serious damage to the stupid Yank. I was off to the course for the final round the next day at an hour well before any signs of life from the restaurant from hell.

Ronan Rafferty was the Scandinavian Enterprise Open defending champion. You had to compose your questions to Ronan with great care or you were dead meat. It wasn't a case of him not suffering fools gladly, rather not suffering press people at all. Forget any leading questions. With Raffs it was pretty well a case of how the course was playing and that was it. I remembered my first-ever gambit to Ronan. That had been at the previous year's PLM Open, my début on tour as a freelance. As he had won the Scandinavian Enterprise Open a little earlier and was leading the PLM Open, could it be a 'Swedish double', enthused I?

'That kind of question doesn't deserve an answer,' sniffed Raffs, looking at me as if I'd just compared one of his best clarets to a glass of gorilla piss.

Eventually, when I started working for Irish newspapers full-time, we did strike up a bit of rapport – founded on our shared love of wine. But Raffs was always a man you approached wearing kid gloves. On this occasion he gave it his best shot but couldn't quite defend his title and finished third, bowing to a remarkable finish by the man with the luxuriant moustache, 'Walrus' Craig Stadler.

It was the usual frantic dash for a plane after the tournament finished on Sunday night. I was just about to dive into the courtesy car which was to take us to the airport when the tournament office called me back up the clubhouse steps to take a call from Radio Telefis Eireann. The Irish station was supposed to have called to take a live broadcast about half an hour beforehand, but was late getting hold of me. It appeared they weren't even ready to put me on air as I returned, so I told the producer he was too late because I was in a desperate dash to the airport. The very kind Swedish courtesy car driver then offered his mobile phone and said I could do the broadcast in the car, if they wanted to ring back. I reluctantly gave the mobile number and told them to call me back when they were ready to get me on air. I put down the terrestrial phone and pushed my way through the throng around the clubhouse entrance. As I made the steps the mobile went off in my hand. 'Is that Norman?' enquired an Irish voice.

'Yes,' I replied, guardedly.

'Oh great; we can get you straight on now.' The news came just as my courtesy car companions, pre-empting missed flights, began gesticulating fairly animatedly, kindly inviting me to 'get into this fucking car right now Dabell or we're leaving without you.' Taking in their message and trying to catch my cue on RTE at the same time proved just a little too much for the Dabell guidance system. I was introduced to my Irish listeners: 'Well, the Scandinavian Enterprise Open has just finished and though it's been a great bid by Ronan Rafferty to keep his title, there's been a quiet outstanding display from the Walrus in Stockholm. Tell us all about it, Norman Dabell.' As I made to speak, my body went into free fall down the clubhouse steps. While the broadcast was not word-perfect, contained several pauses, possibly carried a grunt or two and, I know for definite, at least one moan, I managed to hang on to the phone and get over all the salient information. I clattered down what seemed like 39 steps without one oath. A stream of profanities did happen off air, though, as I was being bundled into my car. Over the years my broadcasts have many times been by the seat of my pants, but only once literally.

The Irish Open is still my favourite event of the year. For the 1990 event at Portmarnock I had splendid digs for the week because, thanks to my great friends at Borde Failte (Irish Tourist Board), I managed a very cheap rate at one of my favourite hotels, the Burlington in Dublin. It does not need me to reiterate that the Irish are the best hosts in the world. A certain young Swede would have agreed with me on the Friday night of a tournament, which José Maria Olazábal won in the teeth of a gale. Mikael Krantz had never tasted the black stuff that causes loss of equilibrium before in his life. On the Friday night he – as the Irish so eloquently put it – gave the liquid that begins life in the Liffey 'a good lash'. In fact, Krantz gave the Guinness such a seeing-to that when he arrived at the course on the Saturday morning his balance was still by no means perfect. On the first tee he made to give the ball a good lash also, but missed it completely, collapsing in a heap onto his golf bag. After remounting the tee, the reeling Krantz staggered off on his round. His golf did not exactly improve. But, encouraged by his playing-partners and the ever-growing band of alerted press corps (all nursing hangovers and thinking 'there but for the grace of God . . .'), Krantz tottered to a round of 83. It was a reasonable score given the circumstances. He was a hero in Irish eyes, but a villain back home, where the Swedish media vilified him. It was hardly surprising that the hapless young player, knowing his exploit had brought him disgrace in his own country, shot an 81 the next day, stone cold sober. It was one of those stories that seemed a great laugh at the time, but it cost Krantz his career, a high price to pay for a few pints of Guinness. Unlike thousands of European Tour professionals, though, Mikael Krantz will never be forgotten for an 83 at Portmarnock, 11 over-par – after one over the eight.

I'd nearly finished paying off the instalments on my Tandy by the time the 1990 Open came along, my first Championship as a freelance. Following on from the Scottish Open at Gleneagles, it was yet another two-week stint away from home. I'd booked in at a motel miles away from the course and it meant a lengthy drive each day at the crack of dawn to beat the crowds pouring into St Andrews, but it was worth it. I had no intention of sharing a rented house this time, as I had had to the previous year in my last few miserable days working for *Golf Weekly*. In a fraught week in 1989, I was nearly involved in fisticuffs when my bottle of Chablis went missing from the fridge. The lowest moment came, though, when three of us returned to the house and couldn't get in. That was because a colleague and his girlfriend were exercising in the bedroom and didn't want to be disturbed. We climbed over the cloakroom roof and gained entry by way of a skylight, not a recommended route after consuming three gin and tonics and a bottle of wine.

St Andrews proved that Faldo was the best golfer in the world. I was lucky enough to watch pretty well every stroke Faldo played as he set the Open aggregate record. And even at that time Faldo's caddie Fanny Sunesson sounded just like a sergeant-major when ordering the crowd around. Probably one of the most poignant memories of the 1990 Open, though, was of meeting up again with Tip Anderson, Arnold Palmer's caddie, who'd helped me greatly with my first book. I took great delight in getting some photographs of Tip and Arnold for my album. Arnold came down the 18th on the second day to tumultuous applause because this was to be his Open swansong. I have his press conference notes still, scribbled down in my shaky shorthand.

Driving up to St Andrews and back from Kent, coupled with a 70-mile round trip each day during the Open, left me glad to be settling back in the seat of a plane the following week, destination Zandvoort for the Dutch Open. There, Stephen McAllister proved his Oporto win had been no fluke. I also learned one little trick from a doyen of freelance golf writing, the first man to juggle five newspaper stories at once, Gordon Richardson. We were terribly tight for time when McAllister came in for his winner's interview, and the prospect of an extra night in Holland was looming. Things weren't helped by earsplitting thunderflashes, dropped by a light aircaft to celebrate the tournament finishing, which continually interrupted the press conference. Gordon had foreseen trouble, though. I wondered how he was able to send over quotes from McAllister when the bespectacled Scot had not spoken to anyone since coming off the final green. Then I understood. Gordon led McAllister by the hand with his questioning – asking the winner just the right things so that he answered with quotes so similar to what Ricko had already put over to his newspapers that any slight discrepancy didn't matter. What a pro! I'll try that some time, thought I. Gordon made his flight. I missed mine.

It was back to Malmo the following week. I'd gone full circle. In fact, I got close to the Arctic Circle. The Swedes were very keen for the press to sample a new course right up in northern Lapland called Bjorkliden. So, after flying in to Malmo we were soon on our way to Kiruna, then aboard a coach up to the course. It was a sensational journey, stopping off to eat dried reindeer meat (just a sample, it was awful) and view the spectacular Lap Gate. I tried to picture what this wonder of the world looked like when it was covered in snow and ice. As it was the miles-long cleft in the mountains where the Laps drive their reindeer in and out to new pastures twice a year was a spellbinding sight. The course was not quite so spectacular, laid out to impossible proportions with holes reached only by traversing ball-gobbling rough. The problem, too, was that we were supposed to play it all night and morning. The attraction had been to play in the Land of the Midnight Sun. We were wined and dined in a huge Lap wigwam until about 10 p.m. and then expected to grab a couple of hours' sleep for a midnight start to the competition. Most stayed at the bar. The tournament was hilarious. We got through hundreds of balls in what was, despite its billing, a sort of half-light. The only thing that kept us going was liberal doses of Akvavit, a life-giving local Swedish liquor that left you not caring whether you were playing golf or lacrosse. Messengers were also despatched at every hole to replenish waning stocks of golf balls. It was the worst golf course I've played in my life – but oodles of fun. Of course we were exhausted when we had to come off the course to have a quick shower and catch the bus to the airport. The PLM Open was almost a non-event after that. Ronan Rafferty won and played so well there was no need to talk about anything but golf. That suited Ronan.

A frantic August and September followed. I flew to Germany three times, Switzerland and France, and drove all round Britain. While the air miles were mounting up, my poor old Sierra had gone round the clock. The Murphy's Cup was an enjoyable experience at Fulford. It was my first experience of our new tour sponsors (Murphy's) who delighted members of the Fourth Estate by setting up a bar alongside the press tent. That drew one golf writer to exclaim: 'I've got to get a proper job so I can get more fresh air.'

With the launch of my book, *How We Won the Open*, at

Wentworth during the World Matchplay Championship, a hectic year was winding down. I still had one fabulous memory to store, though, at the Home of Golf. My name came out of the hat to play in the pro-am of the Dunhill Cup at St Andrews. And I was to accompany Mark James. I'd never played the hallowed links. When my name was called out on the first tee underneath the Royal and Ancient, I looked up at rows of spectators in the stands to my left and lining the fence down to the Swilcan Burn. I should have been terrified. Inanely, I said to myself: 'This is it; you've finally made it, Norm.' I could do no wrong for the first nine holes, just hitting left into the wind and watching the ball fade onto the fairway. Jesse (Mark) was amazed and so were my other partners, Martin Hardy of the *Daily Express* and Colin Callander of *Golf Monthly*. I couldn't maintain it, of course, and the others did most of the work coming in, but I'd played my part and we finished second.

The Dunhill Cup was a strange tournament. For instance, we learned that when a three-man team wins one match and halves the other two it hasn't won 2–0. That was the case in England's quarter-final with Japan. Nippon celebrations at getting into the final were cut short when they were told that the two matches finishing in halves had to go to extra holes because there were no half points. When England won both play-offs they were declared the winners. The unavailing protests of the Japanese were quite understandable. Of course, it just had to be Mark James, my pro-am partner, who won at the fourth extra hole to sink the Japanese.

After the main season ended with Ian Woosnam crowned king of Europe at Valderrama, feeling the furrow on my skull, I returned to El Bosque for the Benson and Hedges Mixed Team Championship. Another pro-am place came my way. My partners were Carl Mason and Trish Johnson. We played reasonably well and both the pros stayed calm when the head of my four-iron spun off on impact during the round, whistling over a spectator's head to avoid fate repeating itself with another split cranium at El Bosque. It was a hilarious tournament. Brian Barnes and Laura Davies played together and probably would have won if Laura had been able to concentrate totally. Brian, imbued with the 'spirit' of the occasion, had promised her a kiss every time they made birdie. It was quite a sight watching Miss Davies flee at the appropriate moments, chased by the determined Barnes.

The following week, the World Cup of Golf at the spectacular Grand Cypress resort at Orlando in Florida brought the curtain down on my most hectic year of all time as a golf journalist.

## FOUR

# COMINGS AND GOINGS IN MADRID

LIFE IS FULL of great mysteries. Why do Portuguese men rarely put their arms in the sleeves of their jackets? Why would anyone in their right mind want to brave bitter cold over the windswept links of Rye, as the members of the Oxbridge golfing societies do in the President's Putter in the first week of January? There I was, listening to 'All Our Yesterdays' from ancient Light and Dark Blues and tussling for the secretary's phone with someone wanting to either tell the world they were through to the next round or put a bet on the two-thirty at Towcester. Rye, on this occasion crusted with frost and flayed by a rapier wind, provided my curtain-raiser to the 1991 season. As I'd found on my three previous visits, 'Lord Ted' Dexter could be relied on for a good yarn, but it was a much younger graduate who took the honours, a plus-two handicapper Light Blue Brian Ingleby from just down the road at Deal. While out watching him win, I managed to slip on a freezing bank and put out my back so badly I had to be almost dragged to the secretary's office in a fireman's lift to write and file my copy. I was in such agony with spasms every time I tried to negotiate the gears in my car to go home, I had to wait for painkillers (as a martyr to misfortune like this I kept a supply with me) to kick in before I could drive, extremely gingerly, the 40 miles or so home. It was a good job my fall came during the Putter final, because I was out of action for ten days. I had aggravated an old war wound, originally incurred when slipping on a soggy cheese sandwich in a multi-storey car park in Nottingham.

While my back had recovered by the time I set out for my first tour event of the year, the Girona Open at Pals on the Costa Brava, the bank manager was far from happy. Trouble was, my mainstay client, UPI, was on the verge of bankruptcy and they had no way of paying me. Dabell was insolvent, too. I had a decision to make, either tell UPI that I couldn't carry on working without pay and risk losing a year's money, or soldier on and hope that I would get paid eventually. I took the latter course and so entered my third term freelancing full of trepidation. Out of the blue (green, as it happened), though, came salvation from Ireland. The *Irish Independent* and the *Cork Examiner* both wanted full-time stringers (week by week freelance reporters), so I took them both on and began a wonderful eight-year relationship that brought great writing rewards and financial rescue.

I had also begun working on the tour for BBC Radio Kent, after I'd visited their Chatham studio to talk about my book. I was grateful for Paul Way, from Tonbridge in Kent, playing well, so I had plenty to talk about on air. Radio Kent (pay of £35 a week) was always a labour of love. The money didn't matter. It was worth more than the peppercorns I picked up just to learn how to ad-lib frantically on-air when things invariably went wrong.

If I had plenty to write and talk about for Ireland and Kent at the opening tournament of the year, then my cup was full to brimming at the next event, the Mediterranean Open at St Raphael on the Côte d'Azur. Ian Woosnam won the tournament, but that was only part of the story. We had no less than six holes in one during the week – and Ireland's Eamonn Darcy had two, both at the same hole, the 15th, the 'Lady of the Lake'. He did it in the first round about 30 seconds before I arrived, breathlessly, from broadcasting miles away in the press room. But then, in the third round on the Saturday, I was there when he did it again. After this one went in, Darce called me across and said: 'There's my car for the hole in one,' pointing down into the depths of the lake where a rusting old Renault lay, about 20 ft under. He never did get any great prize for a remarkable achievement on tour of two aces in three days. The line to Radio Kent buzzed. Mike McLean snatched defeat from the jaws of victory when he let in Woosnam right at the death – typically just after I had put my size 10 in it on air. 'Mike McLean surely has this one wrapped up now,' I'd gushed to my Kentish audience when 'Knobby', as he was affectionately known on tour, held a four-stroke lead with only three holes to go. Over the years, Knobby has had his share of disappointments like that and proved almost as accident-prone on the course as I was off it.

It was at this tournament that I fashioned a reasonable working relationship with the scourge of the golfing press, Ronan Rafferty. I'd missed the chance of talking to him when he came in after his first round at midday, so off to the practice range went I. Not wanting to disturb him, I waited patiently for a good hour, not letting him out of my sight so that I had some kind of interview for that night's papers, even foregoing lunch. When he'd hit his last ball I pounced. 'Have you been waiting all that time for me?' said Ronan. 'Well, I'm impressed.' He was as good as gold with me after that, supplying me with a string of stories – until he felt I'd overstepped the mark a few years later.

My first trip to Majorca followed, where I would stay in a cheapish hotel arranged by our lovely little press officer, Maria Acacia Lopez-Bachiller. The Hotel Rey Don Jaime was full of Spanish wrinklies, so there would be plenty of quiet nights, I hoped. After getting my preview stories done I had a light meal in the hotel before the restaurant got really busy, and I retired to do the *Daily Telegraph* crossword in bed. Within about half an hour the eyelids were drooping, so I switched off the light and settled down for an early night. Within a few seconds I was wide awake, shaken from reverie by the sound of a mosquito with a whine on it that wouldn't have disgraced a Stuka. On came the light. No sign of the enemy. Off went the light. The ear-splitting whine returned and I felt a discernable nip on the back of the neck. On came the light. No sign of the enemy . . . or was there? On came emergency specs (the contact lenses were out). Could that be my tormentor on the ceiling above? Yessss! I leapt from the bed brandishing my *Daily Telegraph*. But the mossie was too quick and made off into infinity, as mossies do, able somehow to become invisible. After a few minutes I gave in, hoping the irritant had gone away. No such luck. Back came the chilling whine as soon as I turned out the light. I switched it back on, by now in a fury. I spotted the mossie in a similar place. It was no good getting up to get at him. I reached under the bed for a trainer and hurled it at my foe. I missed by several inches – but not the ceiling light. It shattered and showered me with glass, plunging me in darkness. The little overhead light didn't work either, and nor did the bathroom light. After scrabbling around in the dark for a time I went back to bed. First, though, I decided I had to confess my errant aim and ask if my lighting might be fixed the next morning.

'Señor, mes apologies,' I said to reception, 'me fuso las luminares.'

'Gratias, señor, for letting us know,' said a commendably patient voice. 'I can tell you that you have fused the lights of the whole floor. We have an electrician fixing the fuses at this moment. Your lights will be back soon.'

I was lucky not to face expulsion from the Rey Don Jaime, or at least a sizeable extras charge, possibly because I went on the attack the next morning and complained about a plague of mosquitoes in my room. I kept the windows closed from then on and suffered the stifling and stale air for the rest of the week. Fate had not finished with me in Majorca, however, and nor had flying objects. The airline I'd flown with, Air Europe, went bust on the Sunday and I was stranded. To add further red to my bank account, I had to buy another ticket with Iberia Airways, which cost three times more for a single to get home than the return had with Air Europe. This might be why they went bankrupt.

I had to stifle a guffaw when I saw a little crocodile of out-of-step army cadets wending its way around the fringes of La Moye in the Jersey Open. Remarkably, only that week I'd been told an anecdote about the inimitable Jack Statter of *The Sun* when he was reporting at La Moye some years before. Jack was totally incorrigible. He had been startled by a similar cadre of cadets marching in the dunes. So, short of a good story, he went with a sensational yarn about the Jersey Open being disrupted by army manoeuvres. A mystified Ministry of Defence was baffled, because no such exercises were scheduled. Sensing a possible public relations disaster, a colonel was sent hotfoot to Jersey to investigate. They couldn't find Jack when the colonel demanded to know who was responsible for the hyperbole. It was his day off.

The affable, but too often self-effacing, Andrew Sherborne completed his maiden victory when we moved on to the Madrid Open, but I found it hard drumming up a good story for my two Irish newspapers, until I unwittingly found a scoop. When I 'doorstepped' Christy O'Connor Junior, following what he'd considered a poor second round, the hero of the 1989 Ryder Cup was beside himself with his inadequacy and stormed 'That's it. If I can't play better than that, I'm packing this game in.' I reported him faithfully. Perhaps I put a little spin on things by saying in my introduction that Junior was so upset with his current form he was even thinking of hanging up his golf bag. But my Irish sub-editor really got the bit between his teeth with banner headlines reading: 'CHRISTY READY TO WALK AWAY FROM GOLF'. That one took a bit of living down when I next saw Christy. But it sold a lot of Irish newspapers.

So did David Feherty's victory in the Cannes Open. In fact, I missed my plane because of having to write so much. But I wasn't as badly off as Feherty's caddie, Harry Tone, who arrived at the Belfast ferry terminal after his master's win to find the back of his car had been blown up. In a panic to catch the ferry after arriving late, he had parked it in an unauthorised spot and run for his boat. The police came across it and thought the car looked suspicious. When they could not contact its owner, they ordered a controlled explosion to blow open the boot. All they found were the mangled remains of the caddie's son's football and football boots.

Spain, Madrid in particular, as you will have surmised by now, has always been a turbulent, though invariably happy hunting ground. So many things happened in Spain, largely because when I first started roaming the fairways that country was hosting more events than any other. In my third year freelancing I still hardly had two pesetas to rub together, especially as I still had not been paid by UPI, who were now nearly 15 months in arrears. But the constant fear of losing a week's profit through extravagant cab fares, or trying, unavailingly, to decipher strange city-centre maps so I could

use the local transport persuaded me often to book in at hotels
which were beyond my means. That was because the players,
and more affluent members of the press, were staying at them
and there were always courtesy cars available, or buses, so you
could rely on a lift to the course and back each day. The trick
was to stay for one night, get the low-down on the bus
timetable and your location – then move into a seedy joint close
by and walk over to where either the buses went from or where
you could pounce on an unsuspecting player on his way to
practice before tee-off. I learned that one from the caddies, past
masters at this particular art, except they never stayed in the
posh hotels (unless they were at least three to a room) and
worked out their routes in and out of the city from the course
far quicker than I could.

One such hotel was the Victoria, set in a grand square which
was one of Madrid's most renowned 'tapas' bar areas. It was a
fairly classy hotel near watering holes once frequented by
Ernest Hemingway. His favourite haunt was a little piano bar
which I liked to visit in the hope that I might either spot his
ghost or at least feel a little of his talent rubbing off on me.
One night's stay at the Victoria with *desayuno*, including bacon
strips with not much lean and a luke-warm paste going under
the guise of scrambled eggs (I thought 'huevos sloppo con
scratchos del porco' would be the perfect name for the dish)
cost over £60. In 1991 I still wasn't even being paid anything
like that for a week's work doing BBC Radio Kent, so a sharp
move to less impressive accommodation was called for. The
Hostal Persal was my choice, just up a little back street from
the square, within a short walk of the Victoria and among
plenty of bars. It was also obviously in the middle of that area's
red-light district, but that was no concern of mine. So I
thought. Come Saturday (an unfortunate choice of phrase), I
was exhausted. From the Wednesday night on I'd hardly had a
wink of sleep. And I'd had to pay for my room for four days
up-front. There were no 'sale or returns' on it. The trouble was
the temporary tenants. Every room but mine was being used as
a knocking-shop. It caused an unbearable noise. Doors crashed
open and shut all night as clients or purveyors went in and out
(another unfortunate phrase). I couldn't tell whether they were
coming or going (third and, I promise, last unfortunate phrase).

Consequently, I walked around the press room and the course that week looking like a zombie. On the Sunday, though, I had to be on my toes. Seve was carrying all before him. Another famous win for the Spanish maestro was on the cards with just a few holes to go. Secretly quite a few in the gallery were hoping Seve would come a cropper. Seve was a big Barcelona football fan. We were in Madrid.

Well, their hopes were realised when Eduardo Romero beat Seve. Not before a tortuous seven holes of sudden-death in a play-off, though. Play-offs are always a bit of a nightmare because they can't be fully written about until they're all over. And they can, of course, go either way. You just don't know who's going to win until sometimes an hour or more after the tournament should have finished. The fat lady keeps going back into her dressing-room until we find her a winner. Sometimes it can go on for ages. Invariably you're rushing for a plane on Sunday night anyway, and the elongation of the tournament means you're really sweating on your flight. With this one being a seven-holer, going on and on from one drama to another, I was sweating 'neaters' by the time the last putt dropped. Unlike my wealthier colleagues who were on expenses, I couldn't afford to miss the flight. The cost of a new flight the next day and an extra night's accommodation would seriously affect the already scarlet bank account. So the customary 600 words for UPI, 800 words apiece for the *Irish Independent* and *Cork Examiner*, plus two radio broadcast wrap-up recordings, were done at breakneck speed. Most of the guts of the stories were already written and just a few words to start the piece off and a few to slot into blank spaces needed to be added – then I was off like a shot. Our press officer was the long-suffering Maria Acacia Lopez Bachiller again. She had very kindly organised a taxi for myself, Tony Adamson (soon to be my BBC colleague and fellow Five Live broadcaster), and fellow freelancer Micky Britten (not wanting extra costs, like me). We scrambled into the taxi, Tony and Micky in the back, me riding shotgun. We couldn't get out. The avenue out of Club de Campo was blocked by a seething throng of cars as punters made for home after the shoot-out. This called for extreme measures. I jumped out of the cab and directed traffic, waving cars aside, ordering catering wagons to pull over and nearly knocking a motorcyclist off his bike. With a path clear at last, I dived back into the car, yelling 'Pronto, pronto, hombre; aeroporto, pronto' in my usual stentorian tones, but the final 'pronto' was offered in a sort of frantic yodel. All the time I was staring bug-eyed out of the windscreen, hoping no more traffic would block our progress, urging on the driver. When we got to the end of the avenue and the road looked clear, I gave a little sigh and turned round to draw acknowledgement and appreciation from my two colleagues, whom I thought had been admirably calm and quiet after the couple of minutes of turmoil. There was no one on the back seat. I looked in horror at the driver, hunched over a steering-wheel he was gripping with white knuckles, terrified of this pidgin-Spanish-speaking deranged hijacker, resigned to following the maniac's orders until perhaps he spotted the Guardia Civil or someone in a white coat. 'Señor, señor, mes apologies,' gibbered I. 'Mistakeo, mistakeo; me accidento cambio machina.' I looked back at the car behind. I could see Adamson had adopted the foetal position with hysterics. Britten looked largely unruffled, his face showing total comprehension: 'Mr Bean' had struck again. As we came to the turning for the dual-carriageway, I flung open the car door and leapt out, still muttering apologies, leaving a relieved private car driver to set off for the wife and ninos he thought he might never see again.

Italy was my next stop, the beautiful Lake Como providing the scenery on the way to Castelconturbia where we were to have quite an Italian Open. We nearly lost one pro, Martin Gates. He inherited his sobriquet that week of 'Pearly'. It was nearly the Pearly Gates that Martin went through after being struck by lightning while leaning on a metal fence during the tournament. He survived, and so did the press corps, although we were taken to the limits by telephone connections that refused to work at optimum times and a mystifying transport system, from down in the lakeland resort to the course, that had its own unique and instantly changeable timetable. Having been left behind on the Friday morning for the second day in a row through no fault of my own, I was still seething when the little Italian lady kindly giving out ice-creams to the press corps left me out. Mischievously, my pal Martin Hardy from the *Express*, whispered loudly behind me 'Awwh, Norm's been missed out again; nobody loves him.' 'Right. That's it. Outside, Hardy,' snarled I. Surmising that Dabell was just blustering, Hardy took up my challenge and we both went marching out of the press centre into the gardens outside the clubhouse. Our press officer, Caroline Owen, halfway through her double-chocolate cornet, came scampering after us. As we two stags readied to lock horns, she stood between us: 'Norman, you're on the air in five minutes; this is not the playground, either of you. Get back inside.' Well, we could hardly duel after that, could we?

It continued to be an uproarious week. Ian Woosnam made the news when we watched him get a hole in one, and win a very expensive car, on a par three which was right outside the clubhouse. Woosie came in but we didn't hear much of his story. That was because the godfather of golf writing, Peter Dobereiner, drowned out most of Woosie's conversation with his heavy snoring at the back of the press conference. Pete had consumed a bottle of red at lunchtime and had relaxed to comatose level after being presented with a lifetime achievement award by the Italian Golf Federation.

Ian Woosnam went back to the top of the world rankings by reclaiming his Monte Carlo Open title. Fog caused me to miss yet another Sunday night flight in Nice. However, the worrying outlay of extra hotel and the expense of a new air ticket was almost forgotten when I arrived home to find that UPI had paid up at last – 15 months' back pay, plus interest. This came just in time to prevent the Dabell freelancing business going under.

At the 120th Open Championship at Royal Birkdale I had a chance to renew acquaintances with the winner's caddie. The gregarious Pete Bender had been on the bag for Greg Norman when the Shark won in 1986 and I'd had a great interview with him for my first book. Now he'd come up with an Oz double by carrying for the 1991 Open Champion Ian Baker-Finch. I had a long chat with Pete, hoping I was going to be able to use his thoughts for a paperback update of *How We Won the Open*. Of course, our Australian customers at UPI wanted copious copy about Baker-Finch. I earned my corn that week – and now I was being paid for it!

The tournaments straight after the Open, Dutch and Swedish

events, can be a bit of an anticlimax, but that was far from the case at the Scandinavian Masters in Stockholm, where Monty won and proved finally he was going to be a force in Europe for many years. However, this year's Dabellism in Sweden happened not at the hosting Drottningholm but down among the beautiful lakes which embroider the city. With the third-round leaders not out until the Saturday afternoon, Jon Bramley of the Press Association and I decided to get in some play ourselves. The press officer kindly fixed us up with a game at Stockholm Golf Club, so we arose at the crack of dawn, forfeited breakfast and met up to take a taxi to the club. We arrived at 7 a.m. Perfect. No members would be about at that time. We could get our round over in about three hours and be back at Drottningholm before any real action began. The trouble was, nobody was around. Certainly no pro shop was open. As the taxi had driven off, we became desperate. We banged on doors and shouted. Eventually someone materialised out of a greenkeeper's shed. He spoke pretty good English and accepted we were bona fide guests and very kindly sorted us out some oldish clubs and a pair of fairly scruffy bags. He could only rustle up half-a-dozen (scuffed) balls, though, certainly no golf gloves and no tee-pegs. Bramley and I, without proper golf shoes either, looked a bit agricultural but we were just grateful we could get on the course. We didn't want to have to wait until the clubhouse opened a couple of hours later. A rake around in the waste bin at the first tee produced a scorecard (in two parts after being torn up by its owner) to help with yardage and pars, and a little scouting provided us with a few broken tee-pegs. And despite our make-do-and-mend equipment, Bramley and I had a pretty good game. I was one-up when we came to the 15th. However, by then, not unnaturally given our flat-soled shoes on heavy dew and lack of course knowledge, we only had one ball left apiece. I hit first and missed the green well to the right with a pond in between. Tough shot to come.

Bramley then actually found the pond. 'Well, that's that then,' he said. 'I'll have to concede. I don't have another ball.'

'Well, let's just check where it is,' said I. 'You might be able to fish it out.' When we peered into the pond we saw Bramley's ball dry but sitting on a little crusty mud-flat. 'You can get at that,' I encouraged.

'Not on your life, mate,' rejoined the cowardly Bramley. 'I'm not chancing that mud. No, I concede.'

Driven by my British sense of fair play, I reminded Bramley there were still three holes to come after this, and I was in a pretty bad spot myself anyway.

'I don't care. I'm not going in,' insisted Bramley.

'Well, I'm not winning that way,' said I, launching myself from the safety of the bank to retrieve his ball. 'See, the mud's dry.' In fact it was beginning to give. And as I moved to within a yard or so of the errant ball, suddenly my feet were sucked under in a slurp of foul-smelling black stuff. I tried to extricate myself and merely overbalanced, causing me to sink deeper. I was stuck fast, and turned back to look to Bramley for salvation. None was likely in the immediate future. He was horizontal with hysteria, no use to man, nor beast. As, thankfully, I appeared to bottom out waist-deep, Bramley eventually regained some control and checked whether his driver might reach me. It was a sand-iron's length short. He went away to scrabble around in the bushes and returned with a tree branch which he manoeuvered towards me. At this juncture the first people we'd seen since the greenkeeper appeared and, after assessing the situation – me slurping to safety, helped by a still giggling Bramley – bellowed: 'Can we come through?' As they approached the green, with me trying to scrape the bulk of the stinking mud off, I heard one of them say: 'Don't worry; I told you they were English.' After a miserable trek back to the clubhouse, I had to buy shirt, trousers and socks from the pro shop. I had much to live down when we made it back to the tournament. Bramley never could keep a secret.

We were approaching crunch time for Ryder Cup selection. The final event to count for points, the German Open at Dusseldorf in late August, was, thus, a tournament within a tournament. But it was a player who didn't even play in Germany who provided me with my most dramatic story. Eamonn Darcy was in what was felt to be an unassailable position in the Ryder Cup table, so he went fishing at home instead. As the results unravelled on the final day, though, Eamonn lost his place to David Gilford by just £58. I was in a terrible flap. It was all right reporting the facts. But I needed to talk to Darcy about missing out at the death. How was I going to get hold of him on a fishing trip? Somehow, through the *Irish Independent*'s tracker system, we managed to locate Darce. By now we were good friends. It was not the sort of story I enjoyed writing at all.

A fortnight later I was in Ireland again, covering the Walker Cup. Stars of the future were on show in the biennial amateur encounter between Britain and Ireland and America, like Phil Mickelson. He got into trouble for a throwaway line about Irish colleens. It was a real storm in a teacup, but the ultra-polite lefthander had to go on national television and apologise. I wrote about it feverishly for UPI. But when I went to send the story and everything else I'd compiled by modem to London, which would be routing urgently to waiting American clients, my laptop showed completely empty files. The gremlins had visited me and wiped my computer of everything. It takes great strength of mind to gulp and start again, I can tell you, especially when you know you don't have time now to rewrite anyway. I had to unscramble my panicking brain and ad-lib everything to a very patient and understanding colleague in the UPI office.

Totally shattered after that experience I went back to my hotel, the Burlington in Dublin. Of course, I was dreadfully late. The restaurant was just closing. 'Sure I'm sorry, sohrr, but my brutther has just had a double by-pass operation and I have to get to the hospital to see him, so we're closing now,' said the head-waiter. 'Oh, I'm sorry to hear that. Couldn't you please ask the kitchen for something for me before you go, though?' With that I slid over five punts I could ill-afford. It did the trick. I was shown to a table. Just as my stuffed garlic mushrooms turned up, an even later client came into the restaurant. My friendly waiter leapt over and said to him: 'I'm sorry, sohrr, but my brutther has just had a triple by-pass operation and I have to get to the hospital, so we're closing now.' With his brother's operation getting more serious by the minute, I guessed he would need slipping ten punts this time.

It turned out that Eamonn Darcy and I were in the same boat. I missed the 1991 Ryder Cup as well. As our American bureau was covering the event, UPI needed me at the Austrian Open, which was taking place at Salzburg around the same time instead. I watched in misery as Bernhard Langer missed the five- or six-footer that denied Europe at Kiawah Island, crowded around the television in the press officer's room. Some were weeping. But Langer is such a resilient man. Within three days he not only agreed to do an interview with me for *The Independent* on the missed putt that earned America the Ryder Cup, but was quite bullish with his reasons. Bernhard was adamant spike marks had diverted his ball – and I wasn't arguing. The incredible German then went out and won the German Masters.

At end-of-term time at the Volvo Masters, the week went slowly downhill, or rather faster than I wanted when my chair collapsed in the press-centre, causing my January back problem to flare up again. Then I was in total disarray as I succumbed to a bout of Costa Collywobbles. I was explaining my tummy trouble on my press room phone to my wife during a quiet moment on Saturday afternoon when I became aware of a furious rapping on the perspex screen of a radio booth behind me. When I looked behind I could see the BBC World Service's John Fenton throwing what looked like an apoplectic fit. Couldn't be anything to do with me, thought I, as I turned around and continued the dissertation on my bowels. The rapping became louder. I decided to end the call and investigate. When I peered behind the curtain it was to find a slumped Fenton, perspiring freely, rattling through his broadcast. After finishing his piece, he slammed down his mike and said (rather gruffly, I felt, to an innocent): 'The world does not want to know that Norman Dabell has the shits.' Somehow, our lines had become inexplicably crossed. My discourse on said bowels had been going out on the World Service.

From bowels to bladders. My final event of the year was most noteworthy for one unfortunate act by Ian Woosnam. In the World Cup of Golf in Rome, Woosie and partner Phillip Price were on the brink of winning for Wales. Then, towards the end of their final round, Woosnam was just dying for a wee-wee. Spotting a course toilet near the green, he picked up his ball and ran for it. The only trouble was, Woosie forgot to mark his ball in his mad dash to the portaloo. There was no free relief. Penalty was incurred. Wales lost the World Cup by a stroke to Sweden. There was an embarrassing few moments for me, too. Each night we journalists met up in the bar of our Rome hotel for a drink before finding a restaurant. I was always last there, of course. On the final night, with all my colleagues gathered and waiting, I swung on to my chair and ordered a gin and tonic from the waiter at the end of the bar. No response. I often thought I could somehow become invisible when asking for drinks at bars, still do. So I raised my voice slightly. Still no action. I was being ignored. Rather angrily I shouted, 'A sodding gin and tonic – *please!*'

At that point Michael Williams from the *Telegraph*, hardly able to contain himself, came over from my doubled-up comrades to tell me: 'You're talking to a mirror, Norman. The barman's away serving a table.' To rest my eyes, I had taken out my contact lenses and I was too vain to wear my standby glasses when I came down from my room to meet the boys. I had been getting upset at my own reflection.

FIVE

# PLASTERED

THE EUROPEAN TOUR and I were both breaking new ground at the start of the 1992 season as we flew to Thailand for the Johnnie Walker Asian Classic. Bangkok wasn't totally new to me, as I'd paid a call there in 1965 on HMS *Falmouth*. When we press men were sitting at lunch on the Tuesday, I rather stupidly informed everyone of my previous trip.

I was asked by Renton Laidlaw, 'What were you when you last visited Bangkok, then, Norman?'

Off my guard, I cheerfully replied: 'A Radio Operator, Second Class.'

'Nothing changes then, Norm,' chuckled Micky Britten.

I've never really forgiven Mr Laidlaw for allowing my arch-rival to get one up on me. Still stinging from derision, I rather backed up Britten's dig when I ended my first broadcast of the week by saying: 'This is Norman Dabell in Bangkong.'

The Asian Classic was quite an experience. When we arrived at the Pinehurst course we were amused to see a huge billboard of Ian Woosnam, considered the top attraction, outside the course entrance. It was not a flattering likeness because Woosie was depicted in this massive portrait as an Asian, complete with almond eyes. Woosie did his best to live up to his hero status, but fell foul of the steam-hammer heat and humidity. Plenty of players suffered and the press were not much better off, sitting two to a desk and actually finding relief by going out on the course to watch golf instead of bickering over elbow-room. Filing the copy and ensuring it had arrived proved highly

68

frustrating as we were eight hours ahead of Britain and Ireland. The *Cork Examiner* never did quite come to terms with the time difference and twice woke me at 3 a.m. to enquire what had happened to my story – filed some nine hours beforehand. And the *Irish Independent* somehow traced me to the gala dinner in Bangkok's plushest hotel at midnight (interrupting me during a live Dionne Warwick big number) to tell me most of my story had garbled in the system and could I file it again? It meant another ad-lib job over the phone and a hope that memory had served me well.

My really uncomfortable moment, though, came during one of the sumptuous clubhouse luncheons laid on for the press. I swallowed a whole red chilli, the really white-hot type. I came close to needing mouth-to-mouth resuscitation, except no one was prepared to get their lips burnt off. It caused Michael Williams from the *Telegraph* great hilarity. Williams had no room to talk when it came to mishaps, however. After the very same lunch, Mike went up to the clubhouse balcony to intersperse watching some of the play at the 18th with reading a three-day-old *Telegraph* while he enjoyed his pipe. When one of the players called up to him, he leaned over to reply, and dropped his specs over the balcony. That evening, when writing his copy, he complained of heavy blurring in his left eye. So he went to a 24-hour optician – who quietly explained, after an eyesight test and check of his glasses, that one of his lenses was missing, dislodged after its fall from the balcony.

If Mike were alive today I'm sure he would have had a similar book as this one in mind. He could have easily matched me with Williamsisms. He was my forerunner. At an Epson Grand Prix at Chepstow, Wales, Mike wrote in the *Telegraph*: 'Here at St Pierre, with the Forth Bridge in the background . . .' When he came in to work that morning, he was asked, 'What's this "Forth" Bridge, then, Mike?' He said: 'Oh God, no. They haven't put a "u" in it, have they?'

Ronan Rafferty really was at the top of his game at the start of the year and Seve had to pull out all the stops to beat him in the Desert Classic at the remarkable Emirates club in Dubai, clawed from desolation and watered by oil millions. Ronan continued to play awkward with the press. I became the official

passer-on of Ronan Rafferty yarns. As he never read papers, so
he said, I wasn't too worried about him wondering how other
publications had got information he'd given to only me. The
interview that sticks in my memory, though, didn't concern
Rafferty but Nick Faldo. Only Micky Britten and I were
around when Faldo came in with a decent second round score
(lunchtime, I guess, and the lunches at the Emirates were
spectacular). Micky, at about 5 ft 2 ins, and me, at about a foot
taller, stood, sweating in shorts, outside the recording tent.
Faldo opened the flap and peered imperiously down at us. 'I
see the world's press has gathered for me, then.' Never one to
take sarcasm like that lying down, Britten turned and walked
off, leaving me to represent the world's press.

It was a week when the sheikhs really looked after the
players and press at the extraordinary oasis that is Dubai. As
well as trips up the Gulf on lavishly appointed dhows, there
was the desert party. This is a fabulous affair enacted every
year in dunes lapped by the waters of the Gulf, with exotic
foods, finest champagnes and wines (no alcohol bans at those
sort of parties), plush carpets to sit on, hookahs to smoke – and
belly dancing. I was given an unexpected feature on the
pleasures of the desert for the *Cork Examiner* when Eoghan
O'Connell and John McHenry decided not only to give the
belly dancing a go, but me permission to write about it. The
two Cork men were for many years my raison d'être for being
an *Examiner* correspondent. There was an ignominious end to
the evening. We nearly had to call up the local fire service to
release Micky Britten, jammed half in and half out of our
locked bus window when we found we had no driver to get us
back to the hotel. And Jock MacVicar of the *Scottish Express*
spent the journey back, when we did get underway, terrified he
was going to have a hand lopped off in punishment after
discovering he had accidentally walked off with his knife, fork,
and spoon in his jacket top pocket.

There was only time for a brief night in a Horsham motel
before returning to Gatwick to fly out to Europe for the
Turespana Masters at the Paradores course in Malaga. I felt a
little like a celebrity when Vijay Singh won. Vijay still
remembered my header at El Bosque every time he saw me. At
his winner's press conference this time, when he walked in to

the interview area he stopped off to pat me on the head and said: 'Looked for you on the 11th.' It was quite a week, not least because of the noisy colony of parakeets at Paradores. I did at least two stories on players claiming they had three-putted and dropped shots because of a sudden screech. And I was actually there when Knobby McLean grumbled at his caddie for not keeping the macaws quiet after he had watched his ball arc into trouble off the tee. Knobby didn't have much luck that week when I was around. On the first day, I swung open the front door of my course apartment to find myself no more than a few feet from the green on which he was putting in the first round. The movement caused him to step back from his putt, which was only about four feet. Yes, he missed it. I'd had no idea my room was so close to the course, having entered it in the dark the night before from a back door.

I was on a lengthy run in Spain. From Malaga I flew to Tenerife, on to Valencia, thence to Majorca and from that island over to Barcelona. By the time I'd come towards the end of this marathon run, I thought my Spanish had marginally improved. Not enough, though. The Hotel Gitar in Salou on the Costa Brava was alive not, for once, with mosquitoes but with tour players and press. And, great news, we were on a peppercorn rate that would help me to show a handsome profit for that week's Girona Open up the mountain at the breathtakingly picturesque Mas Nous – well, beautiful when you looked down on the Costa Brava coastline. I had a very presentable room with balcony and, on finishing my Wednesday previews in good time, decided to sit outside and enjoy a piccolo of Cava. With the sun quite strong I decided to strip to my Y-fronts (pre-boxer-short days, this) and enjoy the fruits of my mini-bar. I did some wandering around on the balcony as well and noticed that we were opposite similar balconies. My activities were interrupted by a bang on the door. It was a male receptionist. From what I could make out, he had come to warn me not to wander about outside naked. I deduced that by the way he kept gesticulating in the testiculatory area. Someone, it seemed, had complained. I protested, but it fell on deaf ears. He went. I could only surmise it was a case of mistaken identity or perhaps the slats of the balcony were covering up my Y-fronts, giving the appearance of me being nude.

On the second night I was conscious of a constant drip-dripping in the en-suite bathroom. I pulled the pillow over ears, but to no avail. Drip-drip it went, a double-whammy. I had it timed at every three seconds. Finally, I couldn't stand it any more and rose. It was coming from the cistern. I wrenched the toilet top off and inspected my torturer. Ah, that was the problem: ballcock too loose and causing a constant flow of water which then found a level and then slowly drained off. Hence the drip-drip. With a flourish I raised the ballcock arm. It snapped off. Water spurted everywhere. I was soaked. The water cascaded all over the bathroom. I slammed down the lid but in a few seconds it overflowed all over the floor. There was no door-step to the bathroom. The very room was threatened – and then what? In a few moments there was half an inch of water covering the floor, with me sticking in my arm and trying to stem the obdurate flow. Nothing could stop it. I could do no more than leave it to gush, beating a retreat from the soggy tiles to recruit assistance. I grabbed the phone and screeched 'Agua, agua, es gone loco; pronto, señor, pronto . . . por favor.'

A voice, obviously belonging to a hall porter rudely awakened from his 2 a.m. siesta, enquired 'Que?'

Frantically searching the bottom of the now closed bathroom door for signs of impending overflow, I again offered: 'Emergencia. Agua, agua, es loco!'

The voice now seemed a little more awake when it said, 'Si señor, si, si.' This time Manuel had surely comprehended my plight. Within a couple of minutes, by which time there was definitely a damp patch forming just under the bathroom door, there came a rap on my room door. I rushed to open it for my emergency plumber. He stood there holding a tray – on which sat a large bottle of water.

The Castelgandolfo course in Rome is set spectacularly in the huge crater of an extinct volcano outside the Eternal City, underneath the Pope's summer residence. It is one of the few courses in the world where you can see every hole (aided by binoculars for some of the distant ones) from the balcony of the clubhouse. And the clubhouse itself is remarkable, built on several levels. To get up and down from the press room in the bowels of the building, you step into a sort of dumb waiter to elevate yourself straight to the balcony. With busy pressmen and players who soon found out it was a short cut to the locker-room, there was plenty of chaos going on most days. There was also outrage when the organisers came in on the Wednesday morning to discover somebody had broken into a storeroom and stolen all the pro-am freebies and prizes, not inconsiderable booty. The Italian press officer was amused until he came in on the Thursday morning to find his beloved press snack and drinks bar had been raided, too. Gone were two dozen bottles of champagne, goodness knows how many bottles of Chianti, Valpolicella and Frascati, and even the fine cheeses we were to have enjoyed during the week.

At the Rome Masters, José Maria Canizares beat Barry Lane in a four-hole play-off, which cost me another missed flight. The short-sighted Canizares, 22 years on tour, was a delightful man to speak to, as always. He had this wonderful knack of getting out all the information you needed, but not necessarily in any order. His conversation was a perfect mix of Manuel from *Fawlty Towers* and Stanley Unwin.

Our next event was the Jersey Open, financed by Blackburn Rovers' great benefactor, Jack Walker. Jack entertained us all week and laid on a sumptuous banquet for the press, delighting the male members when he suddenly made a grab for a squealing Lewine Mair, plonking the diminutive *Daily Telegraph* reporter on his lap during the pudding. The final day of the tournament saw a mass close-down of restaurants in Jersey as every Portuguese waiter on the island turned up at the 18th at La Moye to cheer their fellow-countryman Daniel Silva to victory.

The Spanish Open in Madrid has always provided me with incidents and Andrew Sherborne added to the list when he took the title at the Royal Autombile Club Espana. And that wasn't just because he outdid the best British golfer of all time, Nick Faldo, to do it. I had taken care to book a flight on the Monday morning, given what had happened the previous year after the Spanish Open, so went out to watch the denouement of the tournament. When I left Sherborne with just a couple of holes to go, he was hanging on gamely in the face of a final round onslaught by Faldo. But the outcome of the tournament was so much up in the air, I mentally patted myself on the back as I looked at my colleagues' worried faces, knowing that the

7.40 p.m. to Heathrow waits for no man. To cover all bases, I sketched out two stories, one with the underrated Sherborne overcoming his illustrious compatriot; another on how Faldo had shown his class in Madrid with a final day charge. The other story would be about a second successive playoff in this tournament after the previous year's marathon finish. But that one couldn't be sketched out to any length at all. My fellow pressmen reached boiling point, then, when news filtered through that there was an incident at the death. Sherborne's ball had been stolen by someone in the crowd. It looked as though this was going to be a trial for even me, who was relishing a nice relaxed bottle of Rioja and a slap-up dinner in Madrid. It certainly meant scrapping pretty well everything I'd mapped out. A good half-hour elapsed before the final round finished. Obviously, the missing ball matter had been resolved because the leaderboard signified a Sherborne one-shot victory over Faldo. By this time there was visible panic amongst my colleagues. Thank goodness I hadn't booked a Sunday flight. It seemed to be an age before Sherborne came in for his interview, reporting that a steward had noticed where his ball had landed, out of sight behind a mound, and made a mental note of where it was before the thief took the ball. His word was taken and Sherborne had pulled off one of the biggest upsets in European golf at that time. I goaded my colleagues: 'Shall I go out and clear the traffic for you?'

My radio work was really getting off the ground by now. And I was assured I had a job for life by my Radio Telefís Eireann producer, if I wanted it, after one memorable broadcast a fortnight later. That was at Woburn when Christy O'Connor Junior denied Tony Johnstone a victory in the British Masters the week after Tony had taken the Volvo PGA Championship at Wentworth. It was one of the most emotional weeks of my career. Christy had survived a helicopter crash in the days before Woburn, so already many column inches had been written about him. When he then survived a spiteful sandwich on the Sunday, after the weather had thrown the British Masters into chaos, then won a play-off, it was hardly surprising I got a bit carried away on RTE. The tournament was thrown into a 36-hole finale on the Sunday when bad weather caused chaos. Christy shot a 66 in the morning, then nearly choked on his ham and tomato when turning straight round to play his final round. As he came to the latter holes and clawed his way up to the top of the leaderboard, I was left on air by RTE to commentate on the finish. A nail-biting one it was, too, with Christy somehow conjuring up a shot through a three-inch gap in a tree to force a play-off, all related excitedly by Ireland's man in Buckinghamshire. I was reasonably coherent until it came to the putt which won the trophy, offering in an emotion-laced yodel: 'Yessss. He's done it. He's walked away from a helicopter crash; he's a survivor. And now he's walking away with a hundred thousand pounds. Victory for Christy O'Junior Connor.'

The Lyon Open of 1992 proved a remarkable tournament for David J. Russell, who entered the record book as one of the few winners to complete a week without dropping a shot. It is indelible in my memory, too, and not for being ticked off on the soaking adjacent course early on the Saturday morning by the tournament director for playing with my trousers tucked inside my socks. My chagrin arose from when we were introduced to Jack Nicklaus's Golden Bear cub, his son Gary, who had decided to give the European Tour a try. Press officer Caroline Owen diligently prepared a business-like interview area in Nicklaus Jnr's honour. Gary was very introvert and was carrying out his first press conference in a dull monotone when from the third row of seated pressmen came a crash and a yelp and flash of arms, legs and notepaper. Yes, it was yet another collapsing chair betraying Dabell. I just lay there in the debris and looked up plaintively in apology to young Bear and to Miss Owen for sympathy. 'So sorry, Gary. Damn chair.' Not a flicker of emotion showed on our guest of honour's face as he merely shrugged. Our press officer, on the other hand, had to run from the interview room to avoid disgracing herself.

'I love Paris in the springtime' goes the song and it certainly always is a delight, but 1992 in the French capital also provided me with double agony. Absolutely breaking your neck for a Jimmy Riddle is bad enough. But when you're denied a shopping spree with a free 500 francs, well, that is more than torture.

Before the French Open got underway at Le National course at St Quentin in Versailles, we were invited to a party on the roof of the Galeries Lafayette near the Paris Opera House, during which the tournament's star-turn, Nick Faldo, would hit golf balls off the roof of the department store. I couldn't resist a glass of champagne or two. And there lay the rub. We were generously handed a 500-franc billet-doux by the sponsors Galeries Lafayette and invited to spend it in the store. Trouble was, it was not at our leisure. We had about five minutes to make our purchases before the coach left for the hotel. It turned into a sort of trolley dash as members of the press corps ran around trying to decide on what to blow their 500 francs. Whether it was the pressure of seeing all the goodies in front of me and not knowing where to start, or the champagne, I don't know. The minute we got down into the store I was absolutely bursting for a wee. I had to find a loo, but I didn't want to deny myself my purchase. I ran around frantically trying to find the gents, racing up and down stairs and interrogating sales staff, five of whom sent me to five different floors. My eyeballs bulged. Twice I measured my length while dashing up flights of stairs. I even went up the down escalator. No loo could be found. Then I was hailed by Renton Laidlaw, who had taken on the role of travel courier. I had to get in the bus or it would be leaving without me. But not only had I not made my purchase, I still hadn't had my wee. I then endured an agonising 45 minutes in Paris traffic jams before we arrived at our hotel. Can there be anything more pitiful than a serious shopper doubled up in pain, sitting amongst colleagues showing off proud purchases, bottles of good Armanac, boxes of snotty Brie, Lacoste shirts, even a Panama hat, when all he's got is an unused cheque? I somehow made it to the hotel. Refusing to be beaten, the next day, bright and early, I inveigled a courtesy car driver to take me back to Galeries Lafayette. Having demurred on orange juice and coffee at breakfast, I had an hour to dally over where my 500 francs should be splashed. I invested in a wonderful bright-red, floppy, designer-label cotton pullover, which is still my favourite chill-out garment. When I wear it, though, I always seem to want to spend a penny.

Curiously, in Paris a bowl of spaghetti produced more column inches than did Nick Faldo's defeat in the French Open to Miguel Martin. Mark Roe was the hurler of the spaghetti; Russell Claydon the receiver, along with Bill Malley's wife, who complained and got the pair fined. Roe is ever the extrovert. Him and Robert Lee once played a round with paper bags over their heads (á la Ned Kelly), hitting exploding golf balls. Mark's always good for a story and he will invariably seek me out to portray it, largely, I think, because of being soul mates in the accident-prone stakes. For instance, just before winning the Lancôme Trophy in late-summer of 1992, Mark was stung by a wasp, fell downstairs and sprained his ankle and then put out his elbow practising. He was my first feature piece in *Golf Illustrated* when he came on to the golf scene, having been forced to end a promising career as a high-diver after perforating his eardrum, and we've been good friends ever since.

While Mark Roe had his wasp that summer, Darren Clarke had his bee.

Monte Carlo was always the place to be during the tour year, the glitziest event of the season. We began the week with a tuxedo dinner at the famous Sporting Club and the next night press and players were all invited up to Prince Rainier's palace for a cocktail party. It was a pretty memorable experience looking down from the parapet of the Monaco palace to spot elephants and giraffes wandering around just down below in the Rainier private zoo. But it was a much smaller creature that gave me a cracking story.

I was out on the Mont Agel course during the first round, wandering between a few matches, picking up little bits and pieces about various groups which might prove useful for opening day stories. Keeping alert, I looked away from the green I was alongside to a distant hole. I spotted something that looked like a sizeable whirling dervish. It was a player. I couldn't be sure, but it looked like the burly, by now extremely animated, figure of Darren Clarke. I felt sure all was not as it should be, so I abandoned the match I was with and made for Darren's group. All was calm enough when I got to them, but I was intrigued. I managed to speak to his caddie and said: 'What on earth was going on there?'

'I'd better let Darren tell you,' said the visibly flushed bagman, who then dissolved into a fit of giggles.

I couldn't wait to speak to Darren. But you don't approach

a player for information during the action unless you know him extremely well. We were on friendly terms, but not bosom buddies, so I decided to wait until he'd finished. When he'd signed for a 66, I said: 'What happened at the 14th? You looked as though you'd been shot!'

'I had a lot of trouble with a bee,' explained a smiling Darren. He had been about to tee off when he became conscious of a strident humming and vibration at his waist. A cursory investigation discovered nothing so he played on. Then the problem grew to 500cc Yamaha proportions. There was no way he could continue, especially as there was a very angry note to the buzz by now. So Darren did no more than quickly whip off his trousers. 'It was a bee that had got stuck in the waistband. I couldn't carry on with it like that. And it could have stung me, so I had to get it out of my trousers,' added a scarlet Clarke.

I milked the story for all it was worth. 'DARREN BUZZING IN MONTE CARLO' and 'CLARKE – THERE'S A KIND OF HUM' formed the headlines the next morning. The next day Darren shot a 60 to equal the tour's best score of all time. This time the headlines read: 'CLARKE THE BEE'S KNESS IN MONTE CARLO' and 'CLARKE STUNG INTO ACTION'. The whole world wanted to know about his unwelcome visitor and how he'd disrobed on the course. It gave me quite a buzz, too.

The Rainiers used to really enjoy themselves at the Monte Carlo Open. Princess Stephanie played in the pro-am this particular week and thought nothing of enjoying a meal with the tournament winner and his caddie, Ian Woosnam and Phil 'Wobbly' Morbey, at an outside café. We spotted them, even if the society mags didn't.

July is just about the busiest month of the year, revolving around the Open Championship. This year's was an extraordinary affair as John Cook played a large part in helping Nick Faldo make it an Open hat trick. Faldo was a sight to behold as he first crumpled up in tears when he came back from the dead to defeat the faltering Cook, and then rallied to give everyone a rendition of 'My Way'. Already there had been signs of disenchantment between Nick and the Fourth Estate in Britain. The media centre was outraged when Nick announced: 'I'd like to thank the press from the heart of my bottom.'

As the summer wore on, the circus had a couple of weeks in Germany, calling in at Munich and Dusseldorf. The Arabella Hotel in Munich provided me with a worrying Tuesday night. I enjoyed a few glasses of wine in the hotel restaurant with Mark Mouland and Richard Boxall, whiling away time trying to decide whether the girls in the bar were hookers or not. Often when the tour was in town the 'brass' used to gather. At one Italian tournament, for instance, African hookers in outrageous hotpants and skimpy tops actually waved down the courtesy cars on the way in to the course. I don't know how they thought they could get any business that way. At the Arabella there was one woman who we were certain was on the game, an Englishwoman who said she, curiously, lived in Majorca. She was wearing a ridiculous porkpie hat. The boys egged her on, I was sure, with no intention of trying her wares, just having a little fun. I left for bed.

I must have been fast asleep for about an hour when I was woken by banging (oops, careless use of expression again) on my door. A voice shouted 'Hi. This is Gloria. Let me in.' I looked through the spy-hole. It was Miss Porkpie.

'No, go away, please, I have to be up early.'

'But I was told you were expecting me. You have been paid for,' she said *sotto voce*, the sultry intonation completely destroyed by her bizarre headgear. 'Please let me in.'

'Go away, you've got the wrong room.'

'No I haven't. Let me in [louder banging on the door], you've got an hour's worth.'

'Go away or I'm on the phone to security.'

Miss Porkpie capitulated. But my sleep was fitful. It didn't take much to work out who had put her up to it. Mouland and Boxall had paid the porkpie to come up and see me, not 'sometime' but that night.

In Switzerland, I awoke, up the mountain in Crans-sur-Sierre, a worried man and spent most of the European Masters last round cowering in the press tent, waiting for a tap on the shoulder from the arm of the law. Driving my hire car late on Saturday night, I accidentally turned out of a car park right instead of left. I quickly realised I was going the wrong way up a one-way street. This was pure carelessness and not because of alcohol. As I was in charge of the car I had drunk only pink gins without the gin. But because it was only about 100 metres to the junction where the road turned into two-way, and the whole of Crans seemed deserted, I decided to go for the junction instead of doing a risky three-point turn. I so nearly made it. With just a few metres to safety a car came round the bend. We met head-on, not at great speed but enough to damage the front of the car I'd hit quite badly and cause a large dent in my bumper. I was very contrite, hopping straight out and admitting to the English-speaking motorist that it was all my fault. With a little crowd gathering by now, I said I'd ring the police from a bar the onlookers had come out of. As I was walking across the road, the other car swung round my vehicle and drove off at speed. He must have been drinking and panicked at the thought of the police being called. I waited for a few minutes and then swiftly made my junction to the cheers of the onlookers before shooting off to conceal my car in my hotel's underground car park. The next day I had to come clean with my fellow hire-car passenger Tony Adamson, who was to come with me down the mountain to the airport at end of play. He spent the day almost as worried as me, not sure whether he was going to get his lift. When I escaped Crans without being apprehended, we then got lost trying to find our airport hotel and missed out on a proper evening meal. In the morning, with Adamson scampering away relieved at Geneva airport, the car was returned to the hire company – with a completely straight face. I hoped they didn't notice the dent in the bumper before I could make sanctuary from the French side of the airport. The following year, while waiting for my luggage after coming through immigration at Geneva airport, I froze when a forceful hand grabbed my shoulder from behind. Just Adamson's little joke.

There was always something cropping up to remind me of my fallibility. For instance, I forgot my wallet when trying to impress a brand-new girlfriend by taking her to the best restaurant in Versailles during the Lancôme Trophy. (By this time I was estranged from wife Jennie, who had finally had enough of seeing me for about six days a month.) The new girlfriend paid and saved me a marathon dish-wash.

As my third season treading the fairways and missing flights came towards its end, the thought of spending the last two weeks of it in Spain again, for some reason, filled me with foreboding. Perhaps I was thinking back to the last time we had a double Spanish finish in 1989 when I was nearly swept away by a flood. I don't know, something just rang a warning bell.

I didn't have long to wait for a problem to occur. When I returned to my hotel room on the Thursday night, about £75 in pesetas and sterling was missing from the drawer, where I had left it in between my shirts. I must say, my revelation was treated with utmost suspicion, not only by the hotel manager but by my press colleagues, who just thought Dabell had mislaid his dosh after one-too-many Vina Sols. That was, until Mark Garrod of the Press Association, staying at the same hotel as me, returned the next night to find he, too, had been robbed. An investigation was launched and the thief was eventually caught after a trap had been set. It was our chambermaid – who, apparently, was funding a drugs habit with her thefts.

When the press corps decided to rig up a plank from the grounds of the hotel over a ditch to give quicker access to Puerta Duquesa and the restaurants, I should have known better and had nothing to do with it. But it did save you about half a mile. However, it was one thing walking the plank when you had taken just one little livener at the hotel bar, but another thing altogether after a litre of Rioja. One night, negotiating the plank at high speed instead of inching my way across, I managed about two thirds of the way before finding myself paddling fresh air, then descending into the rock-strewn ditch. The heel didn't hurt too much that night. On Saturday morning it ached profusely and left me limping badly. But there was far worse to come.

After watching Sandy Lyle win the Volvo Masters at Valderrama and Nick Faldo crowned king of Europe for the last time, there was the usual end-of-term party. I went to bed quite late. But I made sure I'd put my alarm on to be up in plenty of time to ablute and meet up with Mark Garrod. I was to accompany him in his hire car to Malaga airport, roughly an hour and a bit away, for a flight to Madrid and the World Cup of Golf.

I was awakened by a telephone call which had no one on the

other end and, within seconds of that, a furious hammering on the door. My alarm hadn't gone off, mainly because I'd set it for 6 p.m. and not 6 a.m., possibly befuddled the night before by over-zealousness with the Tempranillo. 'We're supposed to be leaving at seven; our flight's at nine-thirty,' warned Garrod. 'It's seven now. How long are you going to be?'

'Nearly ready,' croaked I, hoping he wouldn't spot the just-woken-up-thinking-the-world's-come-to-an-end pitch to my voice. Fortunately I had packed almost everything the night before, but it took a few minutes to stuff the remainder of my belongings into my bag, swill face and gargle toothpaste, before I could present myself to reception and a fairly incandescent Garrod. I bluffed as he went back to the car, which he'd drawn up outside the hotel. 'Sorry, señor, but your credit card, it no work' was not the reaction I wanted from reception as I tried to pay my bill.

'Well, there's enough in it, try it again, for God's sake,' I growled, one eye on the revving car at the bottom of the steps. Whirr, click, whine.

'Sorry, sir, but it no good.'

'Of course it bloody good,' squealed I.

'I telephone card company, sir, maybe we do it that way.'

'Do it!'

With that, Garrod ascended the steps and said, quite fairly and understandably but chillingly, 'Sorry, Norm. Got to leave. It's touch-and-go now whether we'll make it.' Off he drove. Almost immediately came a triumphant, 'OK, sir. All okay with the card. You can sign now.' I ran from reception in the hope I could yet halt Garrod on the exit slipway. I suddenly took off, catapulted down the steps after tripping over my luggage. I felt immediate agony. The hotel staff dashed out to help. My trousers were torn and instantly bloodied. A bandage was produced and my knee strapped up. After gaining some kind of composure I knew I still had to try to make my plane and a taxi was called for me to struggle into.

When I arrived at the airport I hopped gamely towards the check-in desk to find my plane had been delayed by over an hour. Somehow I edged through into the departure lounge, where I met up with my colleagues, full of sympathy but rightly disavowing all blame. After a flight spent with my leg prone, taking up all three back seats, I lurched from the plane to arrivals. The pain was excruciating. When Patricia Davies of *The Times* helped me off with the bandage that was causing much of my suffering, my black and blue knee filled out like an inflating balloon. Patricia called for a car to pick me up from the tournament at La Moraleja, mercifully quite near to the airport. I could hardly walk. When a doctor was called I was despatched in another car to hospital. After an x-ray which discovered a dislocated knee-cap and hairline crack, my leg was put in a plaster-cast from groin to ankle. I couldn't go home, despite the fact that I could only hobble with great difficulty, using a crutch. My clients needed servicing. It was hell dragging myself up hotel stairs and in and out the course, while daily heaving myself around La Moraleja.

As I leant uncomfortably on my crutch in the queue at the airport check-in on the Monday morning, another season over but facing the prospect of being housebound for about a month, a thought crossed my mind: 'Why did it have to be the knee I fell on? If it had been my head I might have got away with it.'

# SIX

# A RIB-TICKLING YEAR

I SPENT MOST of the winter trying to get mobile, undergoing further procedures on my knee. It took ten years before it was discovered that the knee-cap had re-located in the wrong spot. As a footnote, after an operation in February 2002 to put it back, I awoke to the sound of my mobile telephone vibrating by my bedside. Even under the influence of the anaesthetic, I understood the emergency security breach message. My burglar alarm was going off. I was 40 miles away in a hospital, fresh out of theatre. My battle of wounded knee had continued for a decade.

In 1993, though, another part of my anatomy was to suffer.

The season began stylishly when, at the inaugural Madeira Island Open, the press corps was invited to stay in the renowned Reid's Hotel, a five-star edifice on cliffs above Funchal Bay. The hotel still retained nearly all its colonial traditions. It was a bit of a bind having to dress formally for dinner, but nice to bask in luxuries from a bygone era, like tiffin and pre-prandials. It reminded me of wonderful times at Raffles in Singapore when I was in the RN, another colonial hostelry that would soon be on the agenda. It was to Mark Garrod's eternal credit, after what happened in Spain the previous year, that he agreed to share a hire car with me in Madeira. The Santo da Serra golf course was halfway up the mountain that looms over Funchal and entailed a very involved car drive for those who had never been there before. Just negotiating Funchal's maze of roads and streets before trying to chose the correct way to the course took us half an hour and then we went in completely the wrong direction. Garrod just managed to halt the car as we swung around a bend that threatened to topple us all the way back down to Funchal. In recent years, the road system has been improved beyond measure to include mini-motorways and tunnels, but for our first visit it was a hair-raising experience, if breathtakingly spectacular. With my reputation, I was surprised anyone would share a car with me.

We were all offered a place in the pro-am, and myself and John Fenton of the BBC played with Mike McLean. It was wonderful to be able to strike the ball a mile in the rarified atmosphere and look down the mountain on the Atlantic. It definitely competes with Crans-sur-Sierre as our most spectacular venue. Fenton, the man who had listened dismayed to my discourse on Spanish upset tummies a few months before, proved he was just as prone to bad and good luck as me. He was rescued from certain death by freelancer Gordon Richardson, who yanked him from the very bumpers of a speeding bus. Fenton, by now a septuagenarian, stepped on to a crossing without understanding that a flashing amber light gave the bus right of way and not him. The doyen of broadcasting was making his first visit to Madeira since his Royal Navy days as a young man with his ship tied up in Funchal Bay. He has always fascinated me with his stories of BBC 'dark ages', times when he used to do the sound effects for radio plays. Mark James took the tournament honours and I proved again that bad luck doesn't always follow me around by winning a 1920 bottle of Madeira for being nearest to the flag on a demonstration par three at the new Palheiro course just being hewn out on the famous Blandy's estate. I have resisted the temptation to drink it and it still commands pride of place in my wine collection.

Before the Dubai Desert Classic got underway we were given a complimentary round over the new Creek club. This is another remarkable expanse of green in the sands, this one defined by huge dhow sails to enhance the skyline and signify its presence as a marina, compared to the massive Bedouin tents that form the buildings at the Emirates course up the road. As a part-time ornithologist, I wasn't too keen on how the gulls were dissuaded from invading the Creek course. One of the sheikhs came along with a falcon which took care of a few of them and frightened the others into the Gulf. I did a bit of frightening myself, of the labourers who were working on the banks of the lake at the 10th and 11th holes. At first they ignored my shout of 'fore' as I made to traverse the first part of the lake from the fairway of the 10th, not even looking up from their task. When my ball did a 'Barnes-Wallis' and skipped its way at speed right into one of the worker's backside, they soon got the message – and passed it on to their colleagues busy at the next hole. When I returned to play the course in 1994, all the workers downed tools and retired to a safe distance the moment I stepped on to the 10th tee.

The Desert Classic at the Emirates course was noteworthy for the emergence of a young South African who was to go on to much bigger things, Retief Goosen. He finished second behind his fellow South African Wayne Westner and it was the first time I remember hearing about Retief's reason for being perhaps the most introvert world-class player of them all. Apparently, he was quite a gregarious soul until being struck by lightning. Then he clammed up. It still takes quite a lot of cajoling to get Retief to open up.

Before we flew on to the Far East for the Johnnie Walker Classic, we played in the usual press and officials competition at the Emirates course. On a sweltering day, Tony Adamson of the BBC and I were drawn together and decided we would hire a buggy. Both of us were playing rather well. Then we lost the thread a little.

'Where's the buggy, Norm?'

'I parked it on top of the h . . . Oh gloom! It's gone. Somebody's half-inched it.'

'Don't be daft. They wouldn't just drive off in our buggy.'

'Well, it's gone.' We nipped back from the green to the top of the cart track and looked back down the other side. The group behind us were waving and shouting. Our buggy was down among them. Somehow it had slipped its brake and trundled off unaided, scattering the players on the green behind. 'How did it get down there?'

'Because you didn't put the brake on properly, silly bugger.'

'I did, too.'

'And you must have had it facing the wrong way.'

'Wrong way?'

'Well, they can't suddenly go backwards, and it hardly did a three-point turn.'

'Oh. No, I suppose not.'

'Well, you can go down and apologise.'

'Oh, all right.' Off I trudged, trying desperately to think up a reasonable story and hoping there were no broken bones.

After Dubai we made the long hop on to Singapore for another Johnnie Walker Classic. Once again it was the Nick Faldo/Colin Montgomerie road show, with Faldo first and Monty second. Montgomerie had by now earned his reputation of being a difficult customer out on the course. He could be a real Tartar with amateur photographers but I remember him walking up to one startled snapper and saying, 'Now be a good boy [he must have been in his 60s] and put that camera in your bag.' With that he took the camera off the punter, closed its pervasive shutter, and placed it in the thunderstruck man's bag.

It was a nostalgic trip to Singapore for me. The last time I had been there was in the '60s (Radio Operator Second Class). It had changed almost beyond recognition. The elite hosting Bukit club was close to where we went to service dances back then, especially to pick off the always-willing nurses for partners. Lots had changed. Bougie Street, where as a 19-year-old I used to drink copious amounts of Tiger chemical lager and watch X-rated open-air floor shows, was now just a mass of open-air cafés. Mike Williams and I took a tri-shaw back to our hotel after a meal in the Street. With such Jonahs on board, it was hardly surprising our conveyor's front tyre got a puncture.

As usual with Tenerife Opens, the press contingent was very light that year. I was covering for many concerns and that led to the usual running back and forth to the recording area from the press room, which was down in the bowels of the clubhouse. I had just picked up a great story from Christy O'Connor Junior, who had had a rules rumpus (they are always termed that way) with the tournament director, and was heading at speed along the clubhouse verandah. As I came to the corner of the building, so, at a trot as he hurried to catch his bus to the hotel, did Martin Rowley, just about the heaviest caddie on tour. We met full bore. Me at 12 stone and him at 18 stone . . . well, no contest. I rebounded off him like a ball in a pinball machine, off the verandah and down onto a fire hydrant. It knocked all the breath out of me. I couldn't even drag myself to my feet. As a stunned Rowley (mentally, not physically) hauled me back on to the verandah, it felt as though I was being played in by a giant barbed hook which had caught hold of me by the ribs. Even pressing the keys on my laptop proved agony that evening and the next morning it was difficult to prise myself out of bed to get to the airport.

I was at a pretty low ebb when my taxi wended its way through the lane leading to my house in Wiltshire. But when Bridge Cottage came in sight I reached a nadir. Outside, my car door gaped open. A drawing room window had been shored up. When I went in the house there were obvious signs of burglary – my music centre and television were missing, CDs were scattered all around. The police had already been in and kindly tidied up, but I was devastated.

There was no way I could turn around and go straight back out to the Moroccan Open so I had to hastily advise my clients I would not be there and give them names of people who might help out at the tournament in Agadir. It did at least give me a chance to get an x-ray done of my ribs. Two were broken and sprung. Not much could be done to relieve the injury, except rest. Rest? What a joke. It was going to be a painful few weeks.

One of those unique stories that pep up Saturday afternoons for the Sunday papers came along at the weekend during the Balearic Open on Majorca. The week before, 13 players, including Bernhard Langer, were fined for taking too much time over their practice rounds at El Saler near Valencia. At Santa Ponsa, Anders Gillner of Sweden, trying to outdo the eventual winner, Jim Payne of England, was told to slow down, he was going too fast! The tournament director David Probyn explained the bizarre command thus: 'It was ironic after last week, but the way things were going, we were only going to get 10 minutes of golf on the television.'

Freezing weather in Cadiz, and then Verona, hardly helped my ribs rehabilitate but there were useful painkillers to be had, like wonderful sherries and the glorious Italian spumante, Berlucci. Our trip to the Berlucci family home in Verona, though, was not as sparkling as it should have been. The bus driver got lost trying to find his way from our hotel near Lake Garda and we didn't arrive at the house of Berlucci until 11 p.m. They insisted we had the full works, though, five courses and numerous wine tastings. We left at about 2 a.m. The driver got lost on the way home. I had less than two hours' sleep before heading back for the Kronenbourg Open. The frosty air belting down from the Alps that stood sentry in the distance soon woke me up.

Italy caused more woe a few weeks later when we returned for the Rome Masters. After Jean Van de Velde and Jamie Spence took the lead (Radio Kent, now £40 per week) in the third round on Saturday, we went off to our respective hotels, me back to the lovely little guesthouse on the lake under the Pope's castle, about two miles from the course. I showered and changed into my gladrags because the Italian Federation were laying on a grand dinner at the clubhouse. It being a balmy evening and having plenty of time, I decided to walk back to the course and arrived ready for aperitifs. I didn't get a chance to walk up the stairs to the clubhouse. Micky Britten, who had stayed at the club because he had too much work to do to go back to his hotel, shouted up from the basement press room, 'You'd better forget about champagne and get down here. Jamie Spence has been disqualified.' It was like a bolt to the heart. I had filed three stories, including a large piece for *The Observer* and my usual copious copy for the agency, UPI, and done two radio recordings, one for the Radio Kent evening sports show and one looking back for that station's morning show. This was déjà-vu; 1990 Tenerife and the Olazábal dismissal. By now it was 8 p.m., four hours after Spence had finished his round and three hours after I'd done my reports. The only saving grace was that the UK was an hour behind. My laptop was back at the hotel so it was a case of scribbling and ad-libbing. One early edition was missed, but a full recovery operation was carried out. We were all in some lather, though, when we finally made it to the Federation dinner. It turned out that Spence had taken a penalty drop from a wrong point at the 15th hole and, like Olazábal three years before, had returned to the course to discover his error. The 15th hole was cursed that week. Van de Velde had the Rome Masters title in the bag but then triple-bogeyed the 15th to throw the tournament into a play-off and my flight home into doubt. After Van de Velde bounced back to claim victory in a sudden-death finish, I went hurtling off down the Appian Way – then found out my flight was delayed for three hours.

I could have done with that kind of delay when I arrived at Nice airport, with copy to file still, following a late finish in the Cannes Open. I had about half an hour to file before my flight was to be called, so I ducked downstairs to the basement where I knew there was a telephone exchange alongside the toilets. A huge virago commanded the exchange, peering down from what she considered was her machine-gun tower. In my schoolboy French I enquired breathlessly, 'Est-ils possible pour un telephon charge de transfere a Ireland, s'il vous plaît?' I didn't have any francs on me at all.

'Oui,' snapped the Amazon. 'Numèro deux,' nodding towards the second of five telephone booths.

'Merci, merci beaucoups,' panted I, hardly believing my luck that I should be so easily understood, as I glanced nervously at my watch.

On picking up the telephone a voice barked, 'Numèro?' I gabbled the number of the *Irish Independent* sports desk, reiterating 'Charge de transfere, s'il vous plaît, madame.' Within a few minutes the welcome voice of Karl McGinty, the chief sports sub-editor, greeted me. He put me through to copy and I read out my nearly illegible story, scrawled in the back seat of my 100 mph courtesy car on the way to the airport. I breathed a sigh of relief when the copytaker had taken it all and the sports desk acknowledged its safe receipt. I put down the receiver, checked my watch, and decided I just had enough time to get the introduction to my story over to the *Cork Examiner*, so they could start work on the piece, then finish it off when I landed. They had a later deadline.

When I picked up the receiver again, the juggernaut growled. 'Oui?'

'Un charge de transfere, madame.'

'Numèro?'

I responded. There was a much longer wait this time. Just

as I was about to give up, knowing my flight must have been called by now, the voice of Tom Ahern, the *Cork Examiner*'s sports editor, provided me with salvation. I explained the situation, passed on a few paragraphs, finished the call and made for the exit, offering my formidable charge d'affaires a cheery, 'Merci beaucoups, madame.' I hadn't had her down for a swift mover but the femme fatale was out of her office quicker than a jacques in a box. My way was barred by her huge frame. She was beside herself (a terrifying thought: two of them) with indignation, demanding 'payee, payee' in a booming tone that might have graced the foghorn on South Stack Lighthouse. I kept saying over and over again, 'Mais j'ai le charge de transfere, madame, charge de transfere. Pas de payee, pas de payee. Je suis skint; pas des francs!' Imagining I had heard the last call for Heathrow, I was by now gibbering almost hysterically. The next thing that happened was that she reached up to her desk and grabbed her telephone, calling the airport gendarmerie, still barring my exit. Within a minute a gendarme arrived, listened to his fellow countrywoman and repeated the exchange overseer's demand in an aggressive tone, worryingly undoing the stud on his revolver holster.

I was in the midst of going through my transfer-charge call paces again, producing little more than a few shrugs and a chilling disinterested look in the gendarme's eyes, when a man appeared from the gents toilette, a very aristocratic homme, and said, 'Monsieur, are you English? Are you in trouble?' I agreed that I was. 'Tres. Tres.' He allowed me to explain, then turned to the gendarme and the virago and treated them to a volley of what I took took to be fairly in-your-face stuff. The opposition backed down. I never found out whether the exchange operator was pulling a stroke or misunderstood me. I was allowed to leave. I raced up the stairs in time to hear my name receiving its final call and a reminder my luggage would be taken off the flight if I did not appear in the next minute. I scampered and slid to the gate, got mightily scolded by the BA attendant, and ran down the corridor into the plane. As I made my seat, I received an embarrassing standing ovation from fellow tour passengers. 'You'll never believe what happened down in the toilets,' gulped I over my shoulder.

'Oh yes we would,' came the chorus.

When the Spanish Open came around, I'd again taken the precaution of booking a Monday morning flight, and right away I was glad I had. Not for the first time, and by no means the last, the rain in Spain stayed mainly over we unfortunate tour followers for a couple of days. It meant play finishing desperately late for both the first two rounds. Nick Faldo, who again lost out in Madrid, this time to Joakim Haeggman of Sweden, was only able to putt out to end his second round with the assistance of the huge, brightly-lit scoreboard alongside the final green. Even though I was not getting work finished until about 9 p.m., dinner was never a problem. The Spaniards don't even think about putting paella past lips until 10 p.m. at the earliest. I found a splendid restaurant that was really a huge banqueting place for the masses and ate there late every night. You sat in huge rows at banqueting tables, and the place specialised in sparkling rough cider, really medieval. The noise in the place was deafening by about midnight and how the waiters managed to keep a check on each individual's *quenta* was beyond me. My hotel was just across the road, which was just as well. I could never handle the 'scrumpy' when I was in the RN, and this hostelry's cider went to my head every time. On the Saturday night it nearly got me locked up. Relaxed and feeling at peace with the world, I swiped my key-card in the door of my hotel room, which was right outside the lift. It refused me entry twice. The sneering little red light that comes on, as opposed to the welcoming green one, when key-cards which are supposed to work but don't, is like a red rag to a bull to me. On countless occasions I have collected my key-card from reception when I've checked in, struggled into a lift with my luggage – or worse, clambered up endless flights of stairs like a disgruntled packhorse – and then found my key, only cut moments before, denies me entry. It sends me wild. My alter-ego takes over. I am capable of any crime in a mad few minutes until I have resignedly made my way back to reception to report a duff key-card. Then you have to repeat the feat all over again. Sometimes you nearly crack when the receptionist insists there is nothing wrong with the card after trying it out on her endorsing machine, and it happens again after you've trundled all the way back to the unresponsive door. That has happened many times too. Well, when my key-card produced red for a third time on this occasion, my rosy feeling from the cider deserted me. Not gradually, but in a fit of thumps and curses at the afflicted key-card. Another forlorn try, and I gave the door a massive kick and turned to take the lift to berate reception. As I did, a diminutive, roly-poly chappie with his glasses not quite in line with his eyes and sporting a precarious looking bath towel opened the door. Whether he had been caught out during an illicit assignation or not, I don't know. But he looked a worried man. I suppose I would have been if some raving lunatic had tried to smash down my door. As he whispered something in terrified Spanish, my eyes shot to the number above him. I had got out of the lift one floor too early.

Talking about whispering, that brings me neatly to David Gilford, the perennial quiet man of golf. In Modena, the week after Madrid, Gilford, paradoxically, caused an uproar with the Italian press. The Cheshireman came in for a press conference after leading the Italian Open second round and the British media, knowing how he talks in whispers, hutched their chairs forward to the interview stage so we could hang off every word. As usual, David gave us his story and then we wrote a different one, based around his dairy farm in Crewe, milking his unique hobby for all it was worth. When we all got up to go after David's conference, there were vacant faces among the Italian press that turned to fury when they realised it was all over and they'd not heard a thing. The interview had come straight after the usual three-hour Italian lunch and, because of David speaking *sotto voce*, la stampa had been jabbering among themselves while it was going on.

At least I disturbed only one guest in Madrid. In Hamburg it was the whole hotel. We were at Gut Kaden, a sprawling venue set in rolling arable land about 20 miles from the port city, for the Honda Open. This was eventually won by Sam Torrance after a four-man play-off, Sam's third win in less than three months. I found a charming little family-run guesthouse in a small market town right in the country called Barmstedt. The week didn't start off well. The media were at first denied the usual facility of courtesy cars by a promoter who was obviously unsure where his bread was buttered. That led to several scuffles when taxis were twice commandeered before getting anywhere near waiting pressmen on the

Wednesday. On Thursday the promoter relented. But there was more bickering when the courtesy car we were allotted had to stop off at three different hotels to drop off the four pressmen. It meant a lot of waiting around until the media quartet were complete each night. Also, my hotel was in exactly the opposite direction to the other three, so I was last drop-off.

This led to me arriving back at my hotel very late on the Friday night. I had retained my key, just as well for there was no night porter at such a small establishment. I fumbled my way along the corridor and inched up the stairs. Not wanting a repeat of my Madrid fiasco, I pressed the nightlight button on the landing so I could identify my room. At its lack of response, I pressed again, a little harder. All hell broke loose. It was a fire-alarm button, rather ambiguously placed, I thought. As I stood with apologetic outstretched arms, the real landing light now beaming accusingly, the be-curlered landlady raced up the stairs as numbed but obedient guests started to turn out of their rooms, ready to muster in the car park. Strangely, after the hue and cry died down and the guests were safely back in bed, the landlord and landlady, despite talking little English and completely bewildered at my stabs at German, almost saw the funny side of it. And they were ready to admit that the fire alarm should really have been placed where Dabell couldn't find it. We had a couple of schnapps to calm the nerves and then, the landlord, springing across to take charge when the night-light suddenly went out, marshalled me to my room. When I came up with a handful of free tickets for the golf the next day the incident was forgotten and I have stayed at the Barmstedterhof on many occasions since. I'm always given a room in the little annexe, though, just in case. It doesn't have a corridor fire bell, only room sprinklers.

I was waiting down at the players' score recording area by the 18th hole at Gut Kaden that week, and watched Joakim Haeggman of Sweden in action on the final green. His putting wasn't any great shakes and you could see he was absolutely fuming as he walked to the recording tent. Perhaps to assuage his anger, before he went into recorders he threw his ball down into the mud, then jumped up and down on it just as you'd imagine Basil Fawlty would have done if he'd three-putted the last. Haeggman would not stop until the ball had been stomped completely under and then he stepped back with a satisfied but wicked gleam in his eye. As he turned to march into recorders a timid voice in broken English, from a totally bewildered young German lad, one of the youngsters that always gather for mementoes from the pros at tournaments, said: 'Sir. I would be asking for your ball. Is not good now?' Haeggman paused, turned back, called his caddie over and pulled out his pitchfork from his bag, then dug in the spot where he had violently laid his ball to rest. He excavated successfully, cleaned the ball on his towel and handed it to the lad, his ire completely evaporated. Jocky was soon boiling again, though. After signing his card he was handed a letter from the tour, telling him he would be fined for swearing loudly the previous week. Accompanying the letter, the tour's proof apparently, was a *Guardian* newspaper clipping with several lines highlighted in marker pen. Dai Davies had written how remarkable it was that a Swede should utter his profanities on the golf course in English. Haeggman strode out of the recording tent and headed straight for the press room to confront the writer who'd shopped him. He was out of luck. Dai was nowhere to be found.

Perhaps the most startling revelation by a golf professional in all my years freelancing came from Brian Barnes at the 1993 Jersey Open at La Moye. The tour's great rebel, and a man who could have drunk Dean Martin under the table, announced he had taken the pledge. 'I've been waiting for this moment,' said Brian after shooting a 65 to share the lead at La Moye. 'I've given up the booze.' Pressmen had to pick themselves up off the floor. Brian went on to tell us how he'd despaired so much because of drink that he'd driven to Beachy Head with the intention of committing suicide. He was just about to release his car's hand-brake, when he pulled himself together and took the most momentous decision of his life. Not a drop would he drink again, insisted the player who once won the Haig Whisky event and nearly cleaned out the sponsors. And as far as I know, he hasn't touched the bottle since, carving out a whole new career on the seniors tours. It was such a remarkable feat and such a radical change that it was, arguably, the golfing story of the year. I thought back to earlier in the year when he'd been proud to talk about winning a play-off after drinking the club bar dry, and to the Lancôme Trophy two years before when he was rumbled for carrying either vodka or gin in his water bottle. I'd still admired him, especially how he could somehow play on autopilot because of pure natural talent. So I'd gone out to watch how he could cope with swigging on his 'water' bottle at St Nom la Breteche and finished up nearly collapsing with laughter at the 17th green. He was being continually interrupted by a noisy child a woman was carrying in her arms, and had to step back from his putt several times. In the end Brian walked across the green, fished a ball out of his bag and walked over to the child and handed it him with a patient smile. The child accepted the ball, Brian said something like, 'Now, little one, I'll get back to my putting.' Whether the gin fumes sparked something in the kid or not, I don't know, but he drew back his arm – and bopped Barnes one right in the middle of the forehead, with the ball he'd just been given.

Bad weather seems to have dogged me since I joined the tour as a freelance. People cringe when I arrive at a tournament on a Wednesday after two days of sunshine, knowing full well that the heavens will be opening soon or there will be a wind come along that will be strong enough to scatter a tented village to all corners of the course. I was jinxed again at the Scottish Open, the week before the major event of the year in Britain, the Open Championship at Royal St George's. Sure enough, it poured down and it blew at Gleneagles. My new girlfriend, Sharon, had been persuaded to join me for three days up in Scotland and it could have proved our first and last trip together but for her fortitude. On the Wednesday night, after she had had to hang around for an age while I worked desperately late because of the rain delays, every restaurant in Auchterarder was closed. We managed to knock up a pub, where sandwiches were rustled up by one of the numerous merry-making guests, Philip Walton. Noticing that Philip was sporting a policeman's helmet (he had withdrawn from the tournament with a muscle-pull), I decided not to worry about drinking after hours.

I waved Sharon goodbye on the Friday, completed the tournament on the Saturday, then set off to join her at a summer ball at Lincoln Castle, leaving Gleneagles at 7 p.m.

Having got lost on leaving the M6, I didn't arrive in Lincoln until 2 a.m., got changed into my tuxedo in a car park, had the last dance, and then sped off again to make for Kent and two days of Open pre-qualification press duties. I needed matchsticks to keep my eyelids open when I arrived at 9 a.m. on the Sunday at Royal Cinque Ports, having had about an hour's kip since Friday night. Open week was gripping, right up to Greg Norman again shooting a 64 in the final round, but this time to win. Again I saw every shot of the 64 played by the Shark. But, unlike 1989 at Troon, this time I knew that every glowing word I wrote about Greg Norman would be printed.

Australian Mike Clayton was always a bit of a loose cannon. At the Austrian Open, he'd keep getting into a challenging position, but for some unaccountable reason kept throwing in a terrible drive every now and then which kept knocking him back down the field. I watched Clayton hit off at one hole and then virtually collapse, dropping his driver over his shoulder as his ball described nearly a full arc and disappeared into the trees. He bent down, uttering a weird growl, picked up his driver and flung it into a quite fast-flowing brook in front of him. With that his caddie, an equally extrovert Canadian called Duncan (when I asked whether it was his first name or surname, he said, 'Either, it doesn't matter, whatever') chucked down the bag and jumped into the stream after the club. The current had dragged the driver quite a distance but Duncan waded gamely after it and recovered it under the next bridge. When he returned to his by now more quiescent master, Clayton said, 'Thanks, mate.' Duncan clutched the driver to his bosom and said 'No. You threw it away. It's mine now.' From what I gathered afterwards, Clayton never did get to use that driver again.

In August, Seve Ballesteros was named as one of the three wild-cards for Bernard Gallacher's Ryder Cup team and the week after he was picked Seve played a shot that has gone down in golfing folklore, just one of his strokes of genius that will stay etched in my memory. It happened in the European Masters at Crans-sur-Sierre on the last hole on the last day. Seve's ball was in desperate trouble, underneath trees on the right, almost hard up against the wall of the club swimming-pool area. Caddie Billy Foster, concerned that Seve was gazing up at the branches and the top of the wall, said something like, 'No good, boss. Just chip out. You can still make par.'

'No, I think I try something,' responded Seve, gauging just how much space he had to get a ball through, about six inches between the forks of the branches. Up went the ball, through the minuscule gap, over the wall, flying over the swimming pool to land in the apron just in front of the green. Everyone went wild. But more was to come. With the cheering deafening from the waiting grandstand and the crowd following up the final fairway, Seve did no more than chip in for a birdie-three. It still left him a stroke short of the eventual winner, Barry Lane, but Seve had added yet another story to his legend. You can't play that shot now, by the way. A plaque commemorating the feat, like the one that used to be at the 10th at The Belfry until it was pilfered, is placed where Seve's ball landed that Sunday.

It was a memorable week for Sharon, who had now felt brave enough to accompany me abroad as well, although it began in less than auspicious fashion. A power cut during the night knocked my radio alarm for six instead of five. I awoke, rather fortuitously, nearly an hour after I had intended. We had an 8.30 a.m. flight. So I had to call ahead on my car phone to alert our travel agent, who scrambled us on to the flight to Geneva with only 20 minutes to take-off after a hairy run up the M4. Then when we arrived at our hotel on Tuesday afternoon our luggage had gone missing. It subsequently turned up two hotels away, having inadvertently been offloaded by the bus driver at the first stop we made in Crans. Still, we had a wonderful night before I got down to work. Sharon was entranced by the stunning view of the mountains from our hotel window and tickled by the swimming pool which was half inside and half outside the hotel, giving warmth if the temperature dipped but also a swim *al fresco* in the sun, too. The Tuesday night was a mixture of delight and dismay. We enjoyed watching some of the players doing a turn on microphone, piano, and break-dancing on their night off. But we were shaken when moving on to Crans' only real night spot. With no wine available, I bought two gin and tonics which worked out to about £20. We had a couple of sips at that price, then danced for a few numbers. When we returned to our table our drinks had disappeared.

We found time to take the cable-car right up to Pleinmont and the wonderful, spectacular glacier, enjoying an Alpine breakfast at 8 a.m. on a very clear and sunny day. As we made for the return cable-car, we were met by a group of people who were kitted out for Everest, huge hiking boots, impenetrable anoraks and woolly hats. We were in shirtsleeves – and I was carrying my laptop.

There was a historic moment for Sharon during the tournament. While taking a break from walking the course, she was employed as drinks supervisor for incoming press interviewees, and she made Seve a cup of tea when he came in.

The next day we both needed black coffee after a bizarre 'dinner' laid on by the sponsors. We were treated to some tasty Swiss white and rosé wines while the usual speeches were made, leaving us all absolutely famished. At last the starter came up; great, Swiss raclette, a very gooey sort of Welsh rarebit. We were plied with more wine and urged to try more raclette, which most of the starving horde did. Plates were cleared away and more wine appeared, then we were urged to eat more raclette. It soon became evident cheese on toast was the only food available that night. After three Welsh rarebits, though, Sharon and I had had enough, especially as it was swishing around inside with about two bottles of wine. It needed a long walk back to the hotel to fend off the nausea and contributed to about a dozen considerable hangovers in the press tent the next day. We ended the week in much the same way as we'd started it – dashing frantically for a plane. When the tournament finished later than planned, we had about three hours before our flight, including a two-hour journey down the mountain to Geneva. Mark Garrod and the Swedish player Per-Ulrik Johansson were our fellow passengers. Garrod sat in the back of our minibus with Sharon, apprehensively awaiting my arrival. Johansson was signing autographs in the front. They were suddenly descended upon by a wild Dabell. I still had a report to write but commanded the driver 'Go, go, go', dismissing the autograph hunters as politely as I could. My story was written while we charged down the mountain, scribble augmented by sudden involuntary slashes as the driver hit a bend or braked. When we arrived at Geneva airport we had about 45 minutes to take-off. The driver had done a sterling job. I had just finished filing my story when I received the final threat by the airline staff that they were going to leave me behind. Our plane took off within a few minutes of our boarding.

After Switzerland, there was a pleasant little interlude in Ireland away from the trials of tour life, as 30 of us travelled to Ballybunion to play the old and the new courses. It proved an unusual couple of days. The weather was so bad when we played old Ballybunion that you could actually lean into the wind without falling over and the gale came with slanting stair-rods of rain that would have penetrated a suit of armour, let alone waterproofs. Apparently that is the only way to play such a legendary course. I don't know. The hot seaweed bath with accompanying whiskey was much more welcome. But everyone was so knackered at battling with the elements that a 'prodder' had to be employed in the evening when we were entertained by the town's corporation in order to jolt people awake. Our hotel gave us a bright start on the first morning at breakfast, when our soda bread, bacon and eggs was accompanied by Christmas carols from the dining-room speakers – in mid-September.

Jock MacVicar, the stalwart correspondent of the *Scottish Express*, was very pleased when one of his fellow countryman, Gordon Brand Junior, won the European Open at East Sussex in the autumn. And I was pleased for Jock. He'd had a trying week down on the south coast.

It was his car, a Marina, that gave him grief that week. When he bought it he was really delighted to have central-locking for the first time. That was until the central-locking kept going on and off while he was driving – quite unnerving, according to Jock. So he took the car to a garage in Eastbourne. The mechanic did a bit of fiddling around and pronounced the problem fixed. At any rate, if it happened again then Jock was shown the box of tricks under the bonnet that would respond to a hefty tap with a blunt instrument to stop it misbehaving.

As Jock drove to the course in terrible weather, the central-locking immediately started zipping on and off again. Jock pulled in to the side of the road. As he stepped out of the car, the wind slammed the door shut – just as the erratic central-locking cycle moved to lock. This time it stayed locked. Jock could do nothing. He hauled on the door-handles all-round, tried to force the hot bonnet to get at the box of tricks. No good. The engine purred on inside. The bonnet release was inside. Now soaked by the lashing rain, he was stymied.

Help was needed. He spotted a house in the distance and went trudging off through the squalls. His knock on the door was acknowledged but Jock got a little more than he'd bargained for. A huge German shepherd dog leapt from behind its owner and pinned him to a wall. Somehow Jock, his chest and shoulders in the grip of the animal, managed to wheeze out his tale of woe. The dog was called off and a mechanic called in. When Jock and the mechanic went back to the car, no spare key would fit. With the engine beginning to race alarmingly now, basic mechanics normally performed by car thieves were called for. A wire coat-hanger forced inside a window did the job. By now the inside of the car was like a sauna. When normally mild-mannered Jock walked into the press centre, steam was coming out of his ears – and his jacket.

The 1993 Ryder Cup proved a quite extraordinary affair, with Sam Torrance in the thick of it. Sam, who can, incidentally, match me for accidents any old day of the week (for instance, walking into a flowerpot five weeks before the Cup match and damaging his sternum), became walking wounded. An ingrowing toenail turned septic and made it too painful for him to walk properly (prompting his great mate David Feherty to call him 'Pus in Boots'). I went out to watch him and Mark James tee off in the heavy dew of Friday morning, little realising that would be Sam's last match. When the news finally broke on the Saturday afternoon that Sam would be a non-starter in the singles the next day, it was right on deadline, too. Nobody expected Sam to make it. But the real story, which came mighty late, with *The Observer* desperate for copy, was that Lanny Wadkins had volunteered, selflessly, to be the player who dropped out of the singles to accept a half with Sam, as per the rules. Saturday was a fraught day altogether as Europe lost their morning advantage in the afternoon. Then

Sunday was a crushing disappointment for the Europe fans, as the home side again let slip a promising position.

The previous year at the Dunhill Cup at St Andrews, I had been one of six winners of the golfing quiz at Dunhill's gala dinner, but lost out on the glittering prize when names were pulled out of a hat to decide the victor. There was a tie this time, too, with a similar amount of names going into the hat, including mine. 'The winner is . . . Norman Dabell,' announced Richard Dunhill. My prize? Nothing less than a Dunhill limited edition centenary oyster watch. It's not all bad luck you see!

Come the autumn, it was a Spanish double finish again to the tour year, although this time it would be rounded off with a visit to Orlando for the World Cup. Madrid was first stop, Puerta de Hierro, where it rained solidly enough all week to throw the event into a Monday finish. Just two of us stayed on to report the denouement, a win for my good friend Des Smyth, just about the most gentle man on tour of all time. I was delighted for him and it made no difference that I'd had to cancel my flight home and reroute myself to Malaga on Monday night and stay on in Spain for the following week's Volvo Masters. It would have been a waste of time going home just for a night and one day with the season almost over. Well, I'm so glad I didn't. Dessie invited me to his celebration lunch at Seve's favourite restaurant in Madrid. Seve's manager Roddy Carr and his wife, and Des's grizzled caddie Johnny O'Reilly also came. 'Reilly', a dead ringer for Albert Steptoe incidentally, was the caddie who is reputed to have been stowed away in a golf bag and placed in the luggage rack of a train which had come to a border crossing. Reilly had mislaid his passport so the rest of the caddies hid him away while theirs were checked by the border guards. He would have got away with it too, apparently, but, thinking he was safe, he broke wind loudly inside the bag, alerting guards who were just leaving the compartment. Des's party left me very merry and I have only vague recollections of getting on a plane at Madrid airport – and then waking up on the settee of Des's Sotogrande apartment on Tuesday morning, vowing I'd never touch a drop of Cava again in my life.

We all like to say we were there when momentous things

happened, so I was pretty pleased that I was at Valderrama when Monty pulled off the Volvo Masters and won the first of his seven consecutive European orders of merit. The plank was still at Duquesa, but this time it was crossed at strictly walking pace. And the Duquesa hotel steps were descended very carefully.

The World Cup at Lake Nona in Florida rounded off another busy season, with Fred Couples and Davis Love winning again. My most vivid memory is of Charlie Mulqueen, Colm Smith and Philip Reid, Irish golf writers all, and I totally destroying the beautiful ballad 'Yesterday' on the karaoke stage.

# SEVEN

# NO-BELL PRIZE

FOG OR, MORE accurately, low-lying cloud which shrouded Santo da Serra in Madeira, heralded in the 1994 tour season. But it was an ill wind which did most of us no good at all after the Madeira Island Open finished early.

The tournament produces extraordinary conditions. For instance, while Sharon (again risking all by accompanying me abroad, this time to her cost) might be sunbathing down at the Savoy Hotel's swimming pool, I could hardly see a hand in front of my face up the mountain.

I was awarded a place in the pro-am and had a very enjoyable morning out with Paul Lawrie, only marred when I came in off the course to work on tournament previews. As they had flown in from London that day and Sharon and I two days earlier from Bristol, the first my colleagues knew of my presence on tour for the year was when a screech went up from the back of the press tent. A dodgy coffee pot lid had betrayed me and I had scalded my hand.

On the Thursday and Friday the first and second rounds turned into a fiasco, with players suddenly looming out of the mist and neither scorers nor press completely clear at what stage of the round they were. It was the first time I'd heard the order go out: 'Hit when it's clear.' That meant that players waited for a break in the fog and then played until being enveloped again. The cloud swirled back and forth, up and down from the higher reaches and across the course in patches. How the field kept its concentration was a mystery, but they stuck it out. I had just spotted Des Smyth appearing up the 18th like a will o' the wisp when there was a terrific din to my left. I could only surmise its origin. When I ran through the shroud I could see a buggy had turned over. Its engine was screaming and its driver was doing pretty well the same. Tournament official Keith Williams was trapped under the cart. But well before I could get to Keith, Des had raced over to rescue him. It was very dramatic and provided quite a story for the Irish papers. Keith recovered quickly but never again trusted the steep and twisting cart paths at Santo da Serra.

In the end, the tournament was reduced to three rounds, finished off on the Sunday morning. Mats Lanner of Sweden won the first of his two Madeira titles and I took my hat off to him for doing it in a kind of style I'd not seen before. On the penultimate hole, a par three, he produced a complete duffer of a shot which I swear didn't go more than 80 yards or so, one that even a club hacker would have been ashamed of. Mats, with his wife and child looking on horror-struck, just collapsed into a fit of the giggles. This was a man on the brink of winning and with little room for error as players ready to usurp the honours were gathering like vultures waiting for him to slip. Perhaps appreciating the funny side of it saw him through. He quickly recovered his composure to drop only one shot, the awful one he'd made off the tee, and then negotiated the tricky uphill 18th in par for victory.

With the afternoon spare now, because we were, like many, on a week's charter flight, the rest of the day was spent getting lost in the hire car in the same fog that had bedevilled us all week. When we awoke the next day, though, a gale was howling. This was obviously going to be a problem. Landing and taking off from Funchal airport is like landing and taking off from an aircraft carrier and anything above a zephyr can cause chaos. Sure enough, the airport was heaving, with massive queues clamouring to get through check-in but going nowhere. Nearly all flights were halted. I say nearly, because some people did manage to wangle their way out on just the one flight that did take off before the airport was completely closed. We stood behind Jasper Carrot and he had a show somewhere that night, so he was whisked away never to be seen again. It took three days before the winds abated enough for the motley mix of European Tour followers and holidaymakers to fly out of Madeira. Forty or so players managed to get over to a small airport on the nearby island of Porto Santo, to fly direct to Morocco for the next tournament after paying for a charter aircraft. We had to tough it out, billeted in a hotel by the sea front in the old quarter of Canico, which would have been rather pleasant had we been able to relax, or even unpack. We were on standby permanently in case the wind dropped and we needed to be on our way to the airport. We were constantly being Tannoyed to muster in the hotel foyer and then frustratingly stood down. Even a traditional Madeiran opera show, kindly laid on for us waifs and strays, was halted unceremoniously. Just as we looked on expectantly for the young swineherd to slay the evil serpent and rescue the farmer's daughter, we were ordered to our rooms to collect our luggage yet again. We never made it onto the bus, as the wind regathered strength.

When we did finally get back to Bristol I had to get Sharon on a train to her office in Nottingham and then immediately make for London to fly to Morocco as soon as I could, via Casablanca and Tangiers. I met up with the tour's executive director Ken Schofield, who very kindly let me share a room with him when we arrived at Agadir in the early hours, the only one left in a fully-booked hotel. My arrival on Saturday morning at the huge Bedouin tent that was our press area was greeted with jeers and cries of: 'Glad you could make it.'

As usual, the trip to Dubai meant flying all night, driving to your hotel absolutely wrecked, grabbing a few hours' sleep and then setting off for the course to find preview stories. When my alarm clock brought me shuddering to half my senses around 10 a.m. I realised I had half an hour before the minibus left for the Emirates course. I didn't want to miss it. Cabs weren't extortionate in Dubai but I was staying at least 20 miles from the course and it would be a needless expense if I missed the bus. After hurriedly showering and dressing I only had a couple of minutes before the bus departure time, so I grabbed my laptop bag and stuffed my rechargeable razor in it, not wanting to miss my transport for the sake of a scrape. I could do that on the way. A few minutes into the journey I brought out the razor and started to shave discreetly, making sure I wasn't offending a couple of female passengers by crouching down in my seat. Suddenly the bus lurched to a halt. Not wanting to give my secret shave away, I immediately switched off my razor. The driver cocked an ear, then shook his head and pulled away tentatively. What was that all about? I went back to my shave, tracing the stubble on my face furtively as I tried to remember which had been shorn and which still needed a going-over. The driver screeched to a halt again. What on earth was he playing at? This time the driver shot out of his door and lowered his head down alongside the engine cowling. He recoiled smartly as he obviously got too close to the bonnet and burned his ear. He clambered back into the bus, again shaking his head. I soon went back to my shave, by now half wondering whether my ablution might have something to do with the driver's curious behaviour. I cupped my hands around the razor to muffle the noise. It did not fool the driver. This time there was an angry stamp on the brakes, which sent passengers bouncing into the seats in front of them, jolting my shaver out of my hand. It buzzed away plaintively on the floor. Imagining a serious engine fault, the driver scrambled out of the bus. With a histrionic flourish, he whipped up the bonnet – just as I finally located my razor under the seat behind. I tried not to look too shifty as I leant down to switch it off. When I straightened back up I saw the driver outside, looking close to eruption with frustration. He listened hard, buried his head inside the engine compartment and stayed hidden for a good couple of minutes. Then the bonnet was slammed down. He returned to the bus, augmenting his head shakes this time with furious waves of the arms. The penny had completely dropped for me. Not wanting to be dumped in the dunes, I put away my razor, deciding to finish my shave in the Emirates locker-room.

The tournament was billed as a 'Clash of Titans', the dangerous Great White Shark, Greg Norman, versus the cool Big Easy, Ernie Els. Well, it was no contest from the moment Ernie shot a 61 in the first round. He went on to crush Norman into second place by six strokes. I was rather glad. I had followed protocol to the letter and arranged a magazine interview with Norman the day before the tournament, through his caddie Tony Navarro. The Shark kept me hanging around all afternoon and then reneged on the interview.

Just like the previous year, it was on to the Far East after Dubai. The trip to Phuket island in Thailand was tortuous, but all that was forgotten on arrival at the beautiful Dusit Laguna resort. I walked straight out of my room on to a beach punctuated by palm trees, fringing an aquamarine sea. The heat and humidity was searing, though, causing my laptop and my tape recorder to become very unpredictable – just like the tournament really. Or should I say, just like Greg Norman. Even on the Thursday morning it was by no means sure the Shark would play. He had a virus that seemed certain to rule him out. He struggled off his sickbed, though, and won the tournament. It proved a miserable week for Nick Faldo. He missed the cut, and with Norman winning, Faldo was deposed by Norman as world number one after a record 81 weeks on top. In his winner's speech Norman said, 'The leaderboard looks like one from the Open Championship apart from Nick Faldo's name not being there. But Nick was out there practising, like the true champion he is, when I arrived for my last round.' A bit 'yah-boo-sucks', if you ask me.

My relationship with Ronan Rafferty could have disintegrated at Phuket. On the final day Ronan had a great chance to win but shot a desperate 81. I knew why. I'd been out on the course when I saw his putter head suddenly fall off on one of the greens. He put it back on and persevered with it but you could see it was affecting him and his scoring. There was suddenly a terrific scramble as Ronan dashed into the clubhouse and emerged with what I was sure was another putter. There was obviously a good story here. When he finished his round I waited patiently at recorders only to be greeted with, 'I hope you're not waiting to talk to me, Norman. I've shot 81. You know the score.'

I said, 'Ronan, I know there's more to it than just you shooting a bad score. I saw what was happening out there. My Irish papers want to know the real story.' Ronan stopped, gave a little sigh, and then told me everything. Yes, his putter head had come loose and he'd been able to borrow Miguel Jimenez's putter within the rules, because his mishap had not been caused by club abuse.

Travel was non-stop at this time. On landing from Thailand, I just had time to stop off at the BBC to get my brief for a new job as a broadcaster for Radio Five before flying out to Tenerife. The Turespana Masters would be a tricky place to begin my BBC career. There were only mobile telephones, which didn't seem to work in the tiny press marquee. Reception was great outside, though, and armed with a few notes, it was easy to get by. It was an exciting weekend, largely because of one man, Brian Barnes. The old warhorse could certainly still play a bit – and he was doing it without needing a drop or two. Reformed alcoholic Brian was happy to talk about the old days, when he once downed 14 pints during and after playing a final round in the 1981 TPC, then found out he was in a play-off – which he then won. That story got a good radio airing on the Saturday afternoon when Brian stormed into the lead. He ran out of steam on the final day but I'll always be in Brian's debt for giving me such a great start to my career with the BBC.

When I arrived in Badajoz the following week I couldn't believe what a squalid place it was. Apparently most of the people of Extremadura didn't back Franco so this particular part of Spain was never developed. You could still see bombed-out ruins from the Spanish Civil War. It proved a hard place to enjoy once work was finished. There was only one decent hotel and one reasonable restaurant, which was always packed with tour players and never had a spare table until getting on for midnight.

I played in the pro-am with Domingo Hospital of Spain. Like his fellow-countryman Ivo Giner, Domingo has a name you have to be a little careful with, in case it might be deduced that you are not being totally serious with him. Domingo, half Swiss, speaks perfect English. So I could have kicked myself after he asked me what I had been doing in the winter. 'I've been in hospital, Domingo.' It was true. I'd had three operations on various parts of my anatomy in the space of about six weeks.

We were not that successful in the pro-am. But then I have rarely been successful right from my very first pro-am, playing alongside a pro called Ronnie Crockford in a Bournemouth Alliance, *circa* 1982. I was a little nervous. Everything was moving for my first tee shot, and that was close to including my bowels. Despite my ungainly swing, the ball sped off the face of the driver like a rocket, but only knee-high, smashing, full bore, into the tee fence about 20 feet in front of me. There was a fearsome ricochet backwards. My ball slammed into the bewildered Ronnie's crutch, his manhood only saved by the ample folds of his golf trousers. From then on, Bournemouth Alliance pros drew lots to be my partner.

It is much the same with European Tour courtesy car drivers. After finishing work on the Thursday night in Badajoz, John Oakley from the Press Association and I were picked up by a courtesy car to go to our hotels. John was staying at the decent hotel. We stopped off outside my place and I disembarked from the shotgun position by the driver, saying, fairly audibly, I thought, 'I'll just get my bag from the back.' In pretty well the same movement I opened the rear passenger seat door where my bag, for comfort during the drive, had been housed alongside John. With that, though, the driver began moving off, not that slowly either, possibly rushing because of a heavy date (though where she'd spend that in Badajoz I shudder to imagine). I was half in and half out of the car as it swept on. I caught a brief glimpse of a lamppost out of the corner of my eye, smack on collision course. Oakers grabbed me by my shirt front and pulled me into the car, knocking all the breath out of himself as I landed on top of him. Not a split second too soon. The car door gave a sickening thwack as it struck the lamppost, nearly tearing it off its hinges. Oakley had almost certainly saved me from more broken ribs. As he and I untangled, the driver lurched to a halt, immediately bursting into tears when she looked back at her misshapen back door, hanging by just a couple of screws at a crazy angle. We managed to heave it into some kind of safe position so that she could gingerly drive Oakers to his hotel. I don't think she would have been on a hot date that night.

The next morning, after going in to the tournament on the players' bus, there was a memo from the courtesy car manager Rob Gethin on my desk in the press room, which read thus: 'Mr Norman Dabell has been barred from using Volvo Courtesy Cars Inc. Mr Dabell, known to his colleagues as "Mr Bean", has a record of incidents, stretching back over a number of years, of consistent damage, destruction and mayhem. Volvo Insurers have therefore refused to indemnify any vehicle that Mr Dabell would wish to travel in and, regrettably, but with great relief, have had to withdraw this courtesy to Mr Dabell. (Without Prejudice.)' I knew Robbie was only kidding and surely she would be impressed by the flowers I'd bought for the previous night's hapless driver – who was down at the garage getting her door fixed.

Extremedura provided the opening event of a four-week run in Spain. After a flight from Seville I suffered a tortuous long bus journey to Jerez, trapped alongside an enthusiastic Swede. He kept my ears busy for a good two hours, going through every shot he'd played the previous week. He was not even fazed by me introducing my mini radio and earpiece into the proceedings. After ten minutes of 'I three-putted twice on the back nine and that really cost me', or 'Then I couldn't believe it was a six-iron to the 10th', I found myself really getting interested in a Spanish phone-in programme dealing with complaints about the lack of olive oil in the region.

The Andalusian Open at Montecastillo was another of those weeks where you were glad you could say: 'I was there.' Carl Mason finally broke his duck when most people thought he'd retired. Carl had been treading the boards for 20 years and he and I had been involved in several escapades in some of that time. For instance, he had been scared nearly witless when I slammed into a plate-glass window next to him one year and another time, as my pro-am pro, screwed his eyes closed in foreboding as the detached head of my four-iron flew at spectators like an exocet missile. Over the winter, though, Carl and I had teamed up a couple of times in a week-long pro-am in Dubai, organised by D.J. Russell, and I had been very impressed by Mase's game. So, when it came to our usual pre-tournament chat about who could win, I plumped for Carl, much to the derision of my colleagues. When he won against a really class field, including course designer Jack Nicklaus, I was delighted for him, and my colleagues were stunned.

It was another week when Mark Roe drew the short straw. We played together in the pro-am for about the fifth time in my freelance career. Secretly, I think he enjoys the experience. He never stops laughing at my efforts on the way round, anyway, but it wasn't a golf shot that had him rolled up at the 18th. It's a vicious, towering, elevated tee shot with a lake down in the valley below. At last Mark's preaching on my stance had reached fruition. I got a thumping peach of a drive away. I scrambled off the tee to catch him up as he marched down the hill, eager to get a plaudit from my tutor. I was too eager. My feet went from underneath me on the muddy path and I tobogganed down the hill on my backside until I did, still prostrate, meet a weeping Roe.

There was no time to change when we'd finished our round because a press conference with the Golden Bear was imminent. To gleeful hoots from my colleagues I walked into the interview area looking like a badger, with a huge muddy stripe down my shirt and trousers. After checking my chair for signs of deterioration – I was anxious for it to not be like son, like father, after what had happened in front of Gary Nicklaus in Lyon – I arranged it so that it caught the sunlight to help crust up the mud on my back. Straight after the Nicklaus conference, Seve came in to tell us about the treatment he had been having on his back in America and what he expected of himself as he rehabilitated. It should have been an engrossing enough story, but it failed to hold me completely. A combination of trekking 10,000 yards (7,000 yards, of course, plus a lot of wandering about looking for my ball) in the pro-am, the sun on my back and a stuffy room meant that my eyes glazed over. Suddenly I got a poke in the ribs from Roddy Carr, Seve's manager and a good friend. 'Whaaa . . . ?' I looked up to see the whole of the press conference grinning at me. Seve was looking down from the desk with a patient smile. Roddy leant back to me and said, 'Seve doesn't mind you having a snooze. But it's a bit off-putting when you talk in your sleep.' Come to think of it, I could have sworn I'd asked Seve a question.

I was glad I was wide awake later. After saying cheerio to some of the players at a pizzeria in Jerez (Pete Mitchell was one of them, I remember) I walked across a park to my hotel. The park was in darkness, but I could see furtive shapes all over the place, so, despite consuming a bottle of red, I was on my guard. Just as well. I was grabbed from behind by a smelly person, screaming something guttural. Here my naval unarmed combat training, which had seemed so tiresome at leadership school, stood me in good stead. I hauled the surprisingly light assailant over my shoulder. As he hit the deck, I discovered he was only a kid, about 14 or 15. Within seconds I was being thumped about my body by a screeching banshee, possibly the distaff side of the lad's family. I pushed her away and shouted loudly at the pair of them in equally guttural Spanish, 'Venga, venga. Policia, policia – Guardia!' It did the trick. They made off into the shadows. It shook me up, but I'd saved my 5,000 pesetas. My hotel warned me not to take the short cut again. Apparently the park was a favourite haunt of kids taking everything from coke to Spanish fly and mugging to pay for it.

Nicklaus had a couple of indifferent rounds and was very upset with himself, actually wiping away tears in his press conference as he apologised for not making it to the weekend. I was able to commentate on the closing moments of the tournament, watching the climax from our vantage point at the top of the clubhouse, and Mason's historic maiden victory was relayed to Radio Five listeners with me hanging out of the window with my handset lead on full extension.

Continuing the emotion, the following week at Torrevieja near Alicante, I saw another player who'd become a good acquaintance, Paul McGinley, throw away the chance of winning. At Villamartin, one of those Spanish resorts with the golf course intertwining through the condominiums, Paul looked as though he had his maiden victory in the bag only two years into his pro career. I knew what a win would mean, particularly to his dad Mick, a real golf enthusiast who helped bring on Irish youngsters back home. They say you shouldn't get too close, though, and stay impartial. I suffered with Paul on the Sunday when, with one hand on the trophy, a couple of bad decisions and inexperience handed José Maria Olazábal the spoils. Ollie won his first Masters shortly after.

By now I had already had my share of gaffes on air, for instance like happily revealing that Gordon J. Brand had 'shit sox under'. On the Saturday night at Son Vida in Majorca I had my wrap-up recording to do for the night sports desk bulletins, following an afternoon's live broadcasting. There was the usual din from journalists filing copy, people coming in and out for scores and next day's start sheets, clanking of photocopiers and Gordon Richardson phoning his copy to copy-takers. The boys usually quietened down a bit when they knew I was on air, however. Except for one. Micky Britten, as you will know by now, was a deadly rival working for opposition Irish newspapers. Micky and I were not on speaking terms, the best way to obviate constant eruptions between the pair of us. Unfortunately for me, Micky cared not whether I was broadcasting and often wanted me to know it.

Saturday in Majorca was one such day and provided the diminutive Britten with a nickname that has stuck, and my colleagues at the BBC with a piece for the Christmas party radio out-takes. The recording went something like this:

> Barry Lane continues to dominate the Balearic Open and today's magnificent third round 66 in perfect conditions at Son Vida has earned the Surrey professional an impressive four-stroke lead to take into tomorrow's final round. Lane is ready to blot out completely his disappointment at last year's Ryder Cup after surging to 15 under par . . . [shouting and banging behind me as Britten loudly and lengthily discourses about the slowness of his fax going through to Paris with the fax operator. Dabell half turns and retaliates] 'Will you shut the fuck up you stumpy little bastard and think about other people in this press room for once . . .?' But there could still be danger to Lane. One of the three players closest to him is last year's winner of this event, Jim Payne, and the lanky Lincolnshire poacher says he's not prepared to give up this title easily.
>
> 'Can you still go with that and cut out the piece in the middle, Nick?'

The Tournoi Perrier event in Paris, a four-ball tournament, was meant to be a relaxing break after a busy start to the season, not only for the pros, largely pairing up with their tour mates, but for journalists, too. However, there was a disappointment. The promoters were new and they hadn't twigged that one of the ways to keep the press happy, especially in France, is to provide a nice meal during the day. Thus it was a week when the expression 'There's no such thing as a free lunch' was interpreted a little too literally for some of my trenchermen colleagues' liking. To make up for it, the sponsors provided copious glasses of their splendid champagne. As it was really just a bit of fun for the players and there was so much happening on the sporting scene elsewhere, the BBC had virtually stood me down for the week and I was told I had no Saturday radio duties. So when Tim Glover of *The Independent* suggested we had a couple of freebie snorters at lunchtime to give me the courage to prise open my freelance wallet and buy my own lunch, I agreed. I only had a very small report to do for UPI at end of play around 6 p.m., so I wasn't too concerned when, as is Tim's wont, he pressed me to stay longer than I would normally at the hospitality unit, and a couple of snorters turned into nearly a whole bottle. When I got back to the press tent I found a note on my desk. 'Gill at the BBC wants to speak to you urgently. Can you call the studio?' The feeling that my head was up in the rafters of the press room and my body was on roller-skates became stronger, particularly when the Beeb's producer said, 'Norman. Can you help us out, please? We've lost most of the racing to the weather and the rugby league's been delayed, so there's very little live sport. We'd like to come to you throughout the afternoon, OK?'

'No problem.' After I had had three attempts at José Maria Olazábal's name, though, and renamed the tournament the Perrier Bore Fall, I wished I'd kept to my pledge of never mixing business with pleasure on tour at lunchtime.

It sometimes proved to be a taxing first year working for the BBC on a regular basis. The World Service and I got off on rather a bad foot at the Italian Open in Rome at the end of May, at a tournament hosted by fashion and perfume supremo Laura Biagiotti on her Marco Simone estate. It should have taught me never to trust a telephone and always to establish communications both ways, no matter how rushed you are. But it didn't.

It was one of those awkward weeks altogether. First my memory let me down. Leaving a Britain lashed by gales, I travelled in just my waterproof trousers – then found when I checked my luggage that I had, in my usual dawn rush, forgotten to pack any other sort of trousers (the excuses I think of to buy more clothes. It's pitiful). So, complete with a rather chic pair of Italian slacks, if I say so myself, I presented myself to the press room on the Thursday morning. Tony Adamson was supposed to be covering the tournament for the BBC, but no one had seen hide nor hair of him. I smelt a rat. I had finally got my telephone installed (communications were not the Italians' best suit) so I rang the BBC. I discovered Tony had been pulled out of the tournament. Could I take over? Also, the World Service wanted a piece.

I rang the World Service to find they wanted their broadcast in the next couple of minutes, '. . . forty seconds on the button.' I gave them my number, then feverishly set to writing some sort of script so that I could time my piece to the required 40 seconds. I expected to be interrupted anyway, because we were due on air. But as the minutes ticked by, the script gained more and more scribblings and crossings-out as the leaderboard changed constantly. After five or six minutes, I angrily screwed up the (by now) completely unreadable script and phoned through to the World Service.

'What the hell are you playing at? I've got better things to do with my life than sit around writing scripts that aren't going to be used.'

An equally hostile voice replied, 'We've been calling and calling you. Your phone just keeps ringing but there's no answer. We've missed the slot now and that's caused a lot of problems with the bulletin.'

'Well, you've probably taken down the wrong number.' As another piece was needed soon, a ring-back test was mooted. Still nothing.

'Well, I'm sitting right next to the bloody phone. You can't be ringing the right number. Check it again.' The number checks out.

'Norman, get a sodding engineer to look at your phone before we go any further.'

'There's nothing wrong with my phone.'

Just to make sure, though, I asked someone to ring me from within the press room. Nothing.

'Get me an engineer. There's something wrong with my bloody phone.'

The engineer is summoned. The phone is checked. 'Ees no good, signore. Der ees no bell in de phone.'

'Oh, great.' This meant a contrite and ingratiating call to the World Service to apologise. But it's an ill wind. Within 24 hours I had an ISDN unit set up in the press room, complete with my own sound engineer. I felt as though I'd won the No-Bell Prize.

To further prove it was not just bad luck that dogged me, though, my name was drawn out of the hat again. This time my canny knack of winning raffles earned me a set of golf clubs after the golf writers' tournament at Gleneagles, during the Scottish Open. But it didn't end up a lucky week. I was moving straight down to Turnberry for the Open Championship pre-qualifying on Sunday and Monday, only a shortish trek from Gleneagles, so Sharon and I enjoyed a relaxed dinner at Crieff. We then set off early next day for Turnberry and I was enjoying the scenery, expecting to arrive at Glasgow Gailes at least an hour before the first player had finished his opening round, to begin in earnest my duties as press officer. As we were going along there seemed to be a greater police presence than normal and there was the odd banner or two. Soon there was the odd elevated bottom or two with legs pedalling like fury. Gradually what I thought was a Sunday morning club meeting turned into a full-scale cycle race. And soon, we were seeing more than the odd elevated bum. We were right in the middle of the race. I had to slow to a crawl, my eyes flicking everywhere to avoid installing a new, flying cyclist mascot on the front of the car. It was as if we were being escorted to Glasgow Gailes. With our outriders turning a 30-minute section into about an hour and a half, I had to alert the main press room at Turnberry of the delay. The mobile telephone conversation went thus: 'Hello, Joe, it's Sharon, calling on behalf of Norman Dabell.'

'Oh, hello, Sharon. How is the old bugger? Out on the course, I suppose?'

'Well, no, not yet. Actually we're still on the road. In fact, we're likely to be on the road for a little while yet. We're stuck in the middle of a cycle race. Norman reckons he's going to be about an hour late getting to Glasgow Gailes. Can you get somebody to nip down and cover for him, please? [almost dropping the phone in fright] For goodness' sake, Norman! How did you miss him?'

The Open of 1994 was one of those great nail-biting tournaments when you really don't know which of the main contenders is going to win until just about the last couple of shots of the week. In fact, Nick Price's name hadn't sprung to mind when I'd been asked to predict the winner on Independent Television when I went up to the Glasgow studios to do my first television interview live on GMTV on the Wednesday morning. My television début did not go smoothly. After driving up from Turnberry I went to bed very late in the Glasgow hotel in which the television company had put me up, still full of butterflies for the next day, despite a soothing bottle of Sancerre. Over the short walk to the studio the next morning I regretted drinking the wine so late at night, as I was nursing a fuzzy head. When I arrived at a much smaller building than I'd envisaged, nobody seemed to be expecting me. I felt like turning tail. Then a wandering producer sealed my fate. He managed to contact someone who had heard of me and I was given a bacon sandwich (not quite what a churning tummy was crying out for, actually) and a coffee. I was told I would be called for in about 20 minutes to have a run-down of the routine before I went on air. We were linking up with the London main studios. No, they had no idea what sort of questions I would be asked.

Soon a slip of a girl came to see me and explained that I would need to be alert and go through the door of the studio exactly when I was called or the continuity would be lost on the link-up. I'd be taking over from someone else who was currently being interviewed and occupying the studio. I stood at the studio door, dry mouthed and perspiring with apprehension. 'Hope they don't ask me something I can't answer,' prayed I with teeth clamped together. A light flashed and a speaker above the door barked, 'Stand by, Norman.' I had to get into the studio immediately the previous interviewee vacated it, through a soundproof door, and then make for the chair with the lights shining on it and a screen in front of it. Well, the previous occupant loomed into view at the door and I set off from the blocks. It turned into a fiasco because this rather haughty looking man with a baggy sports jacket got his pocket caught on the door handle and that arrested both our passages. We waltzed for several seconds before I could force my way past him. I made for the chair, which was exactly the opposite side of the studio to the side I'd been led to believe it would be, a very flustered man. I plonked very unceremoniously into it and then nearly jumped out of my skin as this gruesome picture of a white-faced, sweating, herbert suddenly flashed in front of me. It was me. Then a voice which suddenly reverberated around the room, startled me even more. It was the interviewer, Eamonn Holmes. But it could have been Sherlock Holmes, for all I knew. I could see no picture of him, just hear his voice.

'Ah, yes. I think we really can go to Norman Dabell now. Hello, Norman. Thought we'd mislaid you for a moment.' Eamonn had launched into a glowing build-up as the cameras had zoomed on a deserted chair, making some viewers think they were watching *Mastermind*. 'Well, Norman, it's the 123rd Open Golf Championship. Are we going to have a British winner again?' Quite a big question to get me underway, but one I'd expected to get at some time. I went off like an overwound clock that had had its spring released, gabbling ten to the dozen. Apparently I never stopped swivelling around in my rotating chair. You had to be as quick as a table tennis cameraman to actually catch sight of me. But we got through it, discoursing on how the weather might play a part, talking about previous Opens, and going through next day's draw. When the interview finished and the order came to close down, I knew exactly what my responsibility was – to make a sharp exit. And a clean one.

One subject dominated press rooms in the summer of 1994: what colour would Norman Dabell's hair turn next? An experiment with henna went awry. After finding two grey hairs I decided to invest in a tube of colourant – not dye, you should understand, but colourant. The hair on the model on the front of the box looked just the colour brown I wanted, 'Chestnut' it lied. Foolishly, I shampooed with the magic potion the night before going to the German Open. It didn't look too bad in the light of my bathroom, nor did I suspect anything really amiss the next morning when rising before dawn to drive to the airport for my flight to Dusseldorf, although I did notice under the bathroom light that it was a rather more reddish hue than I'd expected. When I looked at my hair in the toilets at the airport, though, I nearly collapsed. I can only describe it as 'Vivid Rust'. I toyed with the idea of buying a hat, but knew I'd have to brave everybody at some stage, so thought what the hell. As I boarded my aircraft I had to pass several players and caddies, but fortunately no press. It was hard enough bearing Ronan Rafferty's intense stare that continued to bore a hole in the back of my Belisha beacon head, like a laser, even after I'd passed him in Club. I also had to put up with comments thrown at me from about every other seat, such as, 'Well, you can tell you don't wear a syrup, Norm, because you'd never get one in that colour.' As I walked up the gangway to the press centre at Hubblerath, I met John Hopkins of *The Times*, one of my best friends. 'Good God, Norm. You're luminous.' That was it. In the evening I washed my hair with Vanish, in the hope the russet look would disappear. It didn't work. When I returned home I decided to try to cover my embarrassment with a darker henna, this time choosing 'Mahogany'. It merely made my head look like a large aubergine, which shimmered bright purple in a good light. I gave it all up as a bad job.

There was bitter disappointment for Seve Ballesteros when he was dropped from the field of the prestigious World Matchplay Championship, a tournament he had once made his own. We all knew Seve was upset but then he was handed a chance to get into the tournament through the back door when John Daly pulled out of the Wentworth line-up. At the same time, just before the September Lancôme Trophy, I became the latest 'George Stevens' at the *Today* newspaper, the pseudonym under which several of my colleagues had written in the past. When the World Matchplay's tournament director Peter German revealed to me exclusively in Versailles that Seve had been on the phone pleading for his place at Wentworth, when everyone thought that it was the other way around and the promoters had courted him, I couldn't believe my luck. And it held, too. After Seve came in for interview he was sniffing around trying to find the George Stevens who'd let his cat out of the bag. My loyal colleagues closed ranks and didn't give the game away. I nipped out the back door before he asked me.

Seve's surge to second on the European order of merit, and his challenge to Colin Montgomerie, began at Motzener Zee in the countryside outside Berlin. It is deep in the heart of the former East Germany where remains of the old austere regime were starkly evident, like huge cobbled stones instead of tarmac on the roads and signs all over of former command posts. In fact, the old single-gauge railway that used to carry border guards down to the city had been reopened to bring in spectators on a brightly decorated train. I stayed in a hotel that was formerly used by high-ranking East Germans as a weekend retreat. While it was nice to see the waitresses and chambermaids in traditional bonnets and smocks, the hotel was next to a lake and infested by mosquitoes. While I refrained from using shoes as executioners, my rolled up room-service menu eventually produced a gory frieze on the walls that must have needed a complete repaint after I'd gone. Why is it mossies just love some people and not others? By the end of the week I was a mass of swellings and angry red spots inflicted by the ones that got away. At least with the hotel being near to the course I didn't have the same problem as a gaggle of the pros who got disqualified on the Friday morning for missing their tee-off times. They had been stuck in a traffic jam on the autobahn when staying in Berlin.

I had already suffered that fate when coming to the tournament on the Wednesday. After the usual duel with the A1, M25 and M40, I'd turned off for my off-airport car park but then the traffic stalled, jamming up completely at first before turning into a tortoise-like crawl. As I approached the road that should have taken me to my car park, my watch told me my flight would be on last calls. A motorist hooted me on the roundabout. I was at the end of my tether. 'I'm sure you've heard of road rage?' I bellowed. The hooter nodded meekly. 'Well, I've got it, so watch it.' As he slunk off, I came to a police barrier. There had been subsidence and the road ahead was all caved in. I was diverted 10 miles and came to the car park from the opposite direction. I finally arrived at Heathrow an hour after my plane, which had even been delayed 20 minutes, had left.

The tournament saw an extraordinary win by Seve as he came from miles behind to win a play-off. The finish was chaotic, though, because the scoring system had Seve's score wrong on the 17th and we didn't even know at first he was actually in the play-off. It made for some exciting repartee with the BBC studio as everyone wondered what was going on. Like everyone else, I was caught up in an Ernie Els/José Maria Olazábal match behind and had no idea that an excited German official had miscounted Seve's score.

The Dunhill Cup at St Andrews gave me one outstanding memory and it was a cricketer who provided it. Not an ordinary cricketer, but the one and only Geoffrey Boycott. The legendary opener hardly endeared himself to the gathered elite of the golfing world. As guest speaker at the gala dinner, the professional Yorkshireman declared, with a highly visible sneer (these are not exact quotes but not that far off middle peg): 'I hear about you lot being under pressure to win this week. You guys don't know what pressure is. Pressure is being at the other end when somebody like Malcolm Marshall is running in at you!' He really does know how to make friends, does Geoffrey.

As the season drew to a close there was the most remarkable event at Marianske Lazne in the Czech Republic. For a start, there were over a hundred rounds that broke 60. The first three days were chaotic when it was impossible to totally unfreeze the course, caught in the grip of the approaching winter. The reason for the sub-60 rounds was the sub-zero temperature, which reduced the course to only 15 holes with a par of 59 for Thursday, Friday and Saturday. When the thaw came and the course was opened up to its full 18 holes, the coolest man at the old spa town was Per-Ulrik Johansson of Sweden, who took the title. If the tournament was often a bit of a mess then there was a greater debacle going on in the makeshift press room. For a start, there was only one line available at a time, even though five press men each had a telephone. Angry confrontations turned the media room into a menagerie at times as every one of the quintet came up with valid reasons why they should have the line at that moment and not the other four. As communications kept breaking down with only half a story sent, allowing somebody quick on the uptake to dive in and pinch the line, open warfare soon broke out. Once again it was left to press officer Caroline Owen to act as mediator. In the end, the promoters came up with a batch of satellite phones, but they were hardly any better because the satellite signal kept going down. After five or six broadcasts that week where the announcers were left saying, 'Sorry about that. We seem to have lost Norman Dabell,' the Beeb gave it up as a bad job.

# EIGHT

# BIN THERE, DONE THAT

I DECIDED TO spoil myself at the start of the 1995 season when we again took in Dubai before flying on to the Far East. The Jumeirah Beach made a sizeable hole in my bank balance, but the five-star hotel with its own beach and some of the best cuisine in the Middle East was worth it. And after finally getting my troublesome ribs sorted out from way back, I had been given exercises to do to prevent the problem recurring. I took it a stage further and, for the first time in my life, started working out in a gym. The leisure centre at the Jumeirah was the main reason for staying there. I teamed up with my pal John Hopkins from *The Times* in the fitness centre. Within 24 hours he was seeking massages after tweaking his dodgy back again. His muscle strain was, curiously, not the fault of overzealousness but brought about by laughing his socks off at the sight of my frantically jerking legs and buttocks as I tried to stay on the treadmill. I'd defiantly put it up to 6 mph and then tried to avoid breaking into a run to save damaging my Duquesa knee, by now almost permanently swollen with osteo-arthritis.

My only other visit to the Philippines had been to the naval base at Olongapo in the mid-'60s (Radio Operator Second Class). As we touched down at Manila, I wondered if the incredible squalor I'd witnessed years before would still be evident. It was. Our bus journey every day through the shanties to the Orchard Golf and Country Club made many of us feel guilty that we were staying in such splendour downtown and covering a tournament at such an opulent venue. Rather imprudently, even if well meant, Tim Glover of *The Independent* opened a window one night on the way back from the course and emptied some coins out to the hapless beggars that gathered around our bus the moment it stopped. We were instantly surrounded by a screaming mob baying for money. Our driver went crackers, pointing out that there was every chance we might now get ambushed as well, a not unusual occurrence on our route, apparently.

It was a sweltering week. I bought a pair of sandals and wore them to work each day, discarding my usual trainers. On the Saturday afternoon I wished I had stuck with the trainers. Colin Montgomerie had enjoyed two successful rounds and was in a position to win. As usual with Monty, who wears his heart on his sleeve like a supermarket special offer sign, he was bullish on his chances on the Saturday night. But when he slipped down the field with an indifferent final round, his great mood of the previous day had been replaced by the all-too-familiar scowl. With the *Daily Mail*'s Scottish edition needing quotes from Monty for their big Monday spread, I had to catch him after his round and try to persuade him to talk. I knew it would be nigh-on impossible, but Monty often gives some good lines even when he's powering for the locker-room. So, to make sure I might get something, however short, I positioned myself directly on what I was sure would be his flightpath. Sure enough, card signed, he came bursting out of recorders, snarling that he had nothing to say to the gathered journalists. Instead of taking the turn towards the clubhouse I'd expected, though, Monty strode straight over a hedge and was on me before I could completely weave backwards out of his path. As the spikes of his left golf shoe pierced my foot, all thoughts of a quick question to the raging bull were extinguished as I hopped around the club gardens, cursing the Filipino market trader who had sold me the sandals. I still sport a set of puncture-mark scars that look as if I've been attacked by a disorientated vampire.

It was a crazy couple of months' travelling. Straight after flying in from the Far East I was on my way to Madeira. For once we had four uninterrupted days, with Santiago Luna, my pro a couple of years previously in the Dunhill Cup pro-am and a thoroughly splendid fellow, winning his first title. I'd rather thought Paul Broadhurst would be there or thereabouts and made ready to watch my fellow soccer fanatic out on the course. I'd rather wondered if some of the pros considered me a bit of a Jonah. But I was crushed when Broadie, an ardent Leeds United fan who's continually winding me up about my team (Leicester City), came up to me as we were walking down to the first tee at Santo da Serra.

'Norm, are you thinking of coming out to watch our match?'

'Well, yes, I was.'

'Please. Do you have to? Every time you come out with me I seem to play badly. I don't know why. I just do. Couldn't you go out with somebody else?' Mortally offended, I turned round and went back to the press room for a Portuguese custard doughnut. I have to be honest, though, and admit Paul has not been the only one to worry about my presence. At Pals the previous year, Christy O'Connor Junior came up to me halfway round and pleaded with me to go back to the clubhouse. 'I was going really well until I saw you,' insisted Junior. 'The minute you turn up things seem to go all wrong. I know I'm in for it as soon as I see you beside the tee.' Included in the pros with paranoid tendencies who blanche at the sight of my keen and enthusiastic form on the course, I can number Sam Torrance, David Feherty, Richard Boxall, Philip Walton, Roger Chapman and Mike McLean. They all waited until the end of the round to express their view, however. Feherty used to call me 'an accident waiting to happen'. At least I waited.

My first visit to South Africa was interesting. It was no wonder that my body, particularly my sinuses and ears which had taken a battering from the flying, decided to rebel. After running up a remarkable temperature of 104 degrees in Johannesburg, I was diagnosed as suffering from malaria, then tick bite fever, then altitude sickness. I refused hospital tests to avoid being stranded far from home. The result was I perforated my left ear-drum due to pressurisation and depressurisation flying back from Johannesburg with influenza. It left me with what the specialist called 'barro-trauma', a really disturbing heavy muffling of your hearing.

Just what I needed for noisy Spanish press rooms. 'Will you lot keep the noise down? I'm going to miss my cue.'

'You already did, Norman. That went out on air,' reported a rueful producer, who had linked up to me at the Andalusian Open just a couple of seconds too early.

Weekend BBC Radio Five Live work was enhanced for me at this time because Gary Lineker, whom I'd watched at my adored Leicester City right from his first match at Filbert Street, became the Beeb's anchorman on the afternoon sports programmes. We became kindred spirits over the air waves, plugging the Foxes as much as we dared get away with, and it gave me great delight eventually to invite him to our annual golf writers' dinner at the Open. One of my early broadcasts with him was no raging success, however. At the end of the Moroccan Open, having put over a frenetic interview with the winner, Mark James, I launched into my little dissertation on Jesse's victory. I was using a script so that I could be word-perfect and the studio could record the whole lot and use it for later bulletins. Midway through, a Moroccan golf reporter (perhaps 'the' Moroccan golf reporter, come to think of it) came running into the press room, scattering all the papers on my desk as he brushed in front of it, sweeping the script I was reading onto the floor. I followed it down to the floor but had to break stride when it landed upside down. All I could do was finish off the broadcast from memory. Needless to say, it was not recordable.

I try to ad-lib as much as possible. Using prepared scripts can be hazardous. On one occasion I was well into my script on air when the press officer walked past and casually dropped the next day's draw-sheet over the top of it, stopping me in my tracks. Another time I was rattling along quite nicely when a drunken American journalist knocked his full can of Michelob over me and the script, similarly confounding my progress. Recordings can be a trial. Generally you can get through a recording first time but sometimes, for no apparent reason, unless you've rather inadvisably written in a bit of a tongue-twister, you can go through a whole series of restarts. It can just get worse and worse and leave you more and more panic-stricken and feeling that you're never going to get the recording done, especially when, after about six false starts, you're continually wondering where you'll slip up next. The constant halt and restart is fraught with danger, especially if your

127

producer is trying to operate several pieces at the same time in the studio and doesn't register you've stopped and started again. I was once phoned by Patricia Davies of *The Times* and warned that my wrap-up piece had got an interesting preamble on it when she'd listened to Five Live that night: 'Tam Sorrance showing all his . . . Sod it. Sorry, I'll go again . . . Sam Torrance . . .'

Ad-libbing, though, is always open to hazards. In Switzerland once, I was outside using a mobile to do a live piece at the end of the European Masters and was unceremoniously cut short in mid-flow by a fully extended trombone. I'd got a bit too close to one of the members of the Crans-Montana band, which, on the Sunday night, strikes up at the 18th. Then there was a Portuguese Open when the leaderboard was changing so quickly there would never be time to stick to a script if I wanted the state of play to be truly up to date. I decided to just rely on what the board showed the minute my cue came up to go on air. That little ploy was starkly exposed, though, when, just as Ian Payne announced 'Over to Norman Dabell at Penina', the scoreboard operator tripped and sent names and figures flying. Only a mutilated jumble was left. Following a pregnant pause that was worthy of triplets, I then provided an update from memory that was about as confused as the juggling going on in front of my eyes by a sheepish scoreboard operator. Wasps, though, don't care whether you're broadcasting off the cuff or from a script. Also at Crans-sur-Sierre, I had just begun my piece when I felt a tickle on my telephone hand. I casually slapped it – and yelped in mid-sentence when I was stung.

An invitation to attend the Portuguese Open near the beautiful ancient town of Sintra, with a freebie hotel room thrown in, encouraged me to invite Sharon to another overseas tour event. When we were shown to our room, though, we were a little taken aback to find we were sharing an open-plan suite with Mark Garrod and John Fenton. We were moved to a garret room that was so hot we had to throw the windows wide open, and then the traffic noise from below was unbearable. When, at breakfast, we saw a couple of the golf pros ordered to return the bananas they were taking out of the restaurant to eat on the course, it was time for one of my sharp exits. I committed the unpardonable freelance sin and paid for a different hotel out of my own pocket.

This new hotel was spectacular, with a splendid view from our top-floor room of the coast and the Atlantic. On the first morning there, though, around 7 a.m., we were assailed by furious banging and crashing outside the room. I was already up and getting ready to start my day, but Sharon did not plan to rise for at least two more hours. Vexed, I flung open the door to find two workmen hammering away at boarding where a ceiling used to be. I pleaded with them to desist and return a little later. They carried on hammering. So I raised my voice to a roar which would surpass their banging. It so froze one of the workmen that he dropped his hammer, missing my head by about a centimetre. I confiscated one of the hammers, at least. A furious argument broke out, with me bellowing from the door and the workmen bellowing from above – just as a former Portuguese Open winner, Mike McLean, walked past on his way to breakfast. Knobby had been looking for a calm start to the morning, perusing his chances over a quiet cup of coffee. He dodged past smartly in case invited to referee. When he got to the course, he told everybody that he was sure he'd seen Norman Dabell about to attack a pair of Portuguese workmen with a hammer. Eventually, reception was summoned and the ceiling work was postponed until the afternoon. It proved a traumatic day for Sharon. Returning for a room-service lunch, while waiting for it to arrive she gazed down at the sea from our balcony. To her horror, she realised a swimmer was in distress, splashing and waving and screaming. From 24 floors up, what should she do? However, even as she made the emergency call to reception, lifeguards were dashing to the man's rescue and he was hauled out of the sea to be resuscitated and subsequently taken away in an ambulance. Sharon phoned me at the course. 'You'll never guess what's just happened here,' she said.

'If it's those bloody workmen again, I'll be sticking a bloody hammer where the sun don't shine,' railed I.

When we had a mad dash for our plane on the Sunday night, and I was still phoning over copy when we were ordered to board or miss the flight, I felt Sharon might think twice the next time I offered her a trip abroad. And it was a good job I went to Majorca on my own because it was a logistical nightmare and in the end it could have resulted in serious injury for her. We had our press room at one course, Santa Ponsa One, and the tournament took place at another a few miles away at Santa Ponsa Two. It meant filing stories and doing radio reports down in a basement, then racing off a few miles to watch the tournament and talk to players at recorders for interviews. The journey between the courses, over roads that all looked the same, was totally perplexing. It was easy to get lost over the huge maze that was the Santa Ponsa holiday complex, a sort of Milton Keynes with sun. The tournament was won by New Zealander Greg Turner, brother of Test opening batsman Glenn. The incorrigible Mark Mouland was the early story, though. Mark, an inveterate party-goer and connoisseur of fine beers, decided he was going to give up the good life, sign the pledge, and try to cash in on his not inconsiderable talent. I played along with him. After he'd challenged strongly in the first round, I wrote a story for *Today* which, the following Friday morning, headlined: 'MOO'S OFF THE BOOZE.' On the Thursday night at about 9 p.m., as I alighted from my taxi in downtown Santa Ponsa, I spied three figures walking out of a bar. They shouted for my taxi to stop. One of them took a swig of his lager bottle as he got in the cab to go back to his hotel. It was Moo and he was definitely not off the booze. 'Just a little nightcap, Norm.' On the second night, when I was invited by Des Smyth to a cocktail party on his sponsor Ben Dunne's spectacular yacht tied up in the marina near our hotel, the first person I saw in the yacht's lounge was Mark Mouland. He was 'Just enjoying a quiet glass before I have an early night, Norm.'

I'd decided to call into Ben's yacht for just a quiet one myself, before going on to a farewell party for an ex-girlfriend whose family lived on the Santa Ponsa complex. The last time I'd seen Lynda (the girlfriend who'd paid for our supper after I forgot my credit card) was when I'd taken her out for our last dinner two years previously. On that occasion, as Lynda had made for our table, she brushed against a vase of fresh flowers. I'd dived to rescue the toppling vase with rather a nifty catch, but, in so doing, knocked over a couple's bottle of red wine on another table. The last, and only, time I'd seen her parents was in a Majorcan bar the year before. I don't know who had been more startled on that occasion, them or my bar companion, Gordon Simpson of the Press Association, when I lurched up, just a little tipsily, and said: 'Madam, you don't know me, but you've ironed my shirts!' We had never met, but I had recognised the parents from pictures in Lynda's flat.

In Majorca this time I had taken advantage of the promoter Roddy Carr's kind offer of a free hire car for the week, to help with getting backwards and forwards between courses. We were allowed to use the car after hours. I was soon clocking up Roddy's mileage on the hire car because I got hopelessly lost trying to find Lynda's parents' home. I called on my mobile, admitting to being flummoxed at the directions they'd given me. Father decided he would talk me in. We deduced I was at completely the opposite end of the resort to where I needed to be. It was getting very late. No one else was on the road but it was difficult driving while at the same time frantically casting my eyes over avenue names and house numbers. The journey just went on and on. Just as I answered the latest call, enquiring where I was now, I came to a blind corner. I rested the phone so that I had both hands free. But even an octopus couldn't have saved the situation. There was a wheelie bin completely blocking my way. There was no way I could stop in time. I hit the five-feet high, three-feet wide metal container at fairly decent speed, despite frantic braking, throwing an assortment of Coke cans, wine bottles, cornflake packets and potato peelings up in the air like a mortar going off. Down in the car well, where the phone had bounced, I could hear a metallic voice squeaking 'Norman! What the hell's happened?'

'I've hit a wheelie bin, Jack. I'm OK, but I don't think the car is.'

'Well, can you make it here?'

'I'll try.' My suspect ribs were aching ominously from lashing into the seat-belt, but I knew there were no breakages. The car was a different matter. Although the engine, which had stalled at impact, kicked into life, the car would only lurch. It shuddered, staggered forward again valiantly, then there was something akin to a death rattle and motion was arrested

131

permanently. 'Jack, it's no good. The car's completely knackered.'

'Right. We'll come out and find you. Give me some directions.' With that the mobile phone was knackered, too. The battery had died. I had to go to the nearest house to crave use of a landline and find out exactly where I was. The owners were at first nervous at the sight of the dishevelled, shaking, white-faced caller arriving late at night, but then showed admirable concern, even fixing me a glass of Fundador to calm me down enough to give my exact location. Soon my party host turned up, took a look at my car and said, 'It's a write-off. That's going nowhere.' I was taken to my intended destination at last, although the party was over by now. I had a couple of glasses of wine, some understandably tired buffet, and snatched some sleep. At first light we returned to the scene of devastation, hooked up the car and dragged it down to Santa Ponsa One, leaving it, like a badly mauled stranded whale, outside the clubhouse. When I returned to the course on the bus from the hotel, I ducked down in my seat when the car, its bumper hanging off, bonnet buckled and one wheel at a crazy angle, hove into view. Players took bets on its owner. They didn't have to wait long to find out. On seeing me alight from the coach, Roddy strode out of the clubhouse. 'For God's sake, Norman. I thought you said you'd had a little prang!'

There could have been another serious accident when I returned to Spain the following week, this time to an area steeped in traditions of modern art. Not that I've ever either really understood or appreciated the surrealism of Salvador Dali, who came from Figueras where I stayed in a former monastery, my room a converted monk's cell. Many thought that week that I deserved locking up. In fact, the unfortunate audience that suffered my third attempt at karaoke were pleading for the key to be thrown away. Imbued with enthusiasm from my 1993 karaoke début in Florida, I had been tempted onto a Moroccan stage a couple of weeks previously with caddie Martin Rowley and photographer Phil Inglis, where we castrated 'Daydream Believer' nicely for The Monkees. So when another photographer, Steve Munday, suggested we and a little flock of young courtesy car girls gave it a go at a San Feliu club, I was all for it. This time it was the song I loath and detest above all others, 'I Will Survive', that got given a pretty good hiding. We didn't get an encore.

Sunday at the Peralada course, the third round (because we were finishing on a Monday) was ended at 2 p.m. when a storm lashed the course. We were all ordered out of the press tent when play was called to a halt, because of fears it was about to blow down. I had a live broadcast to do with Gary Lineker at 2.15 p.m., so I rather stupidly insisted on going back in. That was because my desk and telephone were directly under a huge chandelier which was rocking violently as the tent was buffeted. I was halfway through my broadcast when there was an almighty groan from above, a crash and then a noise which sounded like a gang of bell-ringers practising badly. The chandelier had come away from its mooring and fallen about ten feet. It swung even more precariously and even nearer my head. Gary had already remarked on how they could hear the wind howling over the telephone and he urged me to flee the media centre right away. I needed no second bidding.

After being blown off my feet at Girona it was rain which decimated the following week's tournament in Cannes. It lashed down, leaving the event to be decided over only 36 holes, won by Swiss Andre Bossert. If that was a curio then so was Paul McGinley's hole-in-one in the third round on the Saturday. Because the round was wiped out due to the deluge, so was the hole in one. Not only did McGinley not get a car for his achievement, but it was struck out of the record books. The ace that never was. The incident that caused most interest, though, was when Monty putted right off the green into the pond in the first round on the undulating and deceptively fast last hole. That was never going to inspire Monty to a warm and friendly, pedestrian, chat. Again I knew I had to take my life – well my feet anyway – in my hands. I was glad I wasn't wearing sandals.

There was quite a story for the Scots when we got to the Italian Open in early May. Sam Torrance had had yet another mishap. Sam's accidents were legendary. They are never just ordinary accidents, either. This was no exception. He'd strained a tendon in his leg just lifting his daughter out of her pushchair in the park the day before coming to Milan. There seemed no way he could play. However, after intensive treatment, he decided to take a chance at the last minute. Incredibly, he put a large bet on himself to win. Sam cashed in because win he did, against the odds. The old adage 'Beware the injured golfer' was certainly underlined that week.

My cosy relationship with Ronan Rafferty was doomed by something I wrote about him in June, during the Jersey Open. To someone who doesn't have any trust in journalists, it was a case of 'Et tu, Brute?' Ronan was doing well at La Moye and I got a story from him on how losing weight was helping his game when he led after two rounds. But for the third round on the Saturday, it was miserable, drenching, and Raffs just didn't go well right from the start. I got absolutely soaked watching him, but stuck it out. Ronan's bad round wasn't going to make him talkative, but I had to have a story, so I followed him into the locker-room, where I thought there would be no escape from me. After all, I'd got drenched on his account. He went out the back door. I was sunk. I did, however, discuss Rafferty's disappearing act in the paper: 'Rafferty, a shrinking violet in every sense – he has shed one and a half stone – is reticent enough when he's had a good day. Yesterday he was positively Garboesque.' I thought no more of the matter. Then the following week at the National course in Paris, I walked out on the course on the Wednesday to talk to Irish players for my preview stories, the normal routine on pro-am day. I spotted Raffs finishing off on the 9th green and joined him at the back of the 10th tee, where there was a pause in play to allow players in front to clear the fairway. Before I got chance to say anything, Ronan suddenly noticed me. He ducked into his golf bag and pulled out a piece of paper. He strode towards me flourishing his *Observer* news clipping like an irate Neville Chamberlain. 'What the hell's this all about, Norman? You as well? I thought you knew better. That's it. Don't ever bother talking to me again.' He turned on his heel and marched back to the tee, ignoring my protestation about him doing a runner the previous Saturday. I knew I was now also going to be *persona non grata*.

'Damn,' I cursed. 'I thought he said he never read newspaper reports.'

The 1995 Open Championship provided a memorable finish

when Costantino Rocca duffed his chip on the final hole, pulled himself together and then rolled in that mammoth putt from the Valley of Sin. John Daly won but there was woe for me. When I went to the press car park on Sunday night after an exhausting day's work, I found gale-force winds had unshipped the metal litter bins and one of them had had several runs at my car. It must have bounced back and forth off it like a pinball because there were dents and gouges in various places that were to set me back a packet when I got home.

I was in Holland the following week but the biggest golfing story of that time was Brian Barnes winning the Senior British Open at Royal Portrush. Watching the rather soulless Scott Hoch win the Dutch Open wasn't a patch on being at Portrush. What on earth was Barnsey going to celebrate with, I wondered?

Travelling to the Austrian Open in early August was like the leadership courses we used to undergo in the Navy. They used to pile us into the back of a covered lorry with no means of knowing where we were going, then, in the middle of nowhere, drop us unfortunates off at two-mile intervals and tell us to find our way back home. The only time I knew my location exactly was on landing at Vienna airport. From then on, through, I have to admit, marvellous countryside, I was like a homing pigeon that had had its radar removed. Fortunately I was picked up in a courtesy car, but as our journey stretched into a couple of hours from arrival at the airport I became more and more disorientated as we went along. Were we even still in Austria, I wondered? It isn't that big a country. Apparently (I say apparently because all week I never saw anything but Vienna airport, the course, an Austrian labour camp which was my digs, and miles and miles of countryside going past) Litschau was near to Bratislava in Slovakia. My accommodation was a collection of log cabins around a great lake, aesthetically marvellous, but there was a regime there that definitely rather smacked of the 1930s. The staff dressed in tight lederhosen and barked a lot, especially in the mornings when Tannoys went off to discourage guests lying in too long. When you ate at night in the four-roomed rotunda restaurant you were ordered to your table rather than getting your preference. The rushing backwards and forwards of grim-faced waiters, stopping off occasionally to ram plates of bratwurst and noodles down, made your head spin. I suppose it wasn't any worse than one of the old British holiday camps, but it took copious amounts of reasonable Austrian wine to mellow out.

The press centre wasn't quite so militarily run. In fact, the two local press officers were not really prepared for visiting overseas journalists. None of the phones, which needed the performing of a perplexing and convoluted routine in order to go through a switchboard in another part of the building, were compatible with our modems. There were only two desks for four reporters to squeeze into and the scoreboard was tucked away so that it was impossible to see it from any telephone desk. It provided a daunting week for someone doing live radio, especially. It caused a lot of disquiet. But after several altercations, an uneasy peace finally descended on our compact little media area, situated in the clubhouse, entered by ascending a couple of flights of stairs, crossing a large landing, passing through a banqueting room and up some more stairs, then past the scoreboard area. The 18th green, where the players' recording tent was, lay about 200 yards from the fairly narrow clubhouse entrance, which always seemed to be choked up with bodies.

On the second day, while picking up a rather good Irish story from Paul McGinley, a call came through on the walkie-talkie to the recorder from the clubhouse scoreboard operator that Norman Dabell was needed urgently on the radio. I knew I had been cutting it fine but that's how some interviews are – grabbed when you can before the players disappear to practice ranges, restaurants, or in transport back to their hotels. It is frequently a case of nipping down for the interview and hurtling back to do live radio. A glance at the watch showed I was supposed to be on air within about 30 seconds. Apologising to Paul and calling back over my shoulder that I'd catch him in the locker-room to finish off our interview if that was all right, I scrambled for the press room. I had to elbow my way through the usual throng at the clubhouse door and scamper up the stairs three at a time, mentally congratulating myself on doing plenty of legwork in my morning exercises. Then I had to fend off further bodies politely, like some gentlemanly wing three-quarter, to gain entry to the press room still at full pelt.

One of the two press officers had set himself up on a small desk near the entrance and was diligently rapping out a story on his laptop for his newspaper as I raced past him. Suddenly his fingers, still working at Padarewski pace and not realising anything was amiss, lost contact with keyboard. Not surprising really. His laptop had, in a blink of an eye, swished off the table from underneath him. It hit the deck with a sickening crack, the lid and screen separating from the keyboard. I had run into his laptop lead, stretched across that part of the room, like a tripwire. He looked up dazed. I looked at him aghast. He waved me away as I tried to pick up the three pieces of his mortally wounded laptop. I don't think, before or since, I've ever seen a man use so much self-control. 'Do not worry, it is insured,' he muttered blankly as he called for assistance from his fellow press officer to help meet his newspaper's deadline.

At least I had a relaxed trip back home. After the German Open in Stuttgart a fortnight later, our return was a long day's journey into night – and morning. After a lengthy wait in the airport, we were told our flight to London would have to be cancelled. That was because the plane, likely to be delayed for at least two more hours, would be contravening local laws governing night-time runway operating if it were to turn straight round and go back to London. A special aircraft was ordered for we European Tour gypsies, but leaving from Frankfurt. We then had to be bussed all the way north. One of the players' wives was pregnant and ill on the way. Several press men stopped the bus, too, after drinking the executive lounge dry in Stuttgart. When we arrived in Frankfurt, we were rushed to departures and told we could sit where we liked on the plane.

Of course, all the astute ones amongst us made straight for the business class seats. A very camp chief steward then ordered us out of these seats unless we had paid for a business class ticket. We howled in protest, pointing out that we'd been told we could sit where we liked. And we'd been messed about so much, a business class seat was the least we deserved. But, after consulting the captain, he told us the plane would not take off until we decamped. It was gone 2 a.m. I ask you.

One by one, players and press men capitulated. I urged them: 'Stay together, chaps. If we all stick together we can win.' The German Open's IMG promoter, aptly named Peter German, then came over and cajoled those of us who remained to vacate our illicit seats. When there was no sign of movement, he resorted to mild threats, reminding the players they were under the jurisdiction of the European Tour. It might not be good for them to stay where they were. Regretfully, the heart had gone out of my comrades. Even my fellow press men, who, unlike me, had had their tickets paid for by their companies and could have been courting trouble, deserted a sinking ship. I was left alone. The affected steward got angrier. I was the red flag. He was a rather unlikely bull.

He disappeared again. When he came back he snarled: 'If *this person* doesn't move, the captain has assured me the plane will not take off.'

Now my comrades turned against me. 'Come on, Norm. Move, for God's sake, or we'll never get home.' Reluctantly, with a single digit inviting our unfriendly steward to enjoy a good swivel, I gave in, but kept shoulders high as I took my seat in economy. I did feel proud, though, when I received a standing ovation instead of rebukes from my former fellow renegades. When we arrived at Heathrow, it was at an ungodly hour, of course, about 4 a.m. We were given the option of a free hotel for the night or a limousine home. I took the latter. Apparently, I talked in my sleep on the way back to Lincolnshire. When the driver had to brake suddenly, I murmured something like, 'Don't move, lads. They can't touch us if we stick together.'

Another harrowing Sunday night experience came in France after Monty won the Lancôme Trophy. There was the usual scramble to get things done in time before facing the daunting journey to the airport. Whether you took the road alongside the Seine or took the 'périphérique', the traffic queues were always horrendous and it was inevitably nip and tuck whether you made your flight. Our courtesy car driver, trusted with getting us to the airport on time, seemed a little brash. He immediately worried me and the other two passengers, Annette Hofmann, the tour's recorder that week, and John Whitbread from the *Surrey Herald*, when he made for a gap at the St Nom la Breteche course exit that really wasn't even large enough to fit in a 125cc Suzuki. Avoiding a shunt more by luck than judgement, he then assured us confidently that we needn't worry about making our planes, because he was local and knew a short cut. We still had about 90 minutes or so before our departure times, so John and I relaxed a bit then, sat back and enjoyed the driver's Gypsy Kings tape. Annette wasn't worried about traffic, as she wasn't flying to Germany until the next morning anyway. Sure enough, we were soon among unfamiliar surroundings, zooming around lanes and roads at high speed, encouragingly passing through what looked vaguely like Parisian suburbs. But after 30 minutes John and I, sitting in the back, looked at each other quizzically when we still couldn't really identify anything that might lead us to think we were nearing Paris.

A further 30 minutes later we were beside ourselves. There hadn't been as much as a hint that we were on the way to Charles de Gaulle Airport and I was certain, even through the back of his head, the driver was panicking.

'Are you sure you know what you're doing?' I challenged the driver.

'Of course,' he said nervously, I could swear. 'Don't worry.'

Then I spotted a signpost. It read: 'St Nom 7 km'. I bellowed from the back, 'What the bloody hell do you think you're playing at? A short bloody cut? We're still only four miles from the course and you've been driving for an hour. Get us to the bloody airport right now – on a proper route.'

With that, the driver turned round, and with a snarl that was accompanied by an indecipherable torrent of vitriol, hit the throttle. It felt as though the front wheels were off the ground. Annette, in the front, whipped round, alarm etched in her eyes, and rebuked me for complaining. From then on she was too terrified to turn, shrinking further and further down her seat as we raced through built-up areas with two wheels on the pavement, scattering pedestrians, then finally swept on to a main road. We slalomed through traffic, ran along hard shoulders, then screamed back into the city. This was now definitely Paris. More pedestrians were put to flight, more pavements were utilised and hardly once did the needle on the speedo drop below 160 kmph, often climbing much higher. This terrifying second phase took a further 30 minutes at least. At last we were on the dual carriageway that we knew led to

Charles de Gaulle Airport. The driver had been berated and ordered to stop by the back seat and cajoled and pleaded with to slow down by the front seat, but had done little but chunter on in a sort of demented lament, about, it seemed, people not trusting his directions or his driving. I obviously couldn't lambast him physically or we really would have been in trouble, but he knew I was not a happy man. As we approached the airport he looked at his watch and began to whine. We pulled up at departures in a screech of burning tyre rubber. The driver flung open his door – and ran off. We never saw him again. Whitbread and I scrambled for our luggage; Annette tottered out of the car. John's flight had been due off 15 minutes beforehand. He had missed it easily. Ironically, mine had been delayed two hours. I went back to the car to find Annette still extracting her luggage, white-faced and on the brink of being very ill indeed. I comforted her. She was thankful she was at an airport hotel and had no more travelling to do that night. I helped her with her luggage. As I did, the Gypsy Kings were still playing on the car's tape deck. Whitbread cannot bear to listen to them to this day.

There was a memorable finish to the season, not just because it was the first time the tour had played in the Republic of China. Getting to, and then leaving, Shenzhen was a struggle, with hours waiting at the Chinese border both ways. The food was stomach churning at times. When we walked into the foyer of our hotel, we were faced by a blackboard offering its succulent special of the day: 'Boiled snake with chicken's feet!' And when Martin Hardy of the *Express* and I decided to jump ship and found a real-life Chinese restaurant, we were asked to choose our snake from dozens of them either snoozing or swirling around in baskets.

The Chinese have a wonderful perception of how golf began life. An extract from the World Cup programme read: 'Golf was originated in Scotland in 15 DC, or earlier. The winter in Scotland was dreadfully cold, so shepherds had to take a bottle of liquor with them. They took one mouthful of wine with the cap of the bottle while they hit a ball. It so happened that a bottle of wine was 18 ounces and one cap happened to hold one ounce of wine. Thus, when they hit 18 balls, all the liquor had gone. This resulted in a rule of 18 holes for a game. The word golf is the combination of the initial letters of the English words Green, Oxygen, Light and Foot.'

Fred Couples and Davis Love of America won the World Cup, broadcasts of which the BBC took from me mostly in the wee hours of the morning back home. I was glad, therefore, that one of my all-time worst broadcasts might have only been heard by a handful of listeners.

It came early in the third round when Couples had run up a couple of bogeys and Love followed up with a wayward drive. My cue was: 'We can now go over to Shenzhen in the People's Republic of China to find out from Norman Dabell what's happening in the World Cup of Golf.' I thought of the perfect introduction: 'Could there finally be a chink in America's armour?' Thankfully, I only thought of it and didn't say it. I then, though, spent the next 45 seconds desperately trying not to burst into a fit of giggles, interspersing my piece with snorts and gasps as I tried to keep my composure. When I explained the reason for my wavering effort afterwards to the producer, he said: 'Oh, damn, Norman. I wish you'd said it. That would have done nicely for the Christmas out-takes.'

Sam Torrance brought down the curtain for the year with yet another mishap. His ball was lost near an unsighted fairway at the Mission Hills course. Sam was fuming because he knew that was going to prove costly not only to him but his Scottish team. He blamed the spectators who, some never having seen a golf ball before, were pretty adept at nipping out and pocketing one as a memento. The headline was irresistible: 'TORRANCE VICTIM OF CHINESE TAKEAWAY.'

On the Sunday night going back to Hong Kong, our road was hit by a massive landslide which would have swept us away to oblivion had we not been delayed leaving the course. My fairy godmother might have a bit of a laugh at me at times, but she was watching over me again that night.

# NINE

# SWEET AND SOUR

TRAVELLING TO NEW parts of the globe is rare for me after a career in the RN and all my years in journalism, but Tobago was a place I had never visited. So when just after Christmas I was offered the job of press officer to the 1996 Tobago Pro-Am at Mount Irvine Bay, I jumped at it. It's a small tournament, but one in which, in January, European Tour players dust off the cobwebs before they start their season. I was also invited to play in the event and choose my pro, so I went for my pal Richard Boxall. When we flew out to Tobago, though, Boxy nearly made me die with embarrassment. There was a plentiful flow of rum on board the plane and Richard was eventually quite a happy chappy, walking around and slapping people on the back, encouraging the odd sing song or two. Richard just wanted to be friends with everyone. Well, we knew Bill Oddie was on the plane, going out to the Caribbean to do a programme on birds. He remained well down in his seat for most of the flight and, somehow, Boxy never spotted him, to everyone's eternal relief. For the whole of the flight I was just waiting for 'Hey, look who it is,' and then a loud and off-key few verses of 'Goodie, Goodie, Yum Yum.'

It was an idyllic week of playing golf in the morning, rushing off to write stories after catching up on all the play and results, sunbathing and swimming, and enjoying barbecues and dinners in the evening. I found a new customer for the coming tour season. The *Trinidad and Tobago Guardian* invited me to do a guest piece during the week and then asked me if I would cover the progress of their only European Tour player, Stephen Ames.

After the tournament finished, all the pros and I made straight off to Singapore, a tiring and lengthy journey halfway across the world. We arrived in Singapore exhausted, so the idea of warming up for the season the other side of the globe didn't seem such a good one. Ian Woosnam won the Johnnie Walker Classic and for 24 hours was as famous in Singapore as the incarcerated Nick Leeson, serving time for his Barings scam.

Woosie was on quite a roll, because he won the following week in Perth, somewhere else I'd never visited before. What a splendid place it is, a vibrant city, great climate with no humidity, and clean. We were staying at the spectacular Burswood Casino, looking down on the Swan River on which there were the famous black swans and giant pelicans. Arriving there a couple of days before the tournament started, there was plenty of time to explore. I took great delight in visiting the Western Australian Cricket Association ground and trying out my new camcorder. It didn't matter that half the ground was dug up to prepare it for the next season, I could smell the atmosphere and pictured Gower at the crease and Lillee running in at him. I actually enjoyed going to work because it was a splendid ride every day to the Vines Resort, passing through such wonderful old settler towns as Guildford, before arriving at numerous vineyards and ranches on the way to the course. It's a remarkable course, too, embroidered with lakes and bush, and abounding with kangaroos and wallabies.

The hospitality in the press room was first-class. There was even a huge bowl of suntan lotion to slap on before braving over 40 degrees of heat. And when the rounds were over, we were treated to red, white, or sparkling wine while we finished off our work by our admirable expat press officer Kathie Shearer, wife of former tour pro Bob. The largesse provided my fellow freelance Gordon Richardson with a bonus. The careful Yorkshireman had been awarded a complimentary deal at the Vines hotel and, with not quite so much work on as usual, finished work well before most of us. On the Thursday night, though, he nipped into the press room, where I was still working, and claimed a glass of red. Fair enough, I thought.

He's probably come back to do a check call on one of his stories with his newspaper. About 20 minutes later he was in again. Another glass of red, by no means rushed, but he didn't hang about. I raised an eyebrow but didn't say anything. Fifteen minutes later he was in again, a glass of red was downed, but this time savoured fully. Then I twigged. The restaurant was close by. Why pay for a bottle when there was a perfectly great red on offer in the press room? And you could stretch your legs, as well, when you were ready for another glass.

I was loath to leave Australia, especially Perth, and when I arrived in Johannesburg on the Monday night, I really wished I hadn't. On my immigration form I'd been perfectly honest when giving my reasons for visiting South Africa. I said I was a sports journalist and broadcaster covering three golf tournaments. Wrong! Apparently I should have written that I was a holidaymaker like the other press men. At passport control I was whisked away by two security men and taken to a holding area. There I was interrogated about the newspapers and radio stations for whom I planned to work. When I listed my clients – the usual suspects: BBC, RTE, UPI, *Daily Telegraph, Irish Independent, Trinidad and Tobago Guardian* – there was a huddle of immigration officers and a mumbled confab took place at the other end of the room. I was told to stay put. The room emptied. Then in walked a fearsome looking woman. She had a build like Big Daddy and had the sort of malevolent look about her that a wrestler has when he's planning a forearm smash. Her questions were spat at me like Bofors bullets.

The one which made my stomach churn was, 'Why haven't you applied for a work permit?' It was no use explaining that I'd gone into all that with my travel agent and been told that neither work permits nor visas were required, just the same sort of immigration form as I'd filled in the previous year when I'd visited South Africa to cover a tournament. She wasn't interested in the fact that I'd been let in before without all this third degree. I tried to fight my corner but I wasn't getting anywhere, neither by being on attack nor defence. She suddenly exploded. 'Right. That's enough. You will not be allowed into the country. You will be put on the next plane back to Perth.' I was mortified. Then my knight in shining

Tommy Armour poked his head in the door. Mark Watson, my travel agent, wanted to know what was going on. Never would his nickname 'Tester' get a more serious examination.

Mark went on the attack and it did look as though he was gaining the upper hand, until a security man and Ronan Rafferty came to the door.

'Tester, there are 40 of us on a coach waiting to go up to Sun City. Some players have been waiting an hour. Let's go right now.'

Mark threw his hands in the air in despair. 'Sorry, Norm. I've done my best. I'm going to have to leave you. Phone me on the mobile and let me know what's happening and I'll try and sort something out later.'

'But she's going to stuff me on the next flight out of here back to Perth!' I wailed.

With that, the dragon suddenly stopped breathing fire, perhaps at the sight of such mortal dread in my face. 'Right. You can go to Sun City as long as you apply for the work permit the minute you get there. We'll be checking within 24 hours. If you haven't applied then you're out of here and back to Australia.'

My humiliation was by no means over, though. As I struggled on board the bus to Sun City, I was reviled by 40 angry golfers and caddies. Dabell was public enemy number one yet again.

And my persecution was not over, either. Sure enough, there was a call to the press room the next morning telling me I had documents to sign for a work permit that could only be granted by Pretoria. A tome as long as the first chapter of *War and Peace* choked up the fax machine for about half an hour, as indecipherable as the Magna Carta and with similar connotations. I was tiring of the red tape, so I just filled in on the appropriate lines, signed and dated it and sent it in a bulging envelope to Pretoria. Every two or three days for the next three weeks, I got a reminder that my application for a work permit had not been received. I sent at least four duplicates and made at least eight telephone calls, until finally, in the third week, having gone from Sun City to Johannesburg and from Johannesburg to Durban, I was told I would not be allowed to *leave* the country until my documentation had been ratified. By the Friday we were still at stalemate. I was supposed to be flying from Durban to Johannesburg and then home on the Sunday. In desperation, I called immigration in Durban. A very kind lady told me to come in on Saturday morning to see her. After a two-hour wait I explained the whole sorry details. That took about five minutes. When I had finished, she picked up a phone, growled something in Afrikaans and told me everything would be taken care of and asked me to take a seat outside. About 15 minutes later I had my work permit, sent to the immigration officer by fax and endorsed by Pretoria.

How I managed to concentrate and do my job during those three weeks is anybody's guess. It wasn't easy doing the job even under normal circumstances. For instance, the Sun City press room had no lights and, when darkness fell, the only way I could type on my laptop was by lying on the floor and working under the glow of the Coke machine. And the scoring system was non-existent, run by a nice enough but totally inept army of unpaid philanthropists. They never did grasp the fact that press rooms needed up to date and accurate scoring. On the first day of the Dimension Data Pro-Am at the Gary Player Country Club, the felt-tip pen hieroglyphics looked more like caveman drawings than a scoreboard and nothing was either up to date or reliable. It made radio work a tad difficult. The only way I could talk about anything on air was by flitting around the course with the tournament director Andy McFee on his buggy, to find out how the star players were doing. We never did have a proper leaderboard report, although late in the round our press room scorers did tentatively put up a one-two-three. Courageously, I tried to go with it on air.

'Nick Price is leading here, allegedly on four under-par, and one of the three Pappas brothers is three-under. I'll let you know soon whether that's Brendan, Deane or Sean. And now Mark McNulty's just moved into the lead. No, his name's being wiped out. Ah, and here's the top British performer just going onto the leaderboard, Micky Wilson. I rather think that should be Ricky Willison. So, to recap, I can be sure the Price is right because we've just checked Nick Price's score and he's four-under, leading by a stroke from either Brendan, Deane or Sean Pappas. And England's Ricky Willison is up there, two strokes off the lead. No. Forget that. Mark McNulty leads here on four under-par.'

Sun City has to be seen to be believed. We had a beach party next to motor-driven waves, there was a fake earthquake with all the sounds and tremors at the same time each day, fake granite rocks, wall-to-wall slot machines . . . in fact it is a monument to garish and vulgar taste. The only thing I found charming was the troop of mischievous monkeys out on the course that was ready to pinch anything the caddies didn't have a hawk's eye on. At night they repaired to the trees outside our rooms, chattering and screeching as they bickered even more than press men being given dodgy scores.

It was thus a relief to base myself at Sandton, a wonderfully modern shopping, hotel and restaurant complex in the suburbs of Johannesburg. All I saw for the first two days from my penthouse room, though, were spectacular thunderstorms. The Houghton course was waterlogged. There was little play to talk about at all for three days.

The tournament ran into Monday but the deluges couldn't dampen the delight of the South African PGA Championship winner, the man who hero-worshipped Bernhard Langer when he was a youngster, Sven Struver.

It meant arriving a day late at Durban, but I still managed to get a game in the pro-am, using up five gloves and six balls in the sweltering humidity as club shafts turned into bars of soap. There was certainly no need to lose any weight but I continued my quest for the body of an Adonis and visited the local gym every morning at the crack of dawn. It didn't occur to me I could be in any danger as I jogged and walked the two miles from hotel to fitness centre, passing the Durban Cricket Ground on the way. I certainly didn't feel threatened at any time and nearly everybody I saw had a cheery 'Good morning' to proffer. When I told my South African press colleagues what I was doing they threw up their hands in horror. But that year and the next time I visited Durban, a bustling resort without the tartiness of Blackpool or the class of Bournemouth, I never had to worry about its reputation.

As if sensing I might need a little fresh air after the humidity of South Africa, it again blew a hooligan at the Catalan Open. Balls were oscillating right off greens and play was suspended enough times to reduce the tournament to only 36 holes. It was Paul Lawrie's début in the winner's enclosure and I was nearly as pleased at that as getting home 12 hours early because of the curtailment of the tournament.

Fresh air, though, is often in short supply in Rabat, the murkiest city after dark I'd been in since Lusaka six years previously. There I did feel threatened when walking out alone. And, for a time, I was on my own in a strange city. We had all been billeted in a seedy complimentary hotel that had a minaret right outside. Of course, the mullah's calling tower was right outside my window. At 5 a.m. on my first morning I was awoken by the mullah fully exercising his tonsils. So I decamped. It meant going from a freebie to a paid-for four-star but it was worth it. No mullahs, but now carpets and a television in the room with a satellite channel. Within 24 hours the rest of my press colleagues in the freebie hotel joined me.

The 1996 Moroccan Open was the one where Seve made his comeback from four months away from golf. I was given full sound equipment for the week so that I could interview him. When I did the interview I was a little apprehensive, more to do with the equipment than Seve, but, perhaps, also because I was under scrutiny from my colleagues, who had gathered around to take notes as I talked to the maestro. And it had been a long time since I used the media interviewer's short-arm jab, the thrust towards the victim with the foam rubber surrounded microphone. I could feel my arm tiring as I continued my interview, and the mike started to wobble. I grabbed my leading arm with my other arm to steady the ship. All I succeeded in doing, though, was poking Seve in the nose with the microphone. Old pro that he is, he didn't break stride.

We finished the interview. Seve said: 'Norman. Why you so nervoose? You know me. You don't have to be nervoose with me.'

The next day when Seve began his round it was going to be different to his last dramatic day at Oak Hill in the Ryder Cup. His caddie Billy Foster had asserted then: 'Seve couldn't have hit a cow's arse with a banjo.' Seve was back refreshed. The bad old swings and wayward drives would be no more. I stood next to him on the tee, drinking in the still morning, listening to waterfowl hooting from the nearby lake, the only sounds to break the silence at Dar es Salam golf course. A turn and typical full body arc, a whip through, the zing of an impact – and Seve's ball sailed into the trees.

Dubai has given me some pleasant memories over the years, but I cannot look back too fondly on the 1996 Desert Classic, apart, of course, from a scintillating win by Colin Montgomerie at the Emirates. I will always remember that year as being the one where I really did have to give up Chinese food – or die!

On the Tuesday night I met up with the two Mikes, Williams and McDonnell, for dinner, and they were keen to eat Chinese. Now I'd been warned off Chinese food several times in the past because of being allergic to the monosodium glutamate used in its cooking. It can attack my nervous system, especially if I take alcohol during the meal. This was discovered by a neurologist in Milton Keynes many years before, and I had been told to avoid monosodium glutamate as far back as the mid-'70s. The previous year it had been Chinese food or nothing when we went to the People's Republic and Hong Kong for the World Cup. Foolishly, I thought I'd beaten my allergy. After the meal, when I went up to my hotel room, my head suddenly started spinning, my lips went numb and I started getting really short of breath. Then I had a panic attack and began hyperventilating. I staggered down to reception and just managed to blurt out what was wrong before collapsing under the desk. The manageress was called and she immediately telephoned Dubai Hospital emergency centre for an ambulance, explaining my condition. Paramedics arrived within minutes and connected me to an oxygen mask, which quickly eased my breathing problems. By now I was shaking uncontrollably. Soon I calmed down, though, probably out of pure embarrassment as I imagined traffic stopping and parting as we bore down on it with a flashing light and wailing siren. I was taken to an emergency ward and connected up to all sorts of tubes. Then, with my windpipe feeling less constricted, the oxygen was withdrawn so I could explain my predicament to a doctor. I was then injected with some anti-adrenalin fluid or other and, eventually, I calmed down completely, being advised to try to sleep. The doctor was apparently on top of the problem. As I started to doze fitfully, there was an almighty commotion. A dishevelled, shrieking, wild-eyed man was taken to the bed opposite and screens immediately drawn around him. I just had a glimpse of a bloodied bandage. Then loud whimpering went on for some time. Eventually it went quiet and the drugs I had been given took effect. I awoke in daylight, feeling absolutely fine. I was told I'd be visited soon by the doctor who had admitted me. The screen in front had been removed and the sedated patient's left arm was in a protective shield. I looked at the young Asian man in the bed two from mine, the only other person in the ward, and he made a chopping motion down on his left hand. 'Dear God,' I thought, knowing some of the Arab countries' method of dealing with thieves. Now I didn't feel too good again. The doctor came and told me his treatment had worked but that I should never chance Chinese food ever again. I was dangerously allergic to monosodium glutamate. I was advised I should stay for the rest of the day for observation and then perhaps go back to my hotel for a full night's rest. I pleaded to be allowed to leave. I had three preview stories to do. I had to sign a declaration that I had released myself against advice. As I went past my young Asian ward-mate, he whispered, 'Him over there. He's a Russian chef who drank a bit too much vodka yesterday. He was chopping meat and chopped off his fingers instead.' It was all I could do to stagger down to the hospital reception and call a taxi. I cannot speak too highly of Dubai Hospital. I was never charged a dirham for my treatment and they had possibly saved me from what would have been the ultimate Dabellism – death by Chicken Chow Mein.

Sometimes, when you've been zooming around the world every week for years, you can forget where you are, certainly where you're going. I once went to a British Airways desk to collect a ticket and, when asked 'Where are you going?', took several minutes of mental panicking before I came up with my destination. 'Oh, I'm so sorry. You must think I'm such a fool. It's not Madrid . . . I'm not in France this week. God. Just calm down. Where were you last week, Norm? Can't remember. Sorry. This is ridiculous. I'll have it in a minute.'

'Well, sir, let me just try you with a few destinations . . . Rome? Berlin? Istanbul? Glasgow?'

'No, stop. You're just confusing me further. What's the date?'

'May 2nd.'

'Ah, we must be getting near Hamburg. No. That was two weeks ago. Got it. Hamburg, then Vienna . . . Barcelona. It's Barcelona. That's where I'm going. It's a flight around 10 a.m. Now I remember.'

I once rounded off one of my broadcasts with 'Norman Dabell . . . Stuttgart,' to be prompted by German Open press officer David Begg: 'Norman, we're in Dusseldorf.' Perhaps my immortal pay-off, though, was: 'Norman Dabell . . . Phuket.' That was before I was hastily advised that the Thai island's name was pronunced 'Phookett'.

You can imagine my consternation when I did my first Madeira Island Open broadcast of the week in the spring, and I was cued in with: 'And now we're going over to Norman Dabell at the Jersey Open. What's happening in the Channel Isles, Norman?'

'Morning, Bob. Actually we're a few miles from the Channel. We're in the Atlantic, at the Madeira Island Open.' After my broadcast had finished I was upbraided by a furious but, in my humble opinion, unreasonable producer for correcting her presenter on air. What, I thought, would she have done if some of our golf fan listeners had decided to drop everything and head for St Helier?

If there was confusion for radio producers then it spread to players at Santo da Serra on the Sunday afternoon. The denouement of the Madeira Island Open turned into a lottery before Jarmo Sandelin won. The hole on the final green was cut at an angle in such a treacherous way that, if it were negotiated from the top of the green, the only way to stop the ball from hurtling down into the valley below was to sink it. Players who were on the brink of winning were actually reduced to tears as they four-putted from nowhere. Poor old Patrik Sjoland actually five-putted and lost his chance. I watched as he phoned home on his mobile, totally bewildered. I couldn't understand what he was saying but I thought I detected Anglo-Saxon.

Having seen all the chaos on the 18th hole and filed several heart-rending stories, with plenty of daylight left, Mark Garrod and I went out and played the course – and both parred the last from below the flag. Hindsight is a wonderful thing.

The next few weeks produced just about the worst spell of weather the European Tour has suffered in all the time I've been freelancing. Jim Payne won the Italian Open over the muddy Bergamo course where the town's favourite son, Costantino Rocca, was supposed to prevail. All the way into the course there were banners saluting the former box-maker and caddie, perhaps the only place in Italy where a golfer is actually counted as a sportsman. If you're not a footballer in Italy, forget about being a sporting hero. Jim won and it should have been the way back for the player who was tipped to be Britain's next Nick Faldo. But his back problems and subsequent operation produced a different Payne. The one that Jack Nicklaus in 1991 had said would be a superstar never got back his wonderful uncluttered way of competing at the top and a decade later bowed out of the tournament scene. The rain caused a 36-hole final day which I'm embarrassed to report had 'Westwood leading, still proceeding' on Five Live until Lee, the player who actually did take on Faldo's mantel, slipped up at the end. Then the following week in Madrid the rain again stayed mainly on a European golf tournament, producing yet another 36-hole finale, won by Padraig Harrington.Yet another plane missed.

After Spain it was the Home Counties of England and the Benson and Hedges International. This was won by Stephen Ames. The *Trinidad and Tobago Guardian* had been getting chapter and verse on Stephen's every move from the start of the season and Stephen and I had a great rapport. We would meet up after every round and dissect it, so I had enough information for a full-length story to the Caribbean newspaper every day. It was always difficult getting copy over to them, in fact at times it nearly drove me crackers, but we got by. When Stephen beat one of the best fields in Europe for his second tour title, though, the *T and T Guardian* wanted me to write a book on him. I duly obliged and, as usual, with Trinidad being four or five hours behind Europe, burned the midnight oil to do so. My attachment to the West Indian newspaper tickled my colleagues and they were delighted I'd got a winner. 'Bet the *Trinidad and Tobago Guardian* want a thousand words on this

one, Norm?' joked Dai Davies of *The* (other) *Guardian*. Never
has a truer word been spoken in jest. The boys back in
Trinidad even came in early that Sunday night to prepare a
huge spread on Stephen and they wanted more words for
follow-up in the Tuesday paper. I wrote a book on Stephen
that week. Oh, and my fee? Still the same, £30 a day.

It was another week when Michael Williams excelled
himself. He was the first press man who went base over apex
when trying to descend the slippery bank from the media
centre. A flight of steps with hand rails was erected. Williams
christened the steps but when he got to the top, he discovered
the green paint on the hand rail wasn't dry. He looked as
though he was wearing camouflage by the time he walked into
the press centre. Mike was matching me for calamities almost
stroke for stroke and colleagues wondered if there might need
to be a play-off. He had picked up Mathias Gronberg's ball,
which he came across in a tunnel during the Cannes Open, and,
thinking it was an orphan, pocketed it. As he sauntered off in
his inimitable fashion, Gronberg, his caddie, a referee, and
several spectators came into the tunnel. Williams realised then
the ball was only a lost sheep and sheepishly handed it over to
the pro. At the same event, Micky Britten knocked a glass of
red wine all over Mike's laptop. Laptops traditionally don't
much care for wine, coffee, tea or water, with which journalists
often try to sustain them. Mike's rebelled and never worked
again. Micky just said: 'Well, you shouldn't have left a glass of
red wine next to your laptop, ya silly old fool.' Within a couple
of weeks of that mishap an attendant came into the Volvo PGA
Championship press centre to report a shunt in the media car
park. Williams had either not applied the handbrake or not
fully engaged it, and his car had rolled down a bank into the
back of Mark Garrod's, causing a fair amount of damage.

Most of the next two or three weeks were spent trying to
squeeze in television time to watch Euro '96 or dodge bad
weather. Colin Montgomerie won hands down in the Irish
Open at Druids Glen. I stayed at the Glenview Hotel in
County Wicklow, a great hotel sporting a brilliant gym and
with splendid accommodation and food. It did have one
drawback, though. My mobile phone wouldn't work as soon as
I got anywhere near the hotel grounds. On the Friday night I

arranged to record a Five Live preview piece for Saturday morning radio so that I could get away from the course a little quicker. I gave the producer my hotel room number and we decided on an 8.15 p.m. call, giving me plenty of time for dinner. I told the switchboard I was expecting a call, but at the arranged time – nothing. I phoned the BBC and asked the producer if he could extract his finger as the kitchen closed at 10 p.m. He insisted he had rung but been told I wasn't answering my phone. I was perplexed, because I'd not moved from the room, so could only imagine the switchboard had called the wrong room. I asked him to set up the recording again and call back in two minutes. I called the switchboard but they insisted they had put my call through. I said I'd been in the room and there was no call, but, anyway, there was a call coming for me in one minute, could they make sure I got it this time? Five minutes went by, no call. I rang the switchboard again. Yes, I'd had a call but I'd not answered it, so the caller had rung off. By now my stomach was growling and so was I. It was impossible they'd put a call through, I reiterated, adding, perhaps a little sarcastically, that I was not deaf and the phone had not rung. I gave in, phoned the studio and did the broadcast on my call, my freelance money. The next evening, I asked Sharon to call me at the hotel, to avoid interrupting her home aerobic session by me calling her. When I'd heard nothing around about 8 p.m. again, I called her. But she had been put through to my room and told I wasn't there. Alarm bells rang now, if my telephone didn't. I summoned the manager and my telephone was checked from the switchboard. The bell was not working; lightning had struck twice. From the Italian no-bell prize to the Irish no-bell prize.

My weather jinx spread itself to Carnoustie the following week as a gale ravaged the tournament, especially on the last day, before Ian Woosnam won the Scottish Open. The strong winds made it a hairy journey down to the Lake District, where I had booked to stay overnight on my way to final qualifying for the Open Championship at Royal Lytham and St Annes. The hotel I was staying at was very old. I couldn't resist a snigger when I overheard at the bar that one of its rooms was haunted. After a fine meal and a smashing bottle of meaty Chilean red, I hit the sack. I was awoken by a terrible screech, followed by a frantic scratching noise in my room. I would be lying if I said there was not a hint of a trembling hand when I switched the light on. A rook was in the fireplace, looking very sorry for itself.

I've decided that Sweden is my second most ill-fated destination. Gothenburg and the Scandinavian Masters was a trial from start to finish. First the hire car I was sharing with John Hopkins became so entrenched in the mud at the Forsgårdens course after a week of heavy rain, we had to abandon it and take a bus. Then the next night, after we had triumphantly extricated the car, we got so lost trying to get back to our hotel from the course that we nearly finished up on the Norwegian border. Of course, everywhere decent to eat was closed by the time we limped into Gothenburg. The tournament was a milestone for Lee Westwood, as he won his first title, but a millstone for me. After I had gone through the x-ray machine to departures at the airport on Sunday night, I was ordered by a stern security lady to open my bag and start up my Tandy laptop. After satisfying her it was genuine, I reached for my bag to replace it − just as another bag came whisking through and bumped my laptop off the end of the belt, sending it crashing to the floor.

The torment of Gothenburg was not over, though. When I got home I was five shirts, a sweat-shirt, and two T-shirts light. I hadn't emptied one of the drawers in my hotel. I phoned the hotel. They would check. No sign of the clothes. The cleaning service manager launched an investigation. There was no report of any clothes being found in my room. Somebody had moved into my room within a couple of hours of me vacating it. The man had pinched my clothes, the hotel reckoned. I had to claim on my insurance, a long and involved process. The man did have good taste, though, and he must have been a 44-inch chest and 17-inch collar.

On returning to Litschau the following week for the Austrian Open, I prayed there would not be the same press officer as the one whose laptop I'd destroyed the previous year. Embarrassingly, it was. I liked to think there were no hard feelings, although I did sense his congratulatory speech, when I won the first prize for forecasting the correct score for the

36-hole cut-off for the tournament, was rather through clenched teeth. My award was a seven-day holiday for two in Austria. I planned to use it for the following year's tournament and made all the arrangements. Next year's event was cancelled. I never did get my prize. The press officer's laptop had been avenged. Paul McGinley won the tournament. I was delighted to share his pleasure as the pair of us made for Vienna airport, carrying out an exclusive interview in the back of our courtesy car.

The wretched so-called 'summer' continued into August with various disruptions, including rain at Collingtree Park in Northamptonshire, where I was making a nostalgic return to the area of my early sports reporting years. It was the start of a hectic few months for me as I began the huge round of interviews with the caddies for my second book, *How We Won the Ryder Cup*. It fell to Matthew Byrne, one of the famous caddying brothers from Bray (Myles Byrne was Ian Woosnam's hapless bagman in the '15 clubs' Open of 2001), to get the ball rolling. Mat gave me a splendid account of his involvement in Christy O'Connor Junior's legendary two-iron shot at the 1989 Ryder Cup, while we enjoyed a drink and a meal in the Collingtree clubhouse. My next two interviewees were Seve's Ryder Cup caddie Billy Foster and his great mate Martin Gray, David Gilford's bagman. We had our chat during dinner at a karaoke restaurant in Versailles during the Lancôme Trophy. We killed several bottles of wine over a hilarious couple of hours and, of course, got involved in the karaoke. The tape of their memories was excellent, but I was careful to erase my rendition of 'Three Steps to Heaven' when the recorder got switched back on by mischievous fingers.

Armed with a new laptop after my damaged Tandy from Sweden finally gave up the ghost, I looked forward to a busy autumn and I could hardly have had it busier at the World Invitational at Loch Lomond. My portfolio that week was eight clients strong. I had to work for some of them on the Wednesday from quite a few miles away from Loch Lomond. On my way up to Scotland the brand-new immobiliser I had had fitted to my car, immobilised me. I had no chance of getting to Scotland in time to do my preview stories. The Invitational press officer Alister Nichol proved a rock in helping me with interview notes from the players. I filed several stories on my mobile, rather sneakily I confess, just as if I had been at Loch Lomond doing the interviews myself. Alister was quite used to Dabell mishaps. He once played with me in a golf writers' competition when I placed my ball in a rotating ball-washer, cranked the handle round and opened the flap – to find nothing there. The ball had obviously got fed up with bouncing around in the rough and gone to ground. We never did find it.

With a promising income in prospect I had one of my rare splashing out sessions and booked into the Cameron House Hotel, just about the most luxurious place in the Loch Lomond area. It would certainly have paid off for a gossip writer to be there when the fire-alarm went off in the hotel on one of the mornings. The ear-splitting noise drove everyone to the muster area, which was the downstairs library and lounge. I was just about to go for breakfast when the screaming alarm started in my room. As I mustered in the library with the other guests, in walked Nick Faldo in his pyjamas, holding hands with his girlfriend of the time, Brenna Cepelak. I had no idea whether their stay was supposed to be secret, nor cared. But Nick did look a little bashful. Not for long. He soon had people fallen in and standing to attention. Within about 20 minutes it was established that it had been a false alarm. At breakfast, with Nick eating his Wheaties, the darned alarm went off again. This time nobody bothered to muster.

I was up to my neck in caddie interviews that week, too. First of all I recorded the words of Phil 'Wobbly' Morbey on his and Ian Woosnam's involvement in the Ryder Cup. Wobbly's interview was all carried out quite soberly at dinner, as was Fanny Sunesson's about Nick Faldo, although we had begun the session over a jive at the Cameron House Hotel disco. But when I recorded Malcolm Mason the following night, Sam Torrance's latter-day Ryder Cup carrier really got into the spirit of the occasion. I've saved all my caddie tapes for posterity and Malcolm's recording takes pride of place. To get him going I bought him a couple of pints to loosen him up, augmenting them with a couple of chasers. As the interview stretched into about two hours over many more pints and chasers, Malcolm went from logical and clear anecdotes, to some fairly excited but staccato remembrances, to a rather incoherent ramble. By the end of the interview his voice was badly slurred and there was a noticeable filling up of emotions, accompanied by a glisten in the weather-beaten Lancastrian's eyes. It was wonderful stuff. When I played Malcolm the tape back the next day to clarify a few unclear parts, he couldn't remember anything at all about the final 20 minutes.

When Denmark took their first honours on the European Tour, Thomas Bjorn had to be the Great Dane that did it, of course. I regret I also had him bringing home the Danish bacon and laughing all the way to the bonnie, bonnie bank.

I had not been allowed to fly to Berlin the previous year, following another operation on a rogue tear-duct, and I was advised to do the same in 1996 after yet more eye surgery. But I didn't fancy another 24-hour nightmare of uncomfortable steamer loungers, shared sleepers and numerous train changes. So I got the all-clear from my specialist and drove to Birmingham airport at the crack of dawn. I felt decidedly groggy, with my third tear-duct op causing my eye to bleed profusely and my head to ache. I had had little sleep for days because of the eye problems and must have passed clean out in my chair in the executive lounge, where there are no flight announcements. I was awoken by a queasy looking British Airways stewardess, asking me where I should be going and if I was all right. My face was glistening with blood and my shirt collar was soaked scarlet. My flight was due to take off any minute. I fled to the appropriate gate but was told gently I was in no condition to fly. They would not let me on the plane despite my cajoling and pleading. My luggage was taken off and my specialist in Nottingham called while I cleaned up and put on my eye patch. I looked a sorry state, Long John Silver in a blazer. After my doctor had given the ground staff an assurance that the eye would eventually heal and dry up, I was allowed on the next flight. I should never have gone. At one stage at the tournament, a German press girl was mopping my eye during broadcasts as I bled on my notes or tried to make out the names on the leaderboard.

Nobody wanted to sit next to me at the tournament press dinner because they didn't want to be put off their rare steaks. And, of course, my eye patch brought endless comments from players and caddies. I did get a little tired of being asked where my parrot was. Darren Clarke won the tournament and Colin Montgomerie clinched his fourth successive order of merit two weeks early.

I was glad of a fairly low-key Volvo Masters for a change, with only minimal work and the Spanish Tourist Board for the Costa del Sol throwing in a free hotel. We even got a chance to play a little night-time golf at Las Brisas, where, at a rough estimate, 20 press golfers lost around 100 golf balls. One Spanish press man blundered into a lake, another was fetched a beauty on his ankle (not guilty) and hobbled for the rest of the week. Golf is a difficult enough game played in broad daylight.

Our hotel car park was always full. Charlie Mulqueen, my great friend at the *Cork Examiner*, often had to drive around for a good 20 minutes looking for a space. 'Why don't you just park here in front of the lobby?' suggested I, when we were pushed for time on a must-attend dinner. 'Nobody's going to be bothered about the car being here for just one night.' When we left the hotel the next morning, the car was gone, towed away, we were told (gleefully, by reception) by the police. I had to cough up the lion's share of the recovery charges.

My 1996 finale gave me a chance to enjoy Puerta Banus restaurants again. I had fond memories of a riotous party in Tony Jacklin's favourite eating place in the port a few years previously when a blow-up doll (bought from a Marbella sex shop by Dai Davies and me) featured largely in the proceedings on the night of fellow scribe Derek Lawrenson's 30th birthday. This year was a quieter affair, but good red and white wine flowed. I relaxed in a wicker chair, lulled by the food and drink and the voice of the *Daily Mail*'s Alan Fraser. I vaguely remember he was hearkening back to his shot to the green at the 18th during the previous night's golf when suddenly he shook my arm. 'You're dropping off, Norm. It's your round.' Quickly I perceived this was going to be a problem. Unconsciously, I'd been fiddling around idly under my chair

# TEN

# OUT FOR THE COUNT

THE TOBAGO PRO-AM provided me with my first hole in one. This monumental moment came at Mount Irvine Bay's seventh hole, an elevated tee with a green 180 yards away, out of bounds right and a large, marshy pond to the left. I hit a four-iron, my ball bounced once, released and leapt forward to enter the cup after two more hops. My pro, Roger Winchester, and my local caddie, Wayne, erupted at the sight. I stood there stunned, hardly able to believe my eyes. It was my first ace since taking up the game in 1972. It cost me nearly £200 at the bar, with many of the local caddies craftily going round several times to collect their pints of Guinness. I was ecstatic. Never mind that the following year there was a £12,000 car on offer for a hole in one at that very same hole.

I had another stroke of good luck that week. The taste of one of the sauces at a swimming pool barbecue made me suspicious on our first night, so I ate no more than the initial mouthful. That was enough to cause me a very mild version of my attack in Dubai the previous year. The sauce must have had monosodium glutamate in it. I awoke in the early hours, sweating despite the air-conditioning, shaking and breathless. I had to get out for fresh air. I decided to walk the Mount Irvine Bay course. I walked and walked, one of the ways I'd discovered when the attacks had first started in the '70s of alleviating the breathlessness and panic attacks. After about an hour I felt much better and headed back to the hotel. As I walked under the palm trees at the ninth there was just the faint *swishhh* above. And then there was a resounding *thuddd* in front of my feet. A very large coconut indeed had parted company with its mother branch and missed me by about three inches.

As with the previous year, there was not much break before I was heading for the other side of the world, this time my destination was Hope Island on the Gold Coast of Australia. There was enough time for a huge setback, though. I was sitting waiting for my taxi to arrive to take me to the station en route to the airport, when the telephone rang. It was UPI. The sports desk were sorry but UPI was closing down its European operation and decamping to the Middle East. We were all out of a job. Thanks very much. There was a hoot outside as my cab arrived. It was a disappointing end to an alliance that had survived through thin and thin. UPI had nearly made me bankrupt at one stage but we'd soldiered on. Now, after eight years, it was all over.

Bad luck struck again when a foolish dive into a swimming pool set my winter ear operation back by about six months. But then there was a little change in fortune. When Ernie Els won the Johnnie Walker Classic, he earned me a huge bottle of Johnnie Walker Blue Label for correctly forecasting the winner and the winning score. It was nip and tuck, though. When Ernie came to the last he was 11 under-par and that would have earned Michael Williams the whisky. We were both glued to the 18th green where Ernie had a putt to save par, Mike puffing away furiously on his pipe, willing the ball into the hole. Ernie obliged me by missing the putt. Mike, whose kindness to me right from when I first came on the golf scene I could never repay, died three months later. I wish so much that Ernie's par putt had gone in at Hope Island.

There followed a fortnight of flying over vast expanses of Australian wilderness, spotting familiar landmarks from the air, and stopping off at several of the major cities as we hopped around that most spectacular country. Perth and the Vines course, out in the Western Australian farming and wine-growing area, was the venue for our next tournament, the Heineken Classic. The temperature kicked up to 44 degrees. It was about the hottest I'd experienced since once frying an egg on the signal flag locker of HMS *Falmouth* at Port Said.

A three-week stint in South Africa followed on immediately from the fortnight in Oz. The hotel laundries were getting good business, although the amount of clothes seemed to be diminishing. I'd have to check my return laundry packages more thoroughly. Still, plenty of excuse to enhance the wardrobe from the Sandton stores in Johannesburg. My old pal from El Bosque, Vijay Singh, won the South African Open. My most interesting interview, though, was with a skinny 16-year-old. Justin Rose had an invitation to play in the city of his birth.

Sun City was the next venue. Many were looking forward to revisiting the resort. Not I. This time, at least, we had a press room with lighting, even if the scoring was still erratic and untrustworthy. I was lucky to be allowed to stay in the press room after an incident on the Saturday. I was diligently monitoring the play on the screen inside the media centre, and relying on it to help when I went on air for the Beeb. Just as Five Live were about to come to me, this person marched in and, with a curse, switched from the golf to a rugby match. He compounded his felony by shouting loudly to all and sundry about what the Springboks were going to do to their opponents. Incensed that I'd lost my golf at such an important juncture I enquired if the person who had interrupted my viewing was a press man. On being told he wasn't, I invited him, although I say it myself, with commendable restraint, to go forth and multiply in front of another television set far away, or put the golf back on. Although visibly shaking with rage, he acceded and I just had time to catch up with the live action before taking to the air. He stomped off out of the press room while I was broadcasting, presumably to find another knob to twiddle. When I enquired who the moron was, I was told, with a certain amount of genuflection from the local hacks, that he was the tournament promoter and all the equipment in the press room, including the television, was his.

We were back in Johannesburg for the third event of the South African golf trilogy and I had a marvellous stroke of luck when working out in the gym at Sandton one morning. In walked the whole of the Australian cricket team. I spent most of my final half-hour picking out the players. Shane Warne was easily spotted. He was the one funking his exercises when the coach's back was turned. The South African PGA Championship saw Nick Price, who'd won in Sun City, take the honours again. I saw two sides to second-placed David Frost that week. First, he provided us with a great story about buying dozens of pairs of shoes for the impoverished Houghton caddies. Then he nearly decapitated his own caddie when hurling his fully-loaded golf bag from some distance into the boot of his car, after losing a play-off to Nick.

Springtime brought another of those memorable occasions for me, when José Maria Olazábal made an emotional comeback from the foot problems that had been cured by a German specialist. There was not a dry eye in the house at Maspalomas on Gran Canaria when Ollie won the Turespana Masters. Just a few months before there had been dismal reports of him having to give up golf altogether. Now he was back and on the winner's rostrum in only his third tournament since returning from those crushing 18 months away from golf.

I was relieved to see the huge rubbish mound that used to dominate the skyline from the La Moraleja Two course had been turned into something a little more pleasing to the eye when we returned to Madrid. In 1992, at the World Cup of Golf, the tip was actually painted green overnight to try to make it more acceptable. Now it looked like a mere hill in the distance, although the gypsy encampment and the wandering cows, whose bells nearly drove some players to distraction, were still at it, dinging and donging and causing the odd three-putt or two. The Spanish Open was played over the two Moraleja courses. La Moraleja One was the old course where Bing Crosby passed away not long after getting one right down the middle. It proved a memorable week for Mark James when, against all odds, he beat Greg Norman in a play-off.

After 1990 at Tenerife I vowed I would never again try to work for two agencies at the same time, but the Press Association were desperate, so I agreed to operate for them at the Italian Open at Gardagolf near the breathtaking Lake Garda. Never, not even in Tenerife seven years before, had I been so stretched. I did get a chance occasionally to feed the swans first thing in the morning from the steps of our hotel by the lake in the ancient town of Sirmione, but that was about all. It was a truly chaotic week all round, starting with an uproarious return to our hotel on the Wednesday night after doing a mass of preview stories. Because Bernie McGuire (an Australian freelancer whose European initiation involved being stranded for an hour with me on top of the 'Big Wheel' at a Munich Funfair) and I were so late, Mario Camichia of the Italian Federation waited to drive us back. We were on the outskirts of Sirmione when we were stopped and directed away from the town by a traffic policeman. Mario, despite sipping quite a few wines while he had waited for us, launched himself out of his car window at the traffic cop and gave him what for. There was no way he was going to be diverted. The policeman shrugged his shoulders in a way which roughly translated said, 'OK, smart-arse, on your head be it.' Mario zoomed off. Within two minutes we were at a crawl and going nowhere – well, going somewhere actually, but we wouldn't reach it for a long, long time. We were in the mass rally celebrating a major anniversary of the Mille Miglia. No amount of berating got Mario anywhere. But my, our escort was a wonderful sight to behold, vintage Bugattis, Maseratis, Jaguars – rubbing wings with a 1997 Fiat.

On the Friday of the tournament, with me wide-eyed under a crushing writing and scores schedule which was constantly interrupted by hourly radio broadcasts, the diminutive Roberto Livraghi, chairman of the Italian Federation, puffed out his little chest when he came into the press room. 'Today we have a presentation to Mr Renton Laidlaw for the 25 years of the covering of the Open Italia.' Roberto likes occasions. He is credited with writing an Italian Eurovision Song Contest number and he is supposed to be a count (rather unkindly nicknamed 'The Count of No Account'). No amount of protesting would dissuade Roberto from holding the ceremony in the tiny and crowded press room. Come the moment of the presentation, Roberto clapped his hands and called for quiet very loudly, totally throwing me in the middle of my Five Live broadcast. I came off the air and carried on with my frantic input of scores I would be soon be passing en bloc to the PA. I had inputted about 75 names and scores for PA and about the same for Reuters, all ready to go when the final score of the morning session arrived in about 10 minutes' time. I switched from scores to a few sentences of running copy. The final morning score came in while Roberto was just finishing his eulogy to Renton. I was just about to send the whole package to London, when the Count of No Account gave an expansive flourish of his tiny arms and moved forward to present Renton with his 25 years service award and a bottle of champagne. As he did so, Roberto stumbled and ripped out all my laptop and telephone lines. I vented my fury, indicating that I could not be held accountable if this charade did not end. At last Roberto saw the folly of presentations in working press rooms. Almost frog-marched by Renton, the count left the room. I was left to pick up the pieces. When I reconnected my lines, every one of my names and scores, which I thought I had saved on file, had been wiped out by the sudden loss of power. I flopped, defeated, in my chair. The telephone rang. 'Sorry to bother you, Norm, but we've got a couple of customers crying out for morning second round scores. Can you hurry them up a bit, please?'

In a week of frantic activity, though, there were lighter moments, like when Sam Torrance sneaked up behind me and nudged me forward into a hedge, completely forgetting it overlooked the 18th green. I had to do the apologising to startled players on the last, while Sam just looked as though butter wouldn't melt in his mouth. And I provided yet another possible Christmas out-take for the BBC: 'Retief Goosen leads but perhaps his bad cold got to him in the end, because the South African dropped a shot on the last. Goosen using up two boxes of tissues on his way to a 66. But no bogeys for Ian Woosnam . . .'

Having heard of me through my Reuters reports, a magazine in Japan contacted me in the early summer to ask me to do a major feature on Katsuyoshi Tomori, the first Japanese to play full-time in Europe. It wasn't going to be easy. I'd had enough trouble over the past couple of seasons trying not to come a cropper on the radio over his first name. But now I'd got to talk to someone for a 3,000-word feature who didn't speak any English. My Japanese, needless to say, is non-existent. After several failed attempts I found an interpreter and arranged for him and Katsuyoshi to meet me in the English Open press centre. It was the second time I'd carried out this type of interview with someone from Japan, having done something similar with the marketing director of Canon Europe some years ago in Switzerland. But this was a full-length affair. My interpreter didn't always comprehend what I was trying to get over, and I'm sure that my questions got rearranged to suit.

'Can you ask what he has liked best so far about playing on the European Tour?'

'Mr Tomori say going home to Japan to see wife and daughter.'

'Hmmm. Not quite what I was looking for. OK, what have been the best points so far of his career in Europe?'

'Mr Tomori say he like Spanish red wine.'

Perhaps I had something to work on here. 'Ask him if he has adapted to European ways and what else does he enjoy, apart from Spanish red wine.'

'Mr Tomori like fish and chips.'

Now we're cooking, I thought. If nothing else, I could tell the Japanese readers about his trips to Harry Ramsden's. Do they have them in Tokyo, I wondered? 'Could you ask him who is the player that has impressed him most on the European Tour?'

'Mr Tomori do not like weather in Europe . . . too cold.'

'Fine.' That will be something new to tell them in Japan. Time to go for the throat, perhaps. 'Ask Katsuyoshi what his ambitions are playing on the European Tour. What sort of goals has he set himself . . . how much does he want to win a title in Europe, for instance?'

'Mr Tomori say he very pleased.'

'Oh good.'

After much beating around the bonsai I did manage to drag out a little lucid stuff, but the interview was over a gruelling two hours or more. When I came to transcribe everything, it was a complete jumble. So I scrapped the tape recording, relying on a few scribbled notes I took of the occasionally interesting quotes. The magazine was delighted with the piece, though, and sent me a copy of my glowing prose – back-to-front and all in Japanese script. I wondered if Katsuyoshi recognised any of it if he read it. He was probably too busy knocking back the Spanish red and gorging himself on fish and chips.

The Volvo PGA Championship represented a milestone in

writing for me; my presentation, with my publisher Bill Campbell, to the golfing press of *How We Won the Ryder Cup*. With it being such an important week, I'd made sure I only had a light workload. The *Trinidad and Tobago Guardian* was my only daily commitment. It could be difficult finding out if copy had landed all right in Trinidad and I often used to easily use up my daily fee of £30 to £40 in overseas calls. It was an involved process trying to get them to accept a transfer-charge call when the service was even available. It almost needed the Trinidad and Tobago telecommunications minister's approval before they would agree. I usually got through to the newspaper's switchboard and then lost them in the ether when they were trying to put me through to the sports desk, or nobody would answer the phone in sport. To double the chance of my fax landing on Stephen Ames' attempt to win the Volvo PGA Championship on Sunday, about 500 words' worth, I sent it twice. Then I called the newspaper switchboard. After two dummy runs when I had to redial and start my gambits all over again, the girl in reception at last got my gist and I heard a number ringing. It rang for an age but finally I got to speak to someone.

'Hi, it's Norman Dabell in England. I've sent you a fax on Stephen Ames. Has it landed, please?'

Confusion. 'Who that again?'

'Norman Dabell. I've sent you the report on Stephen Ames. Do you have it on the fax machine?'

'Oh, wait a minute, man, I'll go and check.' An ominous long wait, then finally, 'No sign here, man, send it again.'

I had to call off and re-send, then went through the whole rigmarole over again, this time sending the fax three times in succession to make sure. Each time my fax modem confirmed that the message had been sent correctly.

'Still no sign, man.'

So I re-send. No joy.

'Not got anything here, man. Perhaps there's trouble on the line.'

Frustrated, I hit the button on my palmtop, sending the piece through three more times consecutively.

'Nothing here, man. Perhaps you could try later.'

I was ready to give in, but thought I might as well regroup

when I'd driven home, as Trinidad was five hours behind. When I called, on arrival back at Grantham, I got the sports editor, who'd just come on duty.

'Jeez, man. We got fax coming out of our ears. I just got in and there is fax paper all round the room. It even knocked a flower-pot over and it's trying to get out under the door. What you playing at, man?'

My first contact had been checking a fax machine in the main news office. My fax had gone through first time to the unattended sports room. All the subsequent 12 faxes, of three pages apiece, had landed successfully, too.

As with most years, in 1997 there were regular winners and surprise winners. Ross McFarlane, the son of a Manchester United 'Busby Babe', had seemed the archetypal journeyman but he confounded everyone when he took the Deutsche Bank Open title in June, doing it the hard way, too, in high winds at Hamburg. All I could think of was a few years previously when Ross used to do the 'levitation' trick to anyone who would watch. I remember him levitating Brian Barnes from an armchair in the Azafata Hotel in Valencia, much to Brian's amazement and amusement. Nobody could believe it was happening and I was just one of a dozen sceptics. So Ross then proceeded to levitate Barnesy from the chair – with a chuckling Laura Davies sitting on Brian's knee! I don't know how that trick works to this day.

It had been a long night. Television pundit, course architect, and golf swing expert Alex Hay had got the bit between his teeth at a dinner at the hosting Druids Glen clubhouse during the Irish Open. We all clambered on board the coach which was to take us to our respective hotels. Alex and I were staying at a hotel only four miles up the road. I was glad of that because it was way past midnight. After we had been driving for about half an hour I started to get a little concerned. Alex was not quite so worried. In fact he was out to the world, not even disturbed by his wife occasionally poking him in the ribs to try to stop him snoring. After another 15 minutes, I had to do something, so I weaved my way past comatose press men, forward to the driver.

'Sorry to bother you, but are we anywhere near the Glenview Hotel?'

'I think so, sohrrr. I'm keeping my eyes peeled.'

Another 10 minutes went by. This time a march to the front. 'This is bloody ridiculous. The Glenview's only four miles from Druids Glen. Where in Christ's name are you taking us?'

'Well, sohrrr, I'm not local and I think I may have taken a wrong turning. I think I'll turn around.'

We were heading in completely the wrong direction. Within another hour we did finally arrive at the Glenview, where five of us disembarked with bad grace. Alex, blithely ignorant of our detour, merely mumbled his goodnights, only bothering to open one eye. By now, the six other pressmen, who still had to go to hotels in Bray, were agitating. I wouldn't have liked to have been in the driving seat, especially as there were more detours to come. A bleary-eyed sextet reported next morning that some of them hadn't got to bed until 4 a.m. After dropping us off, the bus had made endless twists and turns in country lanes and roads, finally finishing up on a housing estate, where the driver had to knock somebody up to find out where he was.

After Monty's second successive Irish win, we were, as usual, in a frantic rush to make flights from Dublin airport, about an hour from the course. It was the same firm that had got lost after the Druids Glen dinner which supplied the coach to take us to the airport. But I noticed, with relief, it was not the driver from earlier in the week. As soon as we entered the dual-carriageway to Dublin, though, he let out a curse. He, too, was heading the wrong way. The trouble was, he had headed straight into a traffic jam. We were stuck solid, with the nearest exit to allow us to turn around some miles away. It took an age, but then we were racing to Dublin. My mobile phone rang. The final recording I'd done in the press centre had accidentally been wiped. Could I re-record? Gathering my thoughts and scrabbling for my tournament finishing scores, I launched into the broadcast, well aware that everyone had stopped talking on the bus. We did the piece in one hit. At the end of it, I was treated to a ripple of applause by my bus-mates. At least it took their minds off their flights. Most of them, including our courtesy car manager Ann Hart, who had actually employed the local bus company that week, missed their planes. I ran on board mine to East Midlands and within seconds it was taking off. Its most famous passenger welcomed me on board, making sure everyone knew who had been keeping them waiting. Not long before I had been telling the Five Live listeners how Lee Westwood had had to settle for second-best behind Monty.

I love the Dutch Open organisers' sense of humour. When Pedro Linhart of Spain had a hole in one, his prize was a Raleigh bicycle. Well, it would be in Holland, wouldn't it? When José Coceres of Argentina had an albatross, I wondered if he'd be presented with a pair of clogs. It was a curious week before Sven Struver won another title. On the Saturday, I had a caller in the press centre, none other than Britain's consul-general in Amsterdam, Mr D.H. Doble. He'd heard me on the World Service and wanted to know if we were related!

Prague is a wonderful city and the Czech Open, two weeks later, was an enjoyable tournament, won by Bernhard Langer in style, at a course overlooking the spectacular fourteenth-century Karlstein Castle. There was a chance again to look around Wenceslas Square and imagine where those brave souls tried to defy their Soviet masters, drink to their memory in gallons of Bohemia Sparkling, and take advantage of three-course dinners that cost peanuts. There was an intriguing start to the week. I could hardly believe my eyes when I saw the name I. Lendl on the entry list. There couldn't be two I. Lendls. It really was Ivan Lendl, the former Czech tennis grand slam-winner. He had been playing golf satellite tour events in America, so he had pro golfer status and his playing was obviously a fine publicity stunt for the sponsors in Prague. I just had time to watch him start his round before going on air. He chipped straight into the hole and made a birdie. I ran back full steam and went straight on air with the news. It couldn't last, of course, and he proved that he was still probably a far better tennis player than a golfer by stacking up a score of 82 on the first day. He was absolutely pig-sick at that and, give him his due, went out and shot a respectable, but unavailing, 75 in the second round. I thought he was a great sport, though, especially as he sat down with me and gave an interesting, full-length interview for the World Service.

After all the acrimony of the 1997 Ryder Cup selection

regarding the injured Miguel Martin, a decision was finally made at the European Masters at Crans-sur-Sierre. Whereas the previous week's BMW International was supposed to be the one which defined the team and therefore had a full BBC broadcasting operation, the tournament in Switzerland was left to me and a phone. I interviewed Seve on a spluttering mobile in the kitchen of the Crans-sur-Sierre clubhouse.

What did it all matter? At the same time, one of the most tragic stories of the century unfolded. In the early hours of Sunday morning in Munich, I had lain wide awake, my usual insomnia having taken a firm hold. I'd switched on the television and was shocked to see that Princess Diana had been involved in a car accident in Paris. Shock soon turned to horror when the television revealed that Diana was dead. The following week, when her funeral was broadcast on the press-room television, I'll never forget the sight of our courtesy car manager Ann Hart watching the cortege and weeping uncontrollably, being comforted by Renton Laidlaw, iron-jawed and silent, but with tears streaking his cheeks. I had walked out to the course to witness the minute's tribute. On that beautiful mountainside there was an awesome silence, enhanced, not interrupted, by the gentle swish of a breeze passing through the firs lining the fairway, and the haunting, plaintive call of a solitary crow.

Mark O'Meara's win in the Lancôme Trophy was to have repercussions, rather extraordinarily, right at the end of the season. A Swedish television commentator noticed, on his umpteenth look at one of the sequences of O'Meara marking his ball, that the American had replaced it nearer the hole. When Jarmo Sandelin, who had finished second behind O'Meara in Versailles, heard about it, he was incensed and demanded that O'Meara should give up the title and he be awarded the first prize. The tour gave O'Meara, who was said to be mortified when proof was provided of his indiscretion, the benefit of the doubt. Even though there was, apparently, video evidence that he did replace the ball nearer the hole, he was not disqualified retrospectively. The row rumbled on from Sandelin's corner until the two players met up the following spring in Hamburg.

The Ryder Cup at Valderrama was always going to be the

highlight of my season and, in many ways, it was the highlight of my career so far. It had everything. The golf was of the highest order, the play dramatic and watched by a huge, enthralled gallery. Can there ever be a better amphitheatre than Valderrama's 17th hole? I was privileged to be invited to the Ryder Cup gala dinner, and sat with my friend Maxine Longmuir from sponsors Johnnie Walker. I was enthralled by the occasion, watching the players walk up to be presented, feeling particularly emotional about Darren and Heather Clarke, looking absolutely stunning together. I remembered the lad who had a bee in his trousers a few years ago in Monte Carlo and filled up with emotion. Soon after the presentation of the players, we ate dinner. I was wearing my cream 'Spencer' tuxedo, a remnant of Foreign Office days. I was pleased I could still fit into it. It was the first time I'd worn the jacket since I'd had it cleaned after a waitress spilled a whole tray of champagne over me at the Johnnie Walker Classic two years previously. It was, regrettably, fated. Maxine had been sitting alongside me when I got drenched by champagne and she was in the next seat to me again when a waitress emptied a chocolate mousse down my neck at the Valderrama Ryder Cup gala dinner. After getting it cleaned again, I gave the jacket to my nephew Adam.

When I awoke on the Friday morning for the start of the Ryder Cup match, it was to the sound of rain beating on my hotel roof. When I descended the stairs of my hotel in Puerta Duquesa, I could see the rain was serious because it was coming in through the door. There was a torrent outside and it was impossible to leave the hotel. I finished up doing radio broadcasts sitting on the hotel stairs, telling listeners that play was not possible and could be lost for the whole day. It certainly looked that way when I did finally make it to the course, where I recognised the Valderrama owner, Don Jaime Patino, as one of the men working feverishly to sweep water off the fairways and greens and out of the bunkers. By some miracle of drainage, play did get underway, but it meant burning the midnight oil again and it was lucky that our favourite restaurant, Mamma's, stayed open until all hours.

There was great rivalry, and often discontent, within the press centre. Several times the American journalists expressed their disapproval loudly of European pressmen and women cheering winning putts. We felt it was sour grapes. 'Cheer when you're winning,' was the motto for we delirious home media as Seve's men prevailed. Mind you, I wish Seve hadn't ordered Monty to take a half with Scott Hoch in the denouement. That cost me a gallon of Johnnie Walker Black Label, which was on offer to those correctly forecasting the winning score.

Setting off from Gibraltar after the match finished, I was elated to be upgraded for my flight home. That elation turned to misery in the end. A 25-stone woman, who could not fit into economy class, was installed next to me, taking up the two seats alongside. She was so huge that she squashed me into the cabin window during take-off. When we arrived at London Gatwick I found out that some luggage had had to be offloaded because of extra weight on board. Could it have been the lady slumped next to me, I wondered? It goes without saying that mine was amongst the unlucky luggage. It still hadn't arrived at my home when I left for Germany and my next tournament. It didn't turn up until the weekend. It was a good job that I had ample spare underwear.

My penultimate event of the year, the Volvo Masters at Montecastillo, was carried out in a frenzy of activity. I had agreed to work for Viewpress, the on-course television broadcasters, which entailed sitting in front of a screen for four or five hours and talking about anything and everything as players came through the ninth hole. It was a sort of stop–gap until the mainstream broadcasters took over in the afternoon. I soon had a name for the service: Groundhog Day. That was because our cameras went through the same routine for hours on end – zoom in on the tee, follow the players up the fairway and then show them putting on the ninth green. Over and over we went. I had to think of something to say about every player we picked out. You had to be like a musician playing three or four instruments at once, with a producer dishing out orders, scores and the state of the groups meant to be on the ninth in one ear of the headset, and your own feedback in the other. One of the things that confounded me a couple of times at first was the on-off control on my broadcasting unit, which I slid on for broadcast and off when I wanted to contact the producer.

It made for a couple of interesting revelations on-air. I wasn't too happy with my performance on the first day and my fears were fully realised when I got back to the press centre. Micky Britten had gone round turning all the monitor television sets off, but then got overruled when reports came in that my commentating was hilarious – not often because of my repartee.

Kiawah Island in South Carolina was my final destination of 1997. The World Cup of Golf proved a triumph for Ireland in the shape of Paul McGinley and Padraig Harrington. It was a memorable week for a traveller. We flew to Washington, stopping off there both ways for me to savour that historic city for the first time. We underwent several climate changes, needing to get de-iced at one stage at Dulles Airport before continuing on to Charleston. We saw myriad spectacles from our aeroplane windows: mountains, forests, coasts, cities; even the industrial areas were a sight to behold. Then there were the spectacular resorts adjoining Kiawah, such as Seabrook Island, where we stayed. There was marvellous wildlife, including fascinating birds, which I appreciated fully as a part-time ornithologist, even the odd rattlesnake might slither past you in the dunes when venturing out on the course. My mind drifted back to what the old Deep South could have been like, when we enjoyed after-work parties and concerts, aperitifs by the water and incredible sunsets. Sometimes, when lost in the landscape as we journeyed to and from the course, I could imagine the roar of cannons and clash of sabres as Confederate Carolina defended itself against its Union foe. It was quite some way to bring down the curtain on an historic season for European golf.

# ELEVEN

# SOMETHING IN THE AIR

I FELT A real buzz when we landed in Phuket at the start of the 1998 season. I'd loved the island when the Johnnie Walker Classic was held at the Blue Canyon club previously. Tiger Woods was playing, returning to his mother's roots. The security surrounding him was unbelievable. Press people are always allowed inside the ropes at events but when Tiger was around, that was definitely not the case. I went out walking the course to see if I could pick up some interesting stories for my previews and casually ducked under the ropes surrounding Tiger's tee when he was practising. I was immediately pounced on by three bodyguards. My arm was grabbed and I was frog-marched unceremoniously back from whence I came, told to 'Piss off' by a distinctly English voice, north-eastern if I wasn't mistaken. Apparently, some former British Army special services men were looking after Tiger and, I can tell you, they were taking neither prisoners nor no for an answer. Tiger wasn't in the best of moods at the start of the tournament but his grouchiness had completely dissolved by Sunday night after he came from miles back to force a play-off with Ernie Els, a tense affair which he won.

I was on a month's trip and flew from Thailand to Australia for the Heineken Classic in Perth and then on to the Middle East. While Dubai is less strict with alcohol, in Qatar it is different. We understood the only way to get alcohol was through a 'source' who had a whole storeroom full of packs of beer and cartons of wine for visiting Westerners. I have no idea who paid for it all, but there was much negotiating by our erstwhile press officer Alister Nicol. It seemed a great idea until I asked myself how I was going to smuggle two large wine boxes, too big to fit into my bulging luggage by far, past security at my hotel. Our source had put me in charge of our group's wine distribution. It needed Alister to go to his room and bring an empty holdall down to me, waiting in the car, so I could get past the doormen unchallenged. Then there was the problem of hiding the cartons. There was a large notice in English forbidding alcohol in the rooms. I didn't want to be flung in an Arab gaol, and I winced at the thought of 100 lashes. I had a brainwave. I took one of the wine bags out of its box. I then tore up the box and crumpled it up enough to secrete it in my laptop case. Then I placed a load of underwear and golf T-shirts around the wine bag in my bottom drawer. Then, when I went down to dinner, I invited every wine connoisseur in the press and players corps I came across to come back to my room and watch the League Cup soccer match on my television, while having a little sustenance. They did roll up, about ten people packing into my room. When we tasted the wine it was awful, certainly not kosher and definitely not the Stellanbosch it purported to be on the label. My guests trooped out disconsolate. I poured the remainder of the box down the sink and hid the evidence, easily enough now it was in its condensed form, in my luggage. I decided to dispose of the other bag of wine. I didn't get a chance to ditch much more than half of it. The bag had punctured in my drawer. I spent the next hour cleaning up, frantic I might now be discovered if the chambermaid smelt the wine the next day. I wasted a whole bottle of Givenchy aftershave covering up. Satisfied with my work I decided to turn in, but by now the noise from a squawking girl band directly below me had grown in volume. I wouldn't be able to sleep until it had abated, so I decided to go down and investigate. It was coming from a *bar*. The *bar* was in an area exclusively for Westerners, totally off-limits to locals. It served alcohol by the bucketful and was full of imbibing press and players.

It was an interesting week. Andrew Coltart finally broke his duck on the European Tour and the flies in the press tent nearly broke everybody's will to live. The place was infested with them. I was broadcasting for RTE on the Saturday when several of them attacked my face at the same time. Trying not to break stride, I whisked angrily at my tormentors, whipping the handset out of my right hand and sending it spinning on to the next desk, catapulting a nearly full bottle of water over a local radio man's notes just before he went on air. When, bowing and scraping and clasping my hands together in a pathetic attempt at supplication, I retrieved the phone, my Irish anchorman had done a brilliant covering job and we slipped straight back into the flow. There were certainly no flies on him. Not long after that, I was summoned to the portakabin tournament office. I wondered what was wrong. Had my Givenchy camouflage been rumbled? Sure enough, there was the sheikh responsible for the Qatar authorities who had underwritten the tournament sitting behind the desk like a magistrate. I could already feel the first lash biting into my tender flesh. 'Ah, Mr Dabell. His Highness would like to show his appreciation for your attendance at the Qatar Masters this week. Here is a little gift for you.' I was handed a smashing looking bag. Inside it was a bundle of Qatari notes, the equivalent of £300, to 'help with your hotel bill'.

The chances of missing a flight after a Spanish Open were, for once, minimal when the event was played at El Prat. That's because the course is right next to Barcelona Airport runway. It leaves telephone broadcasters with a near impossible task of trying to get a piece done before the incessant ear-splitting screams of 737s taking off completely overcome the broadcast. 'Thomas Bjorn on the brink of winning here, Eleanor. He's playing the*********************is two strokes behind.'

'Sorry, Norman, we lost you there. What on earth was that, a plane?'

'Yes, the British Airways four-thirty to Gatwick, to be precise.'

It was a tortuous week in other respects. We were billeted in the holiday town of Sitges, which was miles and miles from the course, down on the Costa Dorada, so that meant crawling in and out of Barcelona on the coast roads every day. Travelling back in the evening was a nightmare, bumper to bumper for hours. Saturday night was lightened up considerably, though, when, after a particularly gruelling journey back, I had enjoyed my supper and was just finishing off a coffee and a Fundador when in scuttled my old cobber Bernie McGuire.

'Yo, Bernie. Where did you eat tonight then?'

'Well, it's a bit of an embarrassing story, Norm. Mel Webb [*The Times*] and I were very late so we didn't bother tracking the rest of you down for dinner and stopped at a nice enough looking place on the way back. We were well into our starters when I looked around the place. At every table there were couples. They were all men – and some were holding hands! We got through the main course bladdy dabble quick, mate, and got out of there even bladdy dabble quicker! I need a bladdy dabble brandy now to recover. Your shout.'

When Gordon Richardson was presented with his award for 25 years' service to the Italian Open, it was a relief that the Count of No Account held the ceremony in the Castelconturbia clubhouse. But he could probably have held the presentation at my desk this time, because there was very little play for the first two days due to rain.

The stoppages did at least enable me to practise a little diplomacy with two Irishmen, who had been friends for many years, but who were at loggerheads over something I'd written. It had all started totally innocently when Eamonn Darcy had revealed he was on a crash diet at the Spanish Open. Darce went through all the nuances of his diet and joked that it wouldn't suit his old pal Christy O'Connor Junior, because you had to give up the booze. It was just a funny line and I thought nothing of it. But, apparently, Christy had not seen the funny side at all. He came looking for me at Castelconturbia, brandishing a press cutting in much the same way as Ronan Rafferty had a few years before. Christy insisted his wife was very upset and that he was worried he was going to lose sponsorships because people thought he was a heavy drinker. I suggested he might be taking it all far too seriously but he would not be mollified, stomping off to find Eamonn after I had to confirm that I had only written what had been said – in jest. The pair must have had a bit of a barney and a little later Eamonn came to see me. He wanted some kind of retraction. I phoned the sports editor and explained what had happened and

179

asked if we might point out that Eamonn had only been joking
and that Christy was not an alcoholic.

By Sunday morning the Italian Open third round still hadn't
started, so the event was cut to 54 holes, won by little Patrik
Sjoland. I remembered back to one of his other chances of
winning when he five-putted the last in Madeira. Because of a
late start on Sunday it looked as though my plans for an evening
flight from Milan were dashed, but the finishing time was just
at that awkward juncture which leaves you feeling you might just
make it if you pull your finger out. I should have done like the
other pressmen and stayed overnight at our hotel by Lake
Maggiore. It was a beautiful setting and it was free. What the
heck was I thinking of trying to make my flight when I could
spend another night on the pasta and Valpolicella? Well, there
was a little matter of an extra £200 for another ticket and the
thought of getting up at 4 a.m. to catch an 8 a.m. flight after a
two-hour journey from the hotel. I decided to go for it.

I was frantic as the tournament came to a close, knowing I
had about two and a half hours before my flight was due to
take off. A few minutes were wasted chasing up my driver
before I dived into a courtesy car, spilling out my laptop,
mobile phone and connectors on to the back seat. I still had
stories to write for the *Irish Independent* and *Cork Examiner*, I
still had to do a wrap-up bulletin for the BBC World Service,
and I had to keep tabs on the scores being sent, in my absence,
from the press centre to Reuters by fax. As we tore along the
clubhouse drive, I saw Thomas Bjorn's caddie Martin Gray, a
fellow Nottinghamshireman and a lad who had never refused
me a favour, arguing furiously. His chauffeur was refusing to
take him to the airport. I told him to hop in my car. While
Martin chatted away in the front seat, I tapped out my *Irish
Independent* story in the back, hitting the keys whenever we
weren't screeching around bends or suddenly braking. I was
interrupted by my mobile phone. After rattling through my
World Service broadcast, despite the car yawing frequently and
once lurching to a stop, sending my laptop sliding to the floor,
I finished my broadcasting for the day. When my first story
was written I connected my laptop to my mobile and, after
three false starts, filed it. I only had time to write about 200
words of my final piece before we pulled in to the airport. My

plane was due off in 40 minutes. There was no time for any more. I rang the *Examiner*. It was OK to send my copy when I arrived back in Birmingham. I was about halfway through the story in the plane, when my battery warning light came on. I cursed, hoping I had enough power left to finish off. Suddenly the screen lit up brightly and died. It meant the story could not now be completed until I landed and found a power source. When we arrived at the Birmingham British Airways Hub, I connected up to the only socket available, halfway up the wall in the luggage arrivals hall, balancing my laptop on top of a rubbish bin. There was no sign of my *Cork Examiner* copy, not a word. The sudden loss of battery power must have wiped everything. I feverishly tapped out while people collected their luggage. Story written, I tried desperately to send, but the mobile signal was non-existent. I'd have to try again outside. The luggage carousel had come to a halt ages before and my bag sat there quite forlorn. I was completely alone in the luggage arrival hall. Stuffing my laptop, phone and laptop bag under my arm and picking up my luggage, I went to the automatic door. It remained closed. I put down my load and cavorted in front of it, trying to persuade it to do the decent thing. It wouldn't budge. I resorted to bashing on the plate glass with my laptop strap buckle. I could see no one beyond the automatic door. After 10 minutes' rapping, at last a perplexed female security guard appeared behind the door. She disappeared and then the automatic door swished open. She reappeared.

'Where the hell have you come from?'

'It's a long story – well, about 750 words, actually. I'm a journalist on a deadline and I wrote up my piece in the luggage hall. When I'd finished, everybody had gone.'

'Well, I don't know what to do with you now because the Hub's closed for the night, everything's locked up down there and I can't get it reopened. You'll have to come back with me to the main arrivals area through the emergency doors.'

'Can I just try to send over my story first, please?'

With utmost patience, the guard stood by while I sent my piece from the Hub information desk via my mobile, which, thankfully, had a strong signal. I checked with the *Examiner*. All was safely gathered in. We trooped off to the main part of the airport from the deserted Hub and I made my way to my car. My mobile rang. It was Sharon. 'Where are you?'

'Still at Birmingham Airport.'

'Oh. Was your flight delayed?'

'No, the flight was pretty well on time. You will never believe what has happened tonight.'

'Oh yes, I will.'


Late spring was brightened considerably by a football stars pro-am Derek Lawrenson of the *Sunday Telegraph* played in with two of his Liverpool heroes, Paul Ince and Steve McManaman. Derek then hit a hole in one and won a £180,000 Lamborghini. Derek thereby lost his amateur status due to the antiquated Royal and Ancient Rules of Golf. But who cares when you're rich? A week after Derek won the Lamborghini, Tim Glover also played in a pro-am, this one to do with a greenkeepers' association. Tim also got a hole in one and also collected the day's star prize. 'Lawrenson wins a bloody Lamborghini and I win a bloody lawnmower,' said Glover the ingrate.

After Mark O'Meara (or Mark O'Nearer, as the caddies now called him) and Jarmo Sandelin made their peace in Hamburg following the infamous Lancôme ball re-spotting the previous year, I enjoyed another wonderful few days of home cooking at my Barmstedterhof guest house. And on the Saturday night the usual spring fair was on, an enjoyable market town knees up, with stalls, roundabouts and open-air dances. Replete from a fine meal at the Barmstedterhof, I decided to stroll into town. As I came to the fair, on sauntering past one of the dances I was grabbed by a jolly looking frau, whom I recognised as a regular at our guest-house bar. She urged me to join in the dancing. Looking at her red face and wiggling ample hips and then glancing behind her at lurching quick-steps taking place on the boards that were covering the Barmstedt high street, I wanted to take flight. But, fuelled by a bottle of nice Mosel and a couple of schnapps, and never wanting to be a bad sport, I allowed her to drag me on to the floor. Within seconds I regretted it, caught in the face by a flying elbow which would have met with Eamonn Darcy's highest approval. I shook my head and regained composure but couldn't rid myself of a distinct blurring of the vision. I knew the syndrome. Not for

the first time, I had lost one of my contact lenses. I pleaded
with the dancing fair-goers to avoid the immediate area and
dropped to my knees to try to find the missing lens. People
wondered if it might be adoration, although the band was not
that good. Soon the penny dropped as I alerted them shrilly of
my plight. A dozen or more dancers were soon on their hands
and knees helping me. It took me back to the early '70s when
I once halted a football match under the Buckingham
floodlights after getting both my lenses knocked out in a
goalmouth skirmish. That time all 22 players, the referee and
linesmen, several club officials and quite a few spectators, who
had climbed over the stand wall, went on their knees on the
pitch. The Barmstedt band stopped. Confusion reigned. People
milled. There were two false alarms that produced a sequin and
a false fingernail. Then I had to give up. The lens had either
gone to ground or had been crushed. Once again I'd be getting
a rather one-eyed view of a European Tour event.

For some reason, the Irish Open has nearly always caused me
broadcasting problems, not least because I have often been
given a desk at the front part of the press room to work for my
publications and a small radio booth at the back, where my
broadcasting unit is, not big enough to house a desk for a
laptop as well. It involves a frantic dash through the media
centre every time the BBC telephone rings in the booth. The
Irish Open nearly always takes place in the second week of
Wimbledon fortnight. My booth phone will ring when a set
looks like it's coming to a close and the Beeb want me on air
soon on the broadcasting unit. I go zigzagging through tables,
à la Basil Fawlty, trying desperately not to trawl up laptop leads
or knock people over. It can be a frustrating business. For
instance, your telephone goes, you scatter the press tent, and
then you spend half an hour or more waiting for a tennis game
to finish. In that time, of course, the leaderboard changes about
20 times. Broadcasting style books go out of the window. 'It is
a type of broadcasting with which I am not familiar,' I
overheard one BBC old stager say. I'm sure it would have had
John Snagg catching a crab. But it is 'live'. Hence an
enthusiastic slip of the tongue by me which referred to Jeev
Milkha Singh being the son of the Flying Sick (Sikh), which is

even now still featured on the internet as a BBC radio bloomer. I've whispered 'It's all gone very, very quiet. Is there anyone out there?' when losing contact, much to the amusement of surprised listeners. And my frustrated cry of 'No. Now I've lost the flipping line,' brightened up one Nicky Campbell show. The repartee between me and Peter Allen and Jane Garvey during the *Drive* programme was even used as a trailer. 'Who is this Norman Dabell? Has anyone ever seen him? I'll bet he's short and fat . . .' 'Excuse me. I'm six foot one, as it happens!'

One of the greatest fears of doing two-way broadcasts, though, is that you get asked a really tricky question that you cannot answer, thus demanding serious waffle. Being bowled a googly you didn't read but scrambling a couple of byes, is about the best way I can put it. I had been waiting patiently to talk about Saturday's play after getting the call to set up the broadcast, tucked away in my little booth at the back of the press centre and unable to see the monitor through my perspex window. I was linking up with John Inverdale at Wimbledon. After a lengthy wait for my cue, a producer cut in to say, 'Hi, Norman. Sorry we've kept you waiting. You're on in 30 seconds. John's going to ask you about the Monty camera incident.' I hadn't a clue what she was talking about. The headset was ripped off as I dived out of the booth, screeching for information on Monty's latest escapade. Thankfully someone had just come in off the course from Montgomerie's match and filled me in at top speed. I dived back into the booth just as John was saying, 'Now it's over to Norman Dabell at Druids Glen, where I understand Monty's on the warpath.'

Monty didn't quite click this time and missed his Irish hat trick when he lost a play-off to David Carter. David and I had something in common that was certainly not an attractive golf swing. He had been rushed to Dubai Hospital the previous year. However, David's condition was much more life threatening than egg foo yung after he had developed fluid on the brain following a waterslide spill in South Africa. Only the speedy action of the friends who found him unconscious in his hotel and the skill of Dubai doctors had pulled him through.

There was great promise from Lee Westwood for the Open Championship when he won at Loch Lomond in style the week before going to Royal Birkdale. I'd gone back to Loch Lomond against my better judgement. I'd vowed I wouldn't return after getting locked in the grounds one night after working late, spending an hour waiting for security to let me out and thus missing supper. The endless trekking around to and from distant car parks and to and from the press centre to locate players had worn me down. But I relented in 1998 and regretted it. It always was a nightmare getting in and out of Loch Lomond but on the Sunday night after Westwood won, it took three hours to clear the area. Play, too, was suspended late on Saturday afternoon and restarted in the evening, a frustrating scenario for anyone trying to write for Sunday's newspapers, and it meant no dinner once again. I had to resort to a dodgy looking tandoori place, living in great dread afterwards in case monosodium glutamate had been used.

The countryside going back and forth from my hotel to the course was spellbinding, though. I was lost in it as I drove back on Friday night after again duelling with the Loch Lomond car-parking system. My thoughts, punctuated by alternate glances at the wonderful view and the road in front of me, were interrupted by my mobile phone.

'Ah, Norman. Glad I've got you. We didn't get round to coming to you to record you for our evening bulletin. Would you be in a position to do a piece?'

It was Irish radio. 'But I'm in the car, on the way back to my hotel. Can it wait until I get back?'

There was a half-muted discussion, then, 'How long will you be before you get to your hotel?'

'Well, about 20 minutes or so. I can be ready to go in about half an hour.'

'Oh, we were hoping you could go on in about five or six minutes.'

'But I'm in the car.'

'Could you do it live on the mobile?'

'Well, obviously not while I'm driving. I'll have to pull over.'

The presenter introduced me as coming from beautiful Loch Lomond. I was actually in a lay-by on the A811 to Drymen.

A home victory at the following week's Open looked remote and the gallery didn't have too much to cheer until young

Justin Rose livened up the weekend. Justin was a hero at 17 and when he turned professional the following week in Holland, it was mayhem in the media centre. Over a hundred media descended on Hilversum just to snatch a minute or two with the lad. It was three people to a one-man desk and phone, and bedlam. Justin's mind must have been in a complete whirl. It was hardly surprising he missed the cut. On Saturday, normality returned to Holland, as Rose fever abated. Justin then went into free fall in his professional career, until the parachute finally opened three years later.

There was a strange start to the Scandinavian Masters. Somebody got the caddies' bibs all mixed up and the Swedish scorers, relying on the numbers they saw on the bibs to cross check with those on their scoresheets, got most of the early first round scores in a total jumble. The hiccup wasn't fully spotted until a couple of hours after the start of the round, by which time, because of the transpositions, I'd already made two wildly incorrect updates of the leaderboard on Five Live.

'Yes, good morning again, Fergus. I have a confession to make. I'm afraid the caddie bibs with the players' numbers on them got all mixed up this morning and that confused the scorers. So you'd better forget everything I said before about the leaderboard. I'm not absolutely sure who's leading, but it could be Colin Montgomerie – providing his caddie Alastair put on the correct bib this morning. Or it could be Darren Clarke, if he didn't. Hope you see what I mean. Anyway, the leaderboard has Montgomerie leading by a stroke on four-under-par. Don't take that for granted, though, Fergus.'

'I see, Norman. I think that's clear. Now, on to tennis . . .'

Unexpected calls by radio stations are an occupational hazard nowadays, with the advent of clear and lucid communications on mobile phones. It isn't very often that a landline telephone can get you into trouble on that score, although I did once get thrown during a World Matchplay Championship. Derek Hobson of the old *Hobson's Choice* programme on one of the London stations arranged to do some pieces with me on the Saturday afternoon at Wentworth. I got myself all ready to go, but the telephone didn't ring at the allotted time. When I checked it, the phone had gone dead. So I dived under the desk to trace the telephone lead. Sure enough, it had been yanked out of its socket. Worse, the connector at the end of the cable was almost hanging off. I pushed it in but it would only stay in as long as I had my finger on it. Above me the phone rang.

'Somebody get that for me,' I bellowed from under the table, to the bemusement of my colleagues who wondered from where Dabell was throwing his voice.

'Hello. No, this isn't Norman Dabell. I'll get him for you.'

The telephone was stuffed underneath the table. I raked it to me one handed.

'Christ, Norman, where've you been?'

'I've had problems with the telephone cable.'

'Well, you're due on in about 30 seconds.'

I had my left hand stretched out to the socket and the telephone in the other hand, crouching on all-fours under a table. I was frozen with indecision. It was, indeed, Hobson's choice. I had to stay put.

I had just enough time to scream out to anyone above me who could hear, 'What's the state of play now in the two matches?' and get a muffled and barely discernible reply, when we were into the programme.

Hobson's choice of introduction would have floored me if I were not already in that position. 'Good afternoon to Norman Dabell, who's watching the drama of the World Matchplay Championship at Wentworth. First of all, Norman, what's the weather like?'

In Berlin we were given mobile phones courtesy of one of the German Open sponsors, because the promoters didn't want to install a series of expensive landlines. They were very good mobiles and reception and reliability of signal was first class. That provided all kinds of benefits. For instance, I know at least one of my colleagues used his back at the course hotel one night to call up German chat lines. As he didn't speak German, I'm not sure what he got out of it, but there you are. The advantage to me was that I wasn't tied down to my press room desk as I can be on Thursdays and Fridays when I can be doing updates every hour on the half-hour. I could go out on the course and, if it were too far to get back, just find myself a course leaderboard at about the half-past mark and take it from there. That was fine until I was put on stand-by when the sports bulletin was delayed indefinitely because of an important announcement coming from Parliament. As time wore on it seemed evident that the bulletin had been dropped. I relaxed and nipped into the on-course loo. Just as I approached mid-stream, my mobile rang. 'OK, Norm. We can come to you now. Keep it tight, though.'

With an early finish on the Saturday in Berlin, the rest of my work was done long before the BBC World Service was going to be ready to do their usual wrap-up of the day's play with a little chat to the anchorman about the golfing world's current affairs. I had been offered nine holes on the adjoining course and was dying to get out and play. I suggested, because I was using a reliable mobile, that we might do the broadcast from the course as most of the chat was going to be flexible stuff. It would largely be about the European chances in the following week's final major, the US PGA Championship. The producer was delighted to oblige. Press officer Gordon Simpson and I were just playing the first when the mobile rang. I had sliced into the rough and was scratching around looking for my ball. 'Hi, Norman, it's Ken. We'd like to do your piece a bit earlier than we arranged. Can we come to you in three minutes?'

'Yes, that should be fine.'

I carried on searching for my ball while listening to reports coming in from around the world.

'Sorry, Norm, but we're running a bit over. It's going to be another couple of minutes more,' said the producer, just as I found my ball.

Two more minutes went by. There came a yell from the group waiting on the tee behind. Gordon shouted from across the fairway. 'Can you just play your shot, Norm, or we're going to have to call them through?'

I checked with my producer. 'Ken. How much longer, please?' There was no reply. A report was in full swing, so I took a chance, placed the phone on the grass and hit my shot. My ball found the stream in front of the green and, fortunately, I uttered just a mild expletive. I scooped up the phone again.

'Well, I told you we were joining Norman Dabell out playing in Berlin. From that reaction, Norman, it sounds as though you're in a spot of trouble.'

Within a short time, we were back in Germany, this time for

the BMW International in Munich. A magazine had asked me to do a feature on what life was like for the losers as well as the winners on the European Tour. It was a touchy subject, but I knew somebody who might talk, one of my favourite sparring partners, Russell Claydon. Russell, an ardent Spurs fan, and I often have a little wager on Spurs versus Leicester City matches and I felt I could embrace a delicate matter with him without rancour. So, on the Wednesday afternoon I sat down with him and recorded an interview on always being the bridesmaid and never the bride. At the end of it, I said: 'Well, the best thing to do now, Russ, is make me scrap this tape. Go out and win, old son.' The 1998 BMW International champion? Russell Claydon. I was never more delighted to lose a feature, nor wipe a substantial amount of egg off my face.

As the season drew to a close, the race to be European number one between Colin Montgomerie and Lee Westwood went right to the wire, that year's decider, of course, being the Volvo Masters at Montecastillo. It was Groundhog Day again for me, but this time I had ensured I was working solely for television. With a reduced workload I had plenty of time to enjoy the trips to the sherry bodegas I'd missed the previous year. We stayed at a hotel actually called the Sherry Park in Jerez. To John Hopkins' chagrin, his bathroom had no soap. He rang down to reception and told them, 'Sopa, sopa, por favor, pronto.' A waiter soon arrived with – a bowl of steaming soup, of course.

The year ended in the sort of style to which we had become accustomed at World Cup of Golf tournaments. I had never been to New Zealand. My trip to Auckland was memorable for myriad reasons, not least through being upgraded and travelling first-class for the first time in my life. That certainly took the sting out of flying for around 24 hours. Before setting off, I chatted to Jean Van de Velde. The very likeable Frenchman was in the same boat, as well as the same plane, as me. We were both sweating on house purchases. His was a little pied-à-terre in Geneva, mine a dilapidated windmill in the Fens. I was delighted to lend Jean my phone to call up his agent and help him clinch his deal. Little did I realise then that *not* winning the Open the following year would pay for his new home. (Jean went on to achieve fame, fortune and legendary status after his memorable failure in the 1999 Open at Carnoustie.) We had a lengthy wait on the tarmac before taking off, during which there were constant head counts of passengers by the flight crew. Several names were called out unavailingly and we looked out to see a whole load of baggage being unloaded. Apparently there was confusion over whether a couple of passengers had boarded or not. 'It would be just my luck if they took my bags off by mistake,' I said mournfully to Jean, sitting across the aisle from me. When we arrived in Auckland, sure enough some luggage had gone missing – Jean's.

Auckland reminded me of Perth: vibrant, clean and brand-new, with spectacular harbours. I had plenty of chance to see plenty of it. I had the most stunning jetlag of my life and I swear I did not sleep for three days. I had to use a sleeping pill for the first time in my life. Our trips to the hosting Gulf Harbour Club each day were spellbinding. One minute you were looking at rugged Scottish heathland, the next, rolling Yorkshire dales, the next, tropical vegetation. At night in Auckland there was a wonderful ambience to the city, enhanced magically by staying at the Sky City Hotel with its own enormous casino. Next to it was one of the tallest buildings in the world, the Sky City Building. We ate in the restaurant on the very top of the tower, causing Martin Hardy of the *Express* to retire just after his starter with vertigo. It was quite a memorable tournament, too. Nick Faldo resurrected a flagging career by winning the trophy with young David Carter, showing touching and unusual humility by cooking his young partner's breakfast every day.

## TWELVE

# BAGS OF WOE

I HAD PAID for an electronic visa to Australia but when I checked in at Heathrow for my flight to Perth and my first tournament of 1999 there was no sign of it on the computer. As I stood dejected at the check-in desk I received the usual salutations from the players and my media colleagues. 'Happy New Year, Norm. What's gone wrong now?' Luckily, my story was believed and a new visa was authorised, but it took an age. This meant boarding the plane when everyone else was seated. I gather there had been two apologies by the crew, blaming a short delay on an errant passenger, whose baggage was now about to be taken off. I seemed to remember something like this happening a couple of months previously when I flew Down Under. I grabbed a stewardess to make sure no luggage had been left behind. I still spent most of the 18-hour flight via Singapore worried about whether I would have a clean pair of socks to wear when I arrived. My bulging holdhall was thus a sight for sore eyes when I arrived in Perth. And sore they were. Foolishly, I had gone to sleep on the first part of the journey while watching the in-flight movie and still wearing my contact lenses.

As usual there was a wonderful welcome awaiting us at the Vines, meeting old friends, especially the redoubtable Kathie Shearer, who runs her press rooms like a mother hen. Certainly eggs were on the menu for the welcome dinner. Thousand Year Old jobs, because there was a culinary spectacular being held at the Vines. We were treated to an extraordinary feast before the tournament, sampling such delicacies as kangaroo and

191

ostrich steaks, braised crocodile, goat curry and several slimy sea creatures boasting suckers and tentacles. I demurred on the suckers and tentacles but, imbued with courage gained from some of Australia's finest fruity wines, gave most of the other tucker a go, although I felt mighty queasy in the morning.

I had felt very nervous during the pro-am. It was tough playing in 40 degrees and when I smashed yet another drive into the woods I was loath to go after it. My pro-am partner Bernie McGuire, never a man to consider a wayward ball a lost cause, persuaded me to search for it. I finally spotted it right under some branches and, after weighing up all my options and judging just where it might emerge, hacked soberly but ineffectively, leaving the ball further embedded. Having tried culture, I then resorted to agriculture and slashed at the miserable object like a mad axe man. The ball stayed put but something did break free, landing with a 'plop' on my shoulder. As my eyes flickered down from a petrified head they lit upon a spider about the size of a bath plug. Imbued with terror and not common sense, I whisked the offending creature off my shoulder and fled for the fairway.

'Did this spider have red blobs on it?' queried McGuire, alerted by Dabell crashing out of the trees.

'It bloody well did, too. Why?'

'Oh, they're absolutely deadly,' offered McGuire nonchalantly.

Thus, when I walked past Padraig Harrington on the verandah of our Vines hotel two mornings later and he took me by the arm, I could tell him straight away 'Oh, that's absolutely deadly,' when he wondered aloud if the spider sitting on the jamb of the top of his closed room door might be dangerous.

'God, what will I do?' whispered an obviously distraught Irishman. 'Caroline [soon to be his wife] is in there. She'll totally freak if I tell her there's a dangerous spider on the door.'

'I think we'd better get somebody, Padraig. You keep a watch.' I returned with a hotel handyman, who said, 'Oh, yes. That is a bit of a dodgy one. I'll take care of it, though.' I wandered off to breakfast, happy in the knowledge I'd saved the day and also saved what might be an endangered species – twice now. As I walked past the Harrington's room, though, I witnessed the outcome of the handyman's version of ecology.

An Attenborough he was not. Above the door was a large, glistening splat mark.

Kuala Lumpur, the following week, was another part of the world I'd last visited as a young sailor in the '60s (yes, Radio Operator Second Class) and I was even more staggered at the changes than when I returned to Singapore. The Kuala Lumpur twin towers were a sight to behold and had to be visited. I was beginning to get my altitude legs after also scaling (by lift, of course) the Sky Tower in New Zealand only three months before. Disappointingly, the restaurant at the top was closed and press officer Gordon Simpson and I had to make do with the dubious pleasures of a downtown 'macchan' stall, sans alcohol, of course, as it was *al fresco*. Before the tournament began we were all expected to play in a press event on the adjoining course. I knew it wouldn't be my day when, in the steam-hammer humidity, my hired driver flew out of my hand on impact and described a graceful arc on its way to the practice green, landing with a thump between two shocked Malaysians. I was mighty relieved it had not travelled further. The Tengku of Malaysia and his queen were sitting in their gold-leaf decorated thrones next to the green, on the clubhouse veranda. I didn't enjoy my golf, but the walk was wonderful. I really did smell the flowers, beautiful tropical ones, kissed and plundered in turn by an array of sensational rainbow-coloured birds. At times I had to be bullied to play, I was so enraptured.

The fact that we had hours and hours hanging around in the hotel bar, waiting for our transport to the airport and onward passage to Dubai, did not prevent me again leaving a cupboard full of clothes behind. Unlike Gothenburg, these were found. But as they were going to cost an arm and a leg to post on, I told the hotel to distribute them among the staff.

I was taught a salutary lesson in the largest cafeteria in Dubai. Nearly everywhere we go, we have to really emphasise the cup of coffee we want, or the brew comes up in all sorts of strange ways in cups that are sometimes about the size of thimbles. So you get into a habit of asking for a large cup of coffee, 'Grande, por favor,' or demonstrating with hands about six inches apart that your need is for great and not small, cup-wise. I went through the usual demonstrative request to my Indian waiter in the City Shopping Centre café. He brought me a coffee in a receptacle I swear was of the proportions of a moderate-sized chamber-pot. 'Large enough, sir?' I guffawed long and loud. That would teach me. The Scots couple on the next table nearly cracked ribs in their hysteria.

The antics of my Reuters photographer, during a week in which young David Howell excelled, were no laughing matter. He was Egyptian, upset at being dragged away from a border skirmish somewhere in the Middle East, and knew nothing whatever about golf. It was tiresome running him through the nuances of the game, but I thought I'd done a reasonable job. That was until a walkie-talkie message came through from a tournament referee, telling Norman Dabell to get the hell out on the course and take charge of his cameraman. My neophyte photographer had managed to upset nearly every player he'd snapped, standing directly in front of them at the first tee and clicking off at all the inappropriate moments I'd warned him against. When I went scuttling up to the course, he was being frogmarched off it. I suggested he might be better off taking war photographs. Not satisfied with nearly making Dabell an outcast, he then spent the rest of the week talking to all his pals from Cairo to Karachi on my Reuters telephone.

As usual, Qatar followed on from Dubai. I was now wise to the sheikhdom's alcohol laws and the first thing I did on checking into my hotel was to find out where the covert bar was. Remarkably, it was two doors away from my room! While the hotel also had a licensed restaurant, its leisure centre was being renovated. We did have the use of a country club a few miles away, though. As I had a day to kill before going to the course to do preview stories, I decided to utilise the facility. I took the shuttle bus and was delighted when I arrived at a sprawling, opulent club with everything from tennis courts to an impressive swimming pool. I spent an idyllic few hours swimming and sunbathing and then decided to head back to the hotel so I could do some shopping in downtown Doha. When I went to open my locker, the key broke in the lock, leaving my clothes imprisoned. After an hour and several pleas to reception, no one had turned up to open the substantial door, which would have needed a jemmy about the size of a boat-hook to force it open. With my shopping trip under great threat, I decided not to wait any longer and travelled back in just my swimming shorts, much to the amusement of a couple of the Spanish professionals' wives, who had also been at the club that afternoon. It was the last I saw of my clothes and my latest pair of sandals. The club insisted they had been sent back to the hotel. The hotel had a vague idea that they'd been sent to my room.

The loss of the sandals provided another sad tale. I had bought their predecessors, some wonderful hessian, beatnik-style jobs, a couple of years earlier and they were just about my favourite footwear. They came in for some heavy stick from my colleagues, who gave me a variety of nicknames when I wore them. John the Baptist was one, and, rather paradoxically, Charlie Manson another. But I let the ribbing wash over me. The previous year in Australia, though, when I unpacked at the Vines I could only find the left sandal. I was beside myself and telephoned my previous week's hotel in Phuket and got housekeeping on the case, offering a small reward for the return of my prodigal sandal. I was quite proficient at chasing up missing apparel. I had left clothes and shoes all over the world in various locker-rooms and hotels, including Germany, Sweden and Malaysia in the past couple of years. The housekeeper thought I was raving mad, of course, and no trace of my sandal was found. I smelt treachery, with the sandals' chief persecutor Bernie McGuire high on the list of suspects. But then again, there had been several visitors to my room to raid my mini-bar the week before. I put out an all-points alert to my colleagues. They only breathed sighs of relief. With all hope lost that it was a mere practical joke, I had to concede the sandal had gone for good. When I packed to leave the Vines, I was heavy hearted that I had to let my siblingless remaining sandal go to the cobbler in the sky. It at least got a respectful farewell from my fellow press men as we saluted it with tinnies and good Oz Chardonnay. A fortnight later, when I unpacked at home and pulled out from my freebie Johnnie Walker bag the numerous gifts I had been given in the month away, I found the other sandal – squashed between some unused polo shirts. I wondered if the Vines bar had emptied its dustbin yet.

Bizarrely, we were given 15-inch by 8-inch wooden galleons to commemorate the week in Qatar. I had no room for mine in luggage bulging with clothes and gifts bought in Doha, so I decided to leave it for the chambermaid. I often did this with gifts that were too bulky to take home. I have bequeathed at least 20 umbrellas and 10 large tomes on the development of European golf courses this way in a dozen years. I packed and took my luggage down to the foyer and went for a bite to eat. When I checked out, there was my galleon standing on the counter.

'Oh, Mr Dabell, you left this in your room.'

'But I'd left . . . oh, forget it. Thank you. You're so kind.' With still half an hour to kill, a dozen or so of us flopped around the foyer waiting for the transport to the airport. I surreptitiously lowered the galleon behind one of the large easy chairs. As we boarded our coach a doorman came running out to us.

'Someone has forgotten this.' Several fingers pointed sympathetically towards me.

'But I don't . . . oh, thank you. You're so kind.' I intended abandoning the proud little ship in the parcel rack above my seat. But our alert driver noticed it before I had even got down the bus steps. I offered it to him for his son. He didn't have a son. He politely declined it for his daughter or his wife. He couldn't accept it for himself. It was more than his job was worth to accept backsheesh. I was beginning to think there was some kind of eastern spell on my gift. But I took a chance and dumped it in a waste-paper bin at check-in. When I took my seat on the plane I nearly fell straight off it. Alongside me, in the lap of someone I recognised as one of the caddies, was a wooden galleon. I didn't realise I was staring at it so intensely.

'Do you like it, mate? Somebody had chucked it, I think. I found it in the dustbin. Great, innit?' I found no rest until our plane had landed safely and I had seen the galleon sail off proudly on top of a luggage trolley – in the opposite direction to me.

I arrived back in the UK at one home after having left from another. While I had been in Perth, my stalwart fiancée Sharon had overseen our removal to an old windmill and cottage that I planned to turn into our dream home. During the week off I ordered a new house sign. There would be no ambiguity this time with a house called 'The Mill'. My previous house was number 28a and called 'Trombones'. I had understood it was going to be number 76 and paid £75 for the house sign, which I installed nonetheless, confusing the postman for five years.

Back on the road, it was a delight to revisit Le Meridien at Penina on the Algarve, where I had enjoyed a couple of winter 'Henry Cotton Championships' in the past. On the first visit, Sharon and I, and two other guests, were picked up by a hotel car at Faro airport after an exhausting day which began with a lengthy flight delay. One of our fellow passengers was eager to talk about a trip he'd made to a Brazilian course and, full of wild enthusiasm, suddenly asked the car to stop and dived into the boot. He produced a glossy course brochure and turned on the car interior light to demonstrate further. By now seething, as well as weary after a long journey, I snapped: 'For God's sake, man. We all enjoy golf courses but will you ever stop banging on about this one? Can we please get to the bloody hotel? I'm dying for a glass of white.' I didn't see him once we got to reception and didn't again until the presentation ceremony of the tournament. He was the managing director of the hotel that had kindly invited me, free of charge, to stay and play.

Since then, I had recovered nearly all lost ground and renewed old acquaintances for the week of the Algarve Portuguese Open. Again I had a wonderful room overlooking the course and a huge umbrella pine that filled with hundreds of sparrows at twilight. Their noisy twittering can drive some to distraction, but not I, who mourns the loss in numbers of that lively little bird in Britain. It proved to be a dramatic finale and the fact that it took a play-off for Van Phillips to beat John Bickerton ruffled not a feather with me either. There was no dash for a plane, because I had a flight booked for the next day. It merely meant another fine meal and several glasses of splendid Portuguese wine.

Within a couple of days, though, I was drinking equally succulent Spanish wine as we visited Malaga for the Turespana Masters. The Spanish Tourist Board were pushing the boat out for the week, so it was the very least I could do to agree to play in the pro-am. I very rarely take my clubs on tour with me because there is so much to carry – my luggage as well as a sizeable bag containing my laptop and all the bits and pieces I need for written and radio work. I arranged, therefore, to borrow a member's set. I was assured they would be ready for me well in advance of my tee-off with that week's unfortunate pro, David Howell. Despite a lot of running around trying to locate my clubs, as well as interviewing players for my preview stories, I still had no weapons by the time my pro-am start drew nigh. I left messages all over the place for the clubs to be brought to me on the tee, but there was still no sign of them when the starter went through his usual preamble.

'Which one is Norman Dabell, please?'

'That's me.'

'Good, and what is your handicap, Norman?'

'Er, well, mainly, I don't have any clubs.'

I had to let my team go off and then catch up with them as soon as I had weapons. I had a brainwave. We were teeing off at the 10th in a two-tee start. Could my clubs be at the first? They were, of course, standing quite proudly in fact, awaiting their new user.

It went down as my worst start to a pro-am, replacing an infamous tee-off at The Belfry. Mark Davis was my unfortunate pro on that occasion. He watched me limber up and admitted he was impressed with the way my swing had improved since the first time we'd teamed up. Of course, the swing collapsed the minute I hit a ball in anger. It had more moving parts than a Meccano set and contributed greatly to my ball whipping smartly to cover-point and rattling into the pro-am registration tent. As I walked over to offer my profound apologies to anyone it may have hit, Pete Mitchell's caddie Deano, who had knowingly waited at a respectful distance until my wild slash was over, strolled past. He drawled a phrase that has become synonymous with Dabell and pro-ams, 'Don't give up the day job, Norm.'

A few weeks further on, the wine was Bordeaux. One of the perks of travelling around Europe is enjoying some wonderful wines in the regions of their source. I have visited up to a dozen Spanish bodegas in my time, in Italy sat down to dinner at the House of Berlucci, visited Tuscan vineyards, and walked the Roman caves in Frascati which first stored that famous wine. But never had I been to a French Chateau. Bordeaux, where Retief Goosen carried off the French Open, gave me that chance. We visited Chateau Lascombes in Margaux, one of the largest estates in Medoc, dating back to the 1600s. As an amateur wine buff, I was spellbound for a couple of hours. Imagine my delight then when my prize in a putting competition was a 1982 claret, a prized vintage. It was a warm week. The press tent reached 100 degrees. More than one person was startled to find a laptop cooling in the fridge among the Cokes, an ideal way, I'd discovered, to prevent it overheating.

I had escaped Ireland without misfortune once that year. Could I do so again, thought I, when flying into Galway airport? The West of Ireland Classic was not the world's biggest tournament but it had great significance for two players: Costantino Rocca, who won it, and Padraig Harrington, who finished second and was thus able to clinch his Ryder Cup place the following week in Munich. The pair provided plenty of excitement during the week, which was just as well. For the whole of the five days we were in the Galway Bay Country Club press room, overriding everything was a 'Best of Van Morrison' tape which filled the room from morn 'til night, the same songs over and over again. No amount of cajoling could end the misery. It was the club's background muzak, and they were not prepared to change it. Everyone else loved it, they insisted. That was because they were not in the building for 10 hours a day.

On the Saturday there was a fairly early finish, so I arranged to meet Irish writers and friends Charlie Mulqueen and Colm Smith in the hotel bar before we went out for a meal down in Galway. It looked as though I was going to be in the chair as I walked into the bar, recognising only players Carl Suneson and Miles Tunnicliff and their families. As I nodded to Carl and Miles, there was a sudden excruciating stab of pain in my right calf, quickly followed by another just a bit higher and then another. I yelped in agony and went dancing around the bar entrance, raking up my trouser leg. That induced yet another piercing stab of pain, higher up and close to my groin. I realised that I had a wasp up my trouser leg, and I hopped out of the bar, whipping my belt undone and clawing off my trousers. That caused Suneson junior, who had been happily tucking into an ice-cream, to run to the arms of his mother, who I expect was averting her eyes. I actually saw the offending beastie fly out – at about the time a gaping and awed Mulqueen and Smith turned into the hotel foyer on their way to the bar. 'Sorry, fellas,' said the dancing and breathless Dabell on the way past the pair. 'Got to get to my room for some ointment. Bloody wasp's stung me. About six times.'

The 1999 Ryder Cup was a crushing disappointment for all who like to see fair play. A week after the match I was writing stories about Sergio Garcia's American caddie Jerry Higginbotham being beaten up by his own fellow-countryman. That was about as sad as it gets. Jerry certainly looked a sorry sight when he arrived at Cologne for the German Masters. I happened to spot him on the practice range with Garcia and he was sporting two lovely black eyes.

I may have incurred a couple of shiners myself that week – or even something worse. My hotel was in the Severinstrasse in Cologne, where there were several really good Italian restaurants. I decided to avoid one of them after the lady of the house constantly stroked the back of my neck and called me 'Richard Burton' when she came to the table. Another trattoria was busy on the Thursday night when I first went into it, but because it was pretty late, the customers thinned out until I was left eating on my own. I was tucking into my calzone with gusto when in walked a swarthy, unsmiling bunch who flopped down at a table and started snapping out orders to the waiters. The man I took to be the owner was transformed from a rather bossy individual to a model of servility, his head nodding frequently in acquiescence to this gang, a bit like one of those dogs you see in the back of cars. The Mark Knopfler album I was enjoying was whipped off without ceremony and on came the track 'Stay', by a group I later learned were called Shakespeare's Sister. It was repeated immediately. I had finished my calzone and needed another quarter carafe of red and some Gorganzola. Could I get the waiter to acknowledge me? Not while me laddos were giving him the run around. 'Stay' had its third outing. I sat neglected in the corner. When 'Stay' came on yet again, I leapt to my feet and collared one of the waiters before he could get away. 'Another carafe of red, please. And can you take that damned record off? You've played it four times now in 20 minutes.' The waiter looked like a rabbit caught in headlights and he gulped, looked over at the table from hell, got a curt nod from the fiercest looking one, and jumped to do my bidding. When he brought me my cheese and wine, he whispered 'Sorry, but that the favourite of friend. Is why we play it lot of times. Sorry.' I looked over at the 'friend'. He was glaring fearsomely at me. I didn't like the cut of his jib and really didn't enjoy my cheese much. As I paid the bill and walked from my table to the exit, this ruffian watched my every move with a dark stare, mirrored by his three companions. I didn't breathe easily until I walked into the foyer of my hotel, half expecting a hitman, perhaps alerted by mobile phone, to suddenly confront me. My suspicion that I'd nearly mixed it with a local protection racket was reinforced when I walked past another Italian restaurant on the Saturday night. The same quartet were slouching around in it, looking just as mean as they had two days before. I hurried past. I couldn't stand the thought of listening to 'Stay' again.

I had a pretty good relationship with Jerry Higginbotham and that came in handy a week later when I drove up to St Andrews, where he was appearing alongside Garcia in the Dunhill Cup, to interview him for my latest book, *Winning the Open*. It took about an hour and a half to interview Jerry and I talked to him in the first place I'd ever carried out a book interview with a caddie 10 years before, the Dunvegan Hotel close to the entrance of St Andrews. In 1989 the interview had been with Arnold Palmer's bagman Tip Anderson and it was great to see Tip still sitting in his usual place at the hotel bar. A real sense of déjà-vu came over me. Jerry really relished his interview and so did his numerous friends who tapped into the Dabell 'slate' over the bar. It needed a trip to the cash dispenser to pay it off, but it was worth it for Jerry's contribution to the book.

There have been enough odd things happen to me on a golf course trying to imitate the players who provide me with a living, to provide material for another book. For instance, in Madeira, I once stood by a green and watched while Mark 'Tester' Watson, the European Tour's travel manager, tried to chip on. Tester took a huge divot. As I looked to see where his ball was bound, an enormous sod of earth fell on my head – and stayed there. I looked like something out of a pagan ritual with mother earth for my headgear. Losing things, though, is generally my forte. I have lost hundreds of balls, numerous gloves and head-covers. In Germany, my prized imitation Rolex (sweep, not tick-tick, sahib) detached itself from my wrist and I didn't miss it until it was too late. I have lost clubs, but only singletons. This includes a driver that once flew out of my hand in near darkness at the wonderful heathland Broadstone club in Dorset. The driver disappeared upwards – and never came back down to earth, even though my partner and I could have sworn we heard it land. After a time spent scrabbling in the undergrowth where we had heard the noise, we were forced to give up and, because it was now absolutely pitch-dark, resort to finishing the match the next morning, when I also hoped to resume the search for my missing driver. When we went back to the spot where the driver disappeared, a look upwards into the pine that stands sentry over the tee revealed the fugitive lying neatly on top of a squirrel's dray. It must have been the startled animal that we had heard hitting the deck, as it deserted its invaded home. A greenkeeper's assistant had to retrieve the driver, using an extended ladder. I have also, while trying to hook out a ball, dropped a sand-iron into a pond, never to be seen again and, in the days when my temperament was a little suspect, hurled a four-iron back to my recumbent bag, to watch in chagrin as the iron ricocheted neatly into an Irish river. But, until Wentworth 1999, I had never lost a whole bag of clubs before. The location was the short 12th on the East Course, where I had hit a nine-iron shot so far right it went deep into the spinney close to gardens. After I urged my partners to play on, I searched in the dense undergrowth and trees. Time was up and, with no sign of the ball, I went to collect my clubs, which I'd thought I'd left leaning against a tree. There was no sign of them either. I couldn't find them even when I ducked into the tangled heavy stuff and crawled around among the fallen leaves.

'Come on, Norm, we're on the tee. Where the devil are you?' My partners were anxious to tee off on the 13th, so as not to call anyone through.

'I can't find my clubs.'

'Can't find your bloody clubs. Don't be such a silly sod. You can't have lost a bag of clubs.'

'But I have, I swear.' They dived into the woods and briefly helped me, but to no avail.

'You are looking in the right place, aren't you, Norm?'

'Well, of course I am.' I had to let them carry on. I resumed the search. While I was in there, I was joined by someone else from the next group, who'd also hit an errant tee shot.

'Are these your clubs?' suddenly yelled my fellow searcher from deep in. 'I was looking for my ball and fell over the damn things.' The bag had obviously toppled from its tree and plunged into a neat little hollow, to be covered by ample foliage. It was, however, at least 30 yards away from where I was looking. My bid for honours was over. My partners were playing the 14th by the time I caught them up.

A return to Malaysia and the World Cup of Golf at the stunning Mines resort in Kuala Lumpur brought the curtain down on the season. But the gremlins put a sting in the tail of the year when Sharon and I went on holiday to Cyprus. On our penultimate day on the island we decided to go to Nicosia from our base at Latchi, via the Troodos Mountains. The outgoing trip passed without incident, even if some of the roads I took in our hired four-by-four were no more than tracks. After an afternoon in Nicosia, I decided to take a different route back, one that looked as though it wouldn't be such a trial and missed out the Troodos Mountains. We came to the new route at about 7 p.m. At first the road seemed fine, marked and pretty new, although the incessant bends kept me on my toes. We saw no one for about two hours and then the road started to get a little older and rougher. After a further hour, during which we made constant checks that there was no other direction we could possibly be taking, we came to a very basic roadside service area, dispensing little but soft and alcoholic drinks and certainly no petrol. Famished, we stocked up with Coke and crisps. Nobody spoke English, but when I pointed to the road we were on and suggested 'Polis?' (the alleged terminus of the route) my query was greeted with enthusiastic affirmation and waves of the arms in the appropriate direction. We travelled on. After a few minutes the tarmac ran out. Within a few minutes more, the stone chips ran out. Within 30 minutes more, a dirt 'road' had narrowed to about the width of our four-by-four and not a lot more. I was worried but dared not show it. Sharon was terrified, thinking of the sheer drop on her side, hundreds of feet down. Suddenly the road ran out altogether as we were faced by a sheer wall of rock. I had to reverse back, gently and hardly daring to breathe in case I put the rear wheels over the edge, until I came to a turn which I had spurned because the road looked even narrower than the one we were on. I took the new path for about half an hour, first buoyed by a tattered sign which confirmed, I hoped, that we were heading down the mountain in the right direction, and then completely lifted when the road widened out a little. That optimism was soon dashed when that road, too, ran out, ending abruptly in a mortifying pile of earth, beyond which lay a rather hastier descent down to Polis than I planned. At least I could turn. I had to head back for the only other option at the earlier junction. Travelling on for another frightening 20 minutes or so, the path became littered with rocks, which threatened to spill us over the mountain edge like a deadly snooker in-off. Sharon was rigid with fear. Then so was I as, directly in front of us, there was a sudden rock fall which completely blocked our way. I ordered Sharon out of the car, on my side, almost hard up against rock-face. I had to somehow turn the car round, and if the back was going to slip over the edge then the calamity would claim only one victim. What sort of predicament that would have left Sharon in did not occur to me. It did to her. She whimpered in terror as I wound down the windows and bellowed out questions, like, how far were the wheels from the edge now? Even using the four-wheel drive, at a rough estimate it proved to be something like a 50-point turn. I shall never know how I got the car around to return from whence we came. I had to drive all the way back past the 'service area' (closed by now) and all the way back up the twisting, tortuous roads to Troodos. There was little fuel left in the tank, and it was around 1 a.m. by the time we arrived in Troodos. I knocked up the night porter at a hotel in the village, toying with the idea of booking in. But I knew I should have to take out my disposable contact lenses to sleep, and I had neither another pair nor spectacles for travelling back. There was also the small matter of making our plane home the next day. It was scheduled for around midday from Paphos, about an hour from our hotel. Almost unbelievably, though, I did find out where there was an all-night petrol station, about 12 miles away. After limping in on mere petrol fumes, I was able to put Cypriot notes into the machine and fill up. We were then faced with a mammoth drive back to our hotel in Latchi. We arrived there around 4 a.m. I had been driving for about 10 hours, around the time I could have taken travelling from St Georges to St Andrews. After a couple of hours of fitful sleep we went to breakfast to discover a notice saying our flight had been delayed indefinitely due to a strike by airline staff.

# THIRTEEN

# DROPPING ANOTHER CLANGER

BEFORE MOVING UP the Gulf to Qatar in early 2000, after my latest trip to Dubai, I had a date in Abu Dhabi to play a new course there. Having lost a bet, Bernie McGuire paid up with a half-bottle of red wine, which he tucked into my flight bag as we made our way onwards to Doha. I forgot all about it. When we landed at Qatar, we were asked if we were carrying anything illegal, especially alcohol. I said I had nothing to declare. Muslim customs officers seem to have a nose for alcohol. I was sent to a cubicle and ordered to empty out my bag. Of course, the first thing my hand felt was the bottle. I went as red as the wine and protested I had forgotten it was there. Three immigration officers went into a huddle and I wondered if this was to be a repeat of South Africa. Was I going to get deported? Worse, was I going to get thrown in gaol? After what seemed an eternity, one of the officers came over and told me I was free to carry on, but my bottle had been confiscated. Cursing McGuire, I had to take a taxi because all the hotel transfer buses had gone. When I arrived at the Sheraton, everyone else had checked in, of course. I was given a similar room to the one I'd experienced two years previously, the one above the screeching girlie group. I would never be able to sleep there, so I went back to reception to request a move. It was the only room available, according to the sympathetic but unyielding receptionist. I pleaded and cajoled. Then, when all hope was receding, I am ashamed to say, I played my only trump card. I was an international journalist known to the sheikh, who had always said he was grateful for my attendance of the Qatar Masters. It did the trick. Pulling out a key on a solid-gold key ring, I was given the sheikh's penthouse suite, used for entertaining VIPs! I could stay there for the night and then the next day I would be found a quieter room. I stayed there all week. Each day I arrived back at the hotel fully expecting my clothes to have been moved and to be going to a new room, but it never happened. I spent a week in the lap of luxury, periodically inviting my colleagues around to see how the unlucky Norman Dabell had, this time, landed on his feet.

I'm surprised the guitarist at the teetotal Italian restaurant at the Sheraton didn't drive total abstainers to drink. He was awful. Undeterred, he strummed and shrieked, until he made his fatal mistake. 'Signores, I will now take requests,' he offered enthusiastically. 'Can you play at the Ramada tomorrow night?' I enquired.

Probably because of the swapping of rooms when I'd arrived, somehow my passport remained in my pigeon-hole at reception and I checked out without picking it up. When I came to go through immigration control at Doha airport, I discovered my passport was missing but didn't immediately twig where it was. I hunted through my luggage, then, with time beginning to run out, realised where it must be. I phoned on my mobile and a thoroughly chastised receptionist agreed to send the document down to the airport by taxi. It arrived in a stretch limo. I made my flight by minutes.

There could have been a bit of a dust-up in the gym at my hotel during the Madeira Island Open the following week, where we had rare perfect conditions. Young Niclas Fasth won the tournament. As is my wont nowadays, I was down in the fitness centre, early doors on Thursday morning. I'd been there about three-quarters of an hour when a girl I thought I recognised as one of the new Swedish pros' wives came into the gym. After a rather haughty look at me pedalling furiously on the bike machine, she walked straight over to the television and turned off the programme I was watching, an old episode of *The Clangers*, and imposed 'MTV' on me.

'Excuse me, but I was watching that.'

'But it's a children's programme.'

'*The Clangers* is *not* a children's programme.'

'Uh? Well, anyway, it's in Portuguese.'

'*The Clangers* aren't speaking Portuguese.' My logic, and a reminder that the early bird catches the worm, defeated her. With an irritated stab of the index finger, *The Clangers* was restored. 'Now where were we? Ah, yes, the Soup Dragon was throwing a party. Two more minutes on the bike and then the weights.'

Following hard on from Madeira there was another first for me. This was visiting Brazil. In fact, I had never been to South America, so when I landed in Rio de Janeiro, it was a wide-eyed Dabell picking out the landmarks, noting the Sugar Loaf, Statue of Christ, and Copacabana Beach. Indeed, my hotel overlooked the Copacabana Beach, with the Sugar Loaf in view from my penthouse window. Dabell had again fallen on his feet. The tournament caused its share of problems, though, from the minute I arrived at the steaming, tiny press room. I was straight off the plane, with the first round about halfway through, following severe delays to my flights. At the weekend, Brazil time was four hours behind the UK, so when Roger Chapman and Padraig Harrington went into a play-off I was already past the time for filing copy to the *Daily Telegraph*. I had to ad-lib the story and then 'tickle' it into shape just before it was placed on the page. The trouble was, the story kept changing. One minute it looked as though Harrington must win, and then the next, Chapman, then Harrington again. By the time Roger won the shoot-out, the *Telegraph* sub was tearing his hair out with all the changes. But you had to be there. Roger, my old comrade from Radio Kent days, had finally won after nearly 20 years of trying, the tour's longest-serving 'bridesmaid'. It proved a heady Sunday night by the Copacabana, with Roger acknowledging the choir of players and caddies, and Padraig, a non-drinker, admirably joining in by toasting Chapman in Coke – when he must have been hurting badly inside.

Padraig soon put it right, though, bouncing straight back to win the following week in São Paulo. Before that, Bernie McGuire and I, and the press officer, Gordon Simpson, did everything you have to do in Rio. We took cable cars and toured the Sugar Loaf and Statue of Christ and ate a wonderful lunch at the Girl from Ipanema Bar. In direct contrast, São

Paulo was an absolute dump, with mile after mile of seedy high-rises and decaying tenements. The traffic was horrendous and the journey to and from the course was a daymare. For two days we lost all communications and the only way I could file stories or do broadcasts was on the tournament director's mobile telephone. We were thinking of having T-shirts made with 'I survived São Paulo' printed on them when we discovered an embroiderer at the airport.

While on the subject of surviving, it's often occurred to me that I can look at life and cock a snook at the misfortunes that tend to litter it. For instance, once when I was allowed out of bed for the first time after a serious operation, I hobbled gingerly to the toilet. As I looked bleakly at the porcelain, my body all aching and racked with pain, I read the words 'armitage shanks'. I whispered to myself mournfully, 'So do I.' This rather absurd thought quite lifted me and, to the sister's total consternation, I was still giggling – and wincing in turn – when I limped back into my room. You need that kind of fortitude to keep going back to Morocco year after year. You need a steadfast nature and a cast-iron stomach to sneer at Agadir Diarrhoea or a dose of Rabat Rumble. Morocco-bound you will rarely be. You need resolve to avoid cracking up when telephone lines fail – if they ever exist in the first place. You can be covered in dust from head to toe when the sand blows in from the Sahara, wreaking havoc with contact lens users. And you need expert knowledge of Moroccan protocol. I once saw one of the king's men and his guest set out for a round of golf at Agadir, ignoring protestations from the tournament director that there was an event going on. When I reported it in the *Telegraph*, I was warned that it could mean instant deportation. Moroccan drivers make up their own rules of the road as they go along. Often there are no roads, just dust tracks churned up by seemingly blinkered moped riders.

But this time it would be different. We were playing at one of those places sung about in hippy ballads that I'd always wanted to visit when I was at the height of my flower power: Marrakesh. Its huge market-place is a sight to behold as a multitude mixes in with numerous floor shows – snake charmers, fire-eaters, fire-walkers, belly-dancers, jugglers. It was all as I imagined it would be. The smaller souks were an

Aladdin's cave. We spent several hours of spare time just being tourists, watching the Gulli-Gulli Man or bartering for satinwood chess sets and – leather sandals. Yes, it was time for my fourth pair of sandals in three years. These lasted more than 24 hours, unlike my purchase the year before in Qatar. The course was raw but boasted a wonderful view of the Atlas Mountains in the distance. Alongside the course were sumptuous villas, one, we understood, belonging to George Michael. We were unsure whether he was in residence but it was reported that a number of guests sitting around his swimming pool were scattered by an errant golf ball during one of the rounds. Roger Chapman, I think, might have been the culprit.

There was one great design fault with the Amelkis course, where Jamie Spence, like Chapman one of my former Radio Kent acquaintances, won so convincingly. At the clubhouse entrance there was a small pool, a trap for anyone not walking around looking down at the ground. I lost count of how many players I saw during the week shaking their soaking feet like Gene Kelly. Believe it or not, I never fell foul of it once, despite hurtling to and from the clubhouse searching for players for interview. The only real blight on a happy week (for once) in Morocco was the press room. Our air-conditioning was commandeered by the VIP tent. Temperatures soared and humidity went off the scale. Micky Britten's laptop power pack blew in the heat. I had only just sold him it. Somehow we managed to stay on speaking terms after burying the hatchet on a 10-year vendetta. Our Moroccan press officer, the enigmatic and callow former Foreign Legionnaire Kamil El Kholti, kept promising new air-conditioning every day, while we melted. On Saturday the unit was, apparently, stuck in Tangiers. It arrived on the final morning, Sunday, and blew up while it was being installed. A workman fixed it during the afternoon and it was immediately taken away to the VIP tent. The final evening saw me in a desperate dash to make the charter flight for players and officials. I filed to the *Telegraph* on the run through the airport. I would have missed the plane if one of the players had not suffered the same fate as me in Qatar and realised, when he was about to go through immigration, that his passport was still in a hotel reception pigeon-hole. Marrakesh or not, you still needed mettle to take the road to Morocco.

Interviews with players after things have not quite gone to plan on the course can be a hazardous business for the press sometimes. I've seen some of the bravest questioners reduced to jelly by an unexpected rebuke in response to what they thought was a perfectly innocent query. Sometimes the questioner does not help himself, though, like the hapless reporter who asked Colin Montgomerie 'Was the wind a factor?' when Monty came in for a press conference after a gale-swept round at Carnoustie. Monty's hair was tangled and plastered around his head and his shirt buttoned right up to his chin after weathering the storm. 'Was the wind a factor? Was the wind a *factor*? *Was the wind a factor*? Have you been any further than the press room today? Was the wind a factor?' Nick Faldo was another to go on the offensive.

'Nick, you rather spoiled your round with those two bogeys at the seventh and eighth.'

'Bogeys? *Bogeys*? Do you think this game's easy? Would you have any idea what it's like playing the seventh and eighth in this tournament?'

It must rankle when you know your interrogator is a hacker. Once in Ireland, Nick described his round at a press conference and after he'd gone there was a good deal of puzzlement because none of the clubs he'd used at particular holes made any sense and some of his shots would have been highly unlikely. We never did find out whether he'd done it for devilment or genuinely got confused. Faldo stories were written that day without much golf analysis in them.

During the 2000 Spanish Open near Girona, Monty was in fiery mood because his putting was getting on his nerves. You could tell that when he marched up to a spectator on the 12th hole, grabbed his camera and handed it to a marshal. When Monty is in that sort of mood, all you are likely to get from him after he's signed his card, is, as he marches past you, 'Not today, thank you,' like someone addressing the milkman. As he was well in contention, despite his putting malaise, Monty did come in for a press conference, however. Ever the helpful soul (sic), Micky Britten dissected his putting stroke and suggested where Monty might be going wrong. 'You stick to your writing and I'll stick to the golf,' blazed Monty at the surprised Britten. But, secretly, Monty might have listened to anything that could change his fortunes on the greens. Nothing would go right and he was easily surpassed by the winner, Brian Davis.

I'm sure Brian had a more relaxed flight home than I did. I had reluctantly flown with 'Easyjet'. The no-frills airline were not exactly my favourites after cancelling a flight to Nice at short notice and causing me all sorts of problems a couple of years before. But I had little option. So I was filled with foreboding when I arrived at Barcelona airport and found my flight had been delayed. When we did finally arrive at Luton several hours late, my luggage took 90 minutes to turn up. I arrived home at 5 a.m., exhausted.

There we were, enjoying a splendid lunch at The Belfry before the leaders went out in the final round of the Benson and Hedges International. Just as my knife cut through a fine piece of sirloin, Canadian freelance Brian Creighton came charging into the dining room. 'Guys, you'd better get back. Padraig Harrington could be disqualified.' As Harrington should, in about half an hour, be taking to the course with a five-stroke lead, our puffing messenger got our immediate attention. Mouthfuls were hastily swallowed, cutlery clattered down on plates and about a dozen journalists repaired at speed to the press room. Soon, the story broke. It had been discovered that Harrington had failed to sign his first round scorecard. The punishment was swift and severe. He was, indeed, disqualified. My sirloin would not be finished. Harrington, somehow staying outwardly cheerful after forfeiting the chance of over £166,000, bravely chatted with me to my Irish radio station RTE about his indiscretion. For the next year, the genial Dubliner would be reminded of the lowest point of his short career. He must have become heartily sick of, 'Have you signed your card this time, Padraig?'

Before I flew to Hamburg, I went for laser eye surgery at Keith Williams' Laservision at Harley Street. Life took on a new meaning. A simple 20-minute op enabled me to awake in the morning and actually see a room instead of a blur. I could see for miles. I was ecstatic. I wanted to tell anyone who would listen how magical my eyesight now was and how I'd thrown away my contact lenses after 30 years. At the BBC, we decided I should produce a short feature, not only talking about my experience but those of the pros who had had laser surgery. A feather in the cap for me would be to get Tiger Woods to talk about his experience after he, too, had the treatment. He was in Hamburg for another Deutsche Bank Open. His management refused my request to talk to him, however, so I rather sneakily introduced the subject into a press conference, where he gave me just what I wanted. When I played my mini recorder back, though, his observations were useless for my feature, affected by a translator doing her stuff right alongside the interview area loudspeaker where I had positioned my mini recorder. It was ironic, then, that I'd got a really good recording from Lee Westwood on the laser subject. Lee had had his eyes lasered as well. He shot a brilliant 64 in the last round at Hamburg to beat Woods for the German title!

I've played golf with many sporting heroes and celebrities over the years, indeed enjoyed a round with Fred Titmus on the very day he was a crossword clue in a national newspaper. And I once played with Max Bygraves and then had to stand in for him as after-dinner speaker when he was called away urgently. But even enduring a couple of frames with Alex Higgins, saving a point-blank header from Ron Atkinson and winning a tenner from Ireland's greatest amateur, Joe Carr, was little compared to the thrill I got at Belton Woods, Lincolnshire, in June, playing golf alongside one of my all-time heroes of sport, Gordon Banks. The nearest I'd ever got to Gordon was standing behind his goal at Filbert Street and gazing up at him at the Royal Garden Hotel from the celebrating crowds in the street in 1966 after England's World Cup victory. Now I was playing a round of golf with him and listening to his anecdotes. It was sheer bliss. My return to Belton Woods reminded me of 1996, when I'd also played in the annual Turkey Federation Charity Event there. The sponsors had provided a huge papier mâché turkey which they had set up at the 18th green. When the Turkish national football team arrived to stay at the Belton Woods Hotel on the same day as our competition, they all came on to the balcony overlooking the 18th. Of course, the first thing they saw was this mammoth turkey's backside. They were outraged, certain that it was a slight on them and their country's chances in Euro '96. Well, nothing would mollify them. The turkey had to be dismantled for the sake of public relations and to avoid the team walking out of the hotel.

Returning to tour was no great hardship, for my destination was Ireland. I flew in to Kerry and, after arranging an interview with Seve Ballesteros for a special feature for the *Daily Telegraph* and getting my preview stories done, took up abode in Ballybunion. While the tournament was hard graft, the entertainment at night was pure joy. The town was throbbing, especially on the Saturday night when the main street was closed to traffic and open to hordes of people. The Irish certainly can party and I was grateful for a trip around the bay on Sunday morning before work, to clear away the excesses of the night before. When the tournament finished, Charlie Mulqueen of the *Examiner* drove me to his home in Parteen, County Clare, just outside Limerick. We saw plenty of Limerick, a particular delight for somebody who had just read *Angela's Ashes*.

Noordwijk is a small Dutch holiday resort on the North Sea coast, full of bright hotels and sea-front restaurants. I had gone up-market to find a hotel that had a gym, but I soon wondered whether I should have spent the extra money. The fitness centre was 'bijou', with just a few pieces of equipment. It did, though, provide me with the shock of my life the first time I used it. I was cycling away, staring idly into the big windows in front of me, which gave a view of a large foyer. Suddenly there was a naked body, then two naked bodies, then several naked bodies. Is there an orgy going on next door, I asked myself? It was not a pretty sight. Wrinkled pensioners in the buff seldom are. Apparently, for I never dreamt of investigating further, next door was a mixed sauna, solarium and steam bath and Dutch holiday-makers have no inhibitions (there's a nudist colony just up the beach from the golf course). I spent the rest of the week trying to avoid looking out of the windows, and actually turned some equipment round to face away.

You could not fault my Munich hotel in the autumn. It was within 30 minutes of the course, had pleasant, sizeable rooms and a gym and was close to several good restaurants. They included two fine pizzerias, where I was able to amend my world's top-20 best calzones. The only fault with the hotel lay with the keenness of its breakfast staff to clean away everything like ravaging locusts. I hate it when the waiters and waitresses are clanging cutlery and clashing plates right next to you, preparing for the next guest but causing your nerves to fray in those very moments when you need to be calm before starting a stressful day. When they take your fruit bowl away before your spoon has actually come to rest in the bottom of it, it's rather unnerving. Incidentally, they are never that quick when you are signalling vainly for a cup of decaff. All waiters and waitresses go to a special school to learn how to cock a deaf 'un and show a blind 'un the minute you actually want anything. But their ability to completely mess up your breakfast routine is the thing that gets my goat. You finish your fruit or cereal and then go off in search of something savoury. When you get back, your place has been cleared. Gone is that lovely, crusty, half-eaten roll. Your orange juice and coffee has been ditched. So you start again after a thunderous glower at the miscreant, who's oblivious to your despair, cocking her deaf and blind 'uns by the cutlery trolley. You can understand it if you're away from your table for some time, like I once was in Hong Kong through having a full-scale argument with a fellow guest who had pinched my toast. But for a quick visit to top up your jam or pick up a croissant, it is not on. Sharon and I once had confiscated during, I swear, a mere one-minute absence, two whole main breakfast courses, eggs, bacon, mushrooms, sausage, tomatoes and baked beans, along with a rack of toast, by an over-eager waitress at the hotel we were staying at for an English Open. Well, something similar happened at my hotel in Munich. I collected juice and fruit, along with two slices of pumpernickel and low-fat spread. I just needed to get my coffee from the table across the room, though, before setting to. When I returned to the table after sending one of the staff off for decaffeinated sachets and waiting my turn for the hot-water urn, nothing! Well, there was something. A body. Not only had my untouched juice, uneaten fruit and bread and marge disappeared, but an imbecile waitress had shown somebody else to my place. I snatched up my room key from the table and remonstrated, but then it was time for the don't understand

215

'un. Shoulders slumped, I started breakfast again. But the fruit bowls needed replenishing now, and there was already a sizeable queue waiting for the new batch. It would be like a rugby maul of knees and elbows when the fresh stuff turned up. See what I mean? Routine completely shot. By now, my coffee must be cold. It didn't matter, though. Someone else had cleared it away from my new table. I decided I would eat breakfast at the press centre.

Crans-sur-Sierre provided the venue for the most emotional win of the year when Eduardo Romero, now at the veteran stage, took the European Masters title in late summer. It once again brought forth the old clichés about 'El Gato' [the Cat] stalking his opponents. In fact, the story that week was about the Cat's dog. Eduardo's German Shepherd had bitten him at the start of the year when he broke up a fight between it and another of his dogs. He was so badly hurt that he missed the first part of the year and it had taken him many months to get back to fitness to play golf properly. Of course, that story was milked for all it was worth. I thought back to the first time I'd heard about Eduardo's feline sobriquet. It was a decade before and I was filing a newspaper story to a copy-taker in the days before I bought a Tandy laptop. It was a slow process because the lady at the other end was neither the sharpest tool in the bag, nor the quickest arrow in the quiver.

I dicatated: 'Romero, spelt R.O.M.E.R.O., is nicknamed El Gato . . .' Before I had chance to go any further, I was interrupted by a playful Gordon Richardson, sitting alongside me, who interposed, '. . . because he looks like a chocolate cake.'

'He looks like a chocolate cake? Are you serious?'

'No, disregard that. It was somebody else messing around. I'll continue . . . that's spelt E.L., new word, G.A.T.O.'

'But isn't Gato spelt G.A.T.E.U.?'

'No, this is G.A.T.O. And, anyway, gateau is spelt G.A.T.E.A.U.'

'Not G.A.T.O., then?'

I was by now terrified of what might appear in the newspaper. 'Tell you what, let's start again. Romero, from Argentina, pounced for victory in fine style, living up to his nickname, The Cat.'

216

'No gateau, then?'

'No gateau, dear.'

Instead of hurtling off down the mountain to try to catch a plane home on Sunday night, most of us opted for the relaxed bus journey and a flight the next morning. Some even enjoyed a glass of wine on the train, which you pick up in Sierre, and an even more laid-back trip to Geneva before flying home on Monday. No more madcap drives, scribbling down copy whenever you're on a straight bit without bumps. Our driver announced, rather in the vein of the misguided individual who had got me lost travelling from Versailles once, that he would take a better route around the towns and villages on the way down, instead of following the auto-route. After we had stopped at our 40th set of traffic lights, when the two-hour journey had already surged to four hours, tempers were sorely frayed. And they were stretched even further when we saw that our colleagues who had taken the train were so relaxed after arriving at our hotel two hours before us that they were positively tired and emotional.

There was no suspicion of trouble when John Huggan, a Scottish freelance friend, and I patiently waited to check in at the Hotel Ibis in Versailles, on the Wednesday evening of the Lancôme Trophy in the autumn. When it was finally our turn, though, the receptionist looked blankly at us when I said I'd booked two rooms. There was no trace of our names. After I had urged the girl to check the faxed bookings, the explanation came to light. I'd booked four days all right – from the next day. They were sorry, but the hotel was full tonight. Huggan looked at me like a hangman eyeing a condemned prisoner. The receptionist took pity on one of us. There was a single room being renovated, with a window that would not close. I had to do the honourable thing and let Huggan have it. As he reminded me, I'd cocked up the booking. I hoped it would rain in the night and soak his ill-gotten room. The receptionist then took pity on me, although she didn't find me a room. She telephoned around every hotel and guest house in Versailles, trying to find digs for me. Apparently, there was some convention going on as well as the golf tournament, and rooms were at a premium. It took well over a dozen calls before she located a room for me. The guest house, about half a mile away by foot and dragged luggage, was old and shabby. It had a surly concierge who did not speak any English and made a great play of not understanding my French. It was late and I was tired after rising at 3 a.m. for my plane to Paris, so I meekly took my key and bounced around with my bags on the way up a flight of narrow stairs that were all corners. The room was tiny, so small that I cracked my knee on the bed as I walked in, and very stuffy. I tried to open the sash window, but it wouldn't budge. I had to have air, so I whipped off my jacket and gave it a mighty heave, nurtured by hours of weight training. With a rending sound like a mating owl, the window finally relented, in fact shooting so far upwards that it would now be impossible to lower it without a jemmy. What was good for Huggan was good for Dabell. I also now had a window that wouldn't close. When I returned from dinner, the room was cool, so it seemed I had a result. That was until 2 a.m. when I was awoken by furiously flapping curtains. I leapt out of bed and swished them back so vigorously they parted company with most of their hooks. The window looked a sorry sight when, with nothing to stop the 5 a.m. light streaming in, I awoke two hours before I'd intended. I just prayed Huggan's window had given him similar trouble.

The most interesting point of the Lancôme Trophy came when Mark James and Nick Faldo kissed and made up. They had been at loggerheads after 1999 Ryder Cup captain James had criticised Faldo in his controversial book *Into the Bear Pit*. Jesse had revealed in the book that he'd put a good-luck note to the team from Nick in the waste-paper bin at Brookline the previous year. We all stood around by the recording tent, knowing Mark was going to speak to Nick when he'd finished his round and arrange a truce. Faldo did a double take when he saw Mark waiting at the entrance to the recording tent. They went into a little huddle and decided to have lunch together. The new treaty of Versailles was then completed.

The season ended with a holiday again, this one my first trip to Sardinia. Sharon and I flew to the north of the island and then travelled down from Alghero to Is Molas, a resort just over the causeway from the capital, Cagliari. It was an interesting tournament, won by young Englishman Ian Poulter to seal Europe's 'Rookie of the Year' award, and an enjoyable holiday afterwards, exploring a wonderful island. However, there was just time for one more Dabellism. It came on the Friday night when we decided to go shopping in Cagliari. I drove round and round the city, trying to find a parking space. Nothing. Cars were even double-parked in places. I thought I was going to be out of luck when, lo and behold, there was a vacant one with nobody fighting to get into it. I couldn't believe my good fortune. I bought the appropriate parking pass from a shop and placed it in the car, with Sharon and I still shaking our heads at our luck in finding a space actually in the city centre. When we returned to the car two hours later, we found out why it had been spurned by everyone else. The car was covered – and I really mean covered – with starling guano. The offending birds were still up there in the trees, making a deafening racket, and at least five of them relieved themselves on me before I had chance to scramble into the car. It was impossible to reverse out, because I just couldn't see through the screens or windows. The washers had nearly dried out by the time I'd cleared away enough excrement to be able to see properly and pick up Sharon, who had fled to safety. It took until Sunday morning to find a car-wash. By that time the guano on the bodywork had caked solid and I had to run the car through the wash three times to get it even respectable.

## FOURTEEN

## MEMORIES ARE MADE OF THIS

THERE COULD HARDLY have been a more emotional start to 2001 than when one of the real gentlemen of golf, Des Smyth, won the Madeira Island Open at the age of 48. Dessie created history as the oldest European Tour winner by 20 days, and I couldn't be more delighted. The last time Des had won I celebrated with him in Madrid. This time it was just a glass of champagne in the clubhouse before he set off back to his lovely home in Drogheda. It once again proved that nice guys do win. I remembered back five years previously when he had been one of several players who had the chance to win this title but fell foul of that infamous pin placing on the final hole. Des had gulped back his anger and frustration but couldn't hide glistening eyes.

Madeira looked as though it was going to be a turning point for Seve. He had been going through a dreadful period but suddenly put three good scores together. I had my fingers tightly crossed that this was it, but, alas, he was flattering to deceive – as press officer Roddy Williams (my old friend Michael's son) and I found out when we went out to watch him. It was just his magical short game that was keeping him going because his driving was still atrocious. At one hole we took cover deep in the woods, just about the most dangerous place to be when Seve was on the tee. A place in the middle of the fairway would have been far safer. His ball came down off a branch above us, like a shot ricocheting off a crossbar in football, and slammed between Roddy's feet. Somehow, though, he conjured the ball on to the green between trunks and branches and, of course, made a big putt to birdie the hole! He couldn't ride his luck every day, though, and sadly he slipped badly in the final round.

I was glad I'd enjoyed Marrakesh the previous year, because we were soon back in Rabat for the Moroccan Open. While the Dar es Salam course in Rabat is a splendid golf course, the city isn't so pleasant, in my opinion, dimly lit, seedy, and claustrophobic, a bit like the press-centre we had to endure that week. The tournament organisers insisted we used pre-paid telephone cards, which kept me on tenterhooks in case I went over my units while transmitting data. Or, worse still, while broadcasting live. Somehow I survived the week without a blip in communications, but it wasn't the same for poor old Andy Redington, the Allsport photographer who was providing picture coverage of the event. Sitting next to me, of course, Andy was the latest to discover laptops don't like any sort of beverage after he emptied a bottle of water over his. No amount of drying out in the sun outside the press room could bring his laptop back to life and he had to resort to darting back and forth to local developers to produce his prints.

Ian Poulter from England won the tournament, but it was another young Englishman who attracted a lot of publicity that week, Nick Dougherty playing as an amateur still. Keen to see just how good Dougherty was, I went out to watch him on Saturday, with my old sparring partner Martin Rowley caddying for him. There was only one other spectator, a wiry looking gent with a 'crew cut', dark glasses and a backpack. After the group, which also included Stephen Gallacher, the former Ryder Cup captain Bernard's nephew, had played the first hole, my fellow spectator dropped back to check with me who else was who in the group. He was a Scot and he told me he was there to watch Stephen play because he was from Stephen's home town, Crieff. I chatted away to him between shots, happy to air my not inconsiderable knowledge of Crieff.

At the halfway stage my companion excused himself while he went to find some bottled water. Rowley came over while the group was waiting to tee off. 'Do you know who that is you're talking to?'

'No. Just some Sweaty [Sweaty Sock, Jock] who's watching his townie, Stephen Gallacher.'

'It's Ewan McGregor.'

'Who's he?'

'Have you never heard of *Trainspotting*? He's a well-known actor.'

I certainly hadn't recognised this bloke with a shaven head. I had to make amends. When my fairway companion rejoined the group, I did a bit of crawling. 'Hi, Ewan. I'm so sorry I didn't recognise you. It's because I'm wearing sunglasses and I'm not used to your new hairstyle!' It wasn't a problem. He was a genuinely nice chap. It transpired that they were shooting Ridley Scott's *Black Hawk Down* not far away and Mr McGregor had nipped over to watch the golf on his day off.

It wasn't the first time Rowley had rescued me over a celebrity, and in similar vein. A few years previously, I had undergone my usual frantic dash from a tournament to catch a plane, still with copy to file. I hammered it out in the airport executive lounge and then went to send it from my laptop to my newspaper, via a modem. The story would just not go through, breaking down halfway each time and causing me great anxiety because I was on quite a tight deadline and boarding time was fast approaching. I wouldn't be able to file when I arrived home. Each time, as the line cut and consigned my story to the ether instead of its base computer, I let out a frustrated groan and thumped the desk. When the line broke down for the fifth time, I leant back on my chair and vented my agony with a resounding cry of 'Bollocks'.

A grinning hairy and bearded individual poked his head into my cubicle. 'Bollocks, indeed. Got a problem?' Totally deflated, I apologised for my outburst and explained why I was so mad. 'You know, I've often felt like shouting something like that out in an airport lounge,' said my new friend. 'Why don't I get you a drink? That'll calm you down a bit and you can try again.' He duly came back with a small bottle of champagne and a glass. I thanked him, drank the contents almost in one, and tried again. This time I just got the story through before the line went. 'Yessss.' I looked out of my cubicle, but my very understanding pal had gone.

Rowley, who had watched the whole scene, walked over and said, 'You know who that was, don't you?'

'No. Some very nice Sweaty. He fetched me some champagne.'

'It's Marti Pellow of Wet Wet Wet.'

I went out the next week and bought their latest album.

There was one star I certainly knew when I bumped into him. It was after a tournament in Germany. That same weekend, Robert Plant and Jimmy Page, the old Led Zeppelin rockers, had done a revival concert. I'd have loved to have gone to the gig, being a keen fan of the original band and a regular headbanger at their concerts in the '70s. When I queued to board my plane home I couldn't believe my eyes when Plant, Zep's former lead singer and 'the' voice of the '70s for me, came dashing up and joined the queue alongside me. I felt like a schoolboy, delving into my bag and pulling out a tournament programme, proffering it to him and fawning, 'You were a rock hero of mine, Robert. Can I have your autograph, please?'

'Certainly, mate. Oh, have you been at the golf? I'd have loved to have found time to go.'

'Well, I wished I could have come to see you in concert.'

'Really? Yes, it was quite a good gig. I've left Page still at it. Are you a golfer?'

'No, I'm a writer and broadcaster. Are you keen on golf?'

'Yes, love it. Who do you broadcast for?'

'The BBC, mainly Five Live.'

'Oh, yes. What's your name?'

'Norman Dabell.'

'I thought the voice sounded familiar. I've heard you on the radio. Nice meeting you.'

'Not as nice as meeting you, Robert.' As Le Plant headed for business class and I took my rightful place in economy, I was already flying. 'Robert Plant! Robert Plant! Robert Plant knew my name!'

Morocco was determined not to let me off lightly. As I flew home on the Monday I felt rather lethargic when writing my follow-up stories for Reuters and filing from Casablanca airport. By Tuesday I had an ominous tight chest and sore throat. When I woke up at 4 a.m. for my flight to Valencia on the Wednesday, I felt dreadful, aching all over and convinced

I had a temperature. On arrival at my hotel near the El Saler course, where the Spanish Open was to be held, I just wanted to get to bed after dragging myself around to do preview stories. But there was to be no immediate respite. Reception had no record of my booking, which had been made some two months earlier. I was distraught, especially as there was not a room left, according to a severe looking male receptionist. I would have to try elsewhere, in Valencia itself, perhaps. As my shoulders hunched I pleaded for a room, explaining how ill I felt, unsure that I could even survive a taxi journey into town. It was cutting no ice with reception. Then came my salvation. Seve Ballesteros came up and asked what my problem was. When I explained, he rapped his hand on the desk and rattled out something completely incomprehensible to me in Spanish that hit the receptionist like a burst of machine-gun fire. The receptionist turned to me in abject apology, scraping before he even had time to bow. Seve said: 'Now you have a room, Norman. Hope you get well soon.'

It was not soon. In fact, I couldn't make it for my first couple of broadcasts because I had to see a doctor at the course on the Thursday morning. He diagnosed just about every 'itis' known to man – laryngitis, pharyngitis, tonsillitis, bronchitis and sinusitis. I had the nap hand. That week I rattled with all the pills I had to take. It was quite extraordinary, though, that when I went for a health check-up with a company that was promoting its mobile 'Well Man' clinic, I passed with flying colours!

The Algarve Portuguese Open proved to be a trying week for Colin Montgomerie and, on a couple of occasions, for me. Monty had kick-started his career at Quinta do Lago in 1989, winning his first tournament by a handsome margin, so he was looking forward to reliving old memories. It didn't work out that well, though. Before the tournament started he was refused entry to the course in his car when the security guard at the gate didn't recognise him. When he then missed the cut by a stroke, it meant anything but happy returns.

I, too, was looking for another good result in a Portuguese Open. The previous year I was delighted, and my colleagues dismayed, when my name was drawn out of the hat after a press golf tournament, with my prize an expensive driver. The

reason my colleagues were miffed was because I was the only
one who didn't actually play in the competition. I was too busy.

So I hoped my luck might hold. When I visited the sports
centre just down the road from my hotel early on the Saturday
morning, the gym was closed, but I found a back door open,
so decided to work out, anyway. I could see what I was doing
and I thought I'd square it with the centre staff when they
came on duty. As I worked the bench-press weights, I heard
the back door slam. On investigation, it had either been locked
by somebody peeved I was in there before opening time, or,
somehow, blown to and locked itself. I couldn't hear anyone
out in the front foyer. There were no windows, so there was
nothing I could do but continue working out until someone
showed up. It was just about my longest fitness session of the
year. Having entered the gym illegally at around 7.45 a.m., I
was released by a nonplussed fitness centre receptionist at 9.45
a.m. She was shocked to find me there and scolded me
passionately in Portuguese. I held up my hands and took my
punishment, grateful she wasn't going to call the police. I had
to skip breakfast and only just made the 10.30 a.m. transport
to the course. My day of misfortune had, thus, been planned
out by fate and it spread to my Saturday radio broadcasting. In
2001 my updates no longer had to rely on manual scoring at
every tournament. For the Portuguese Open I was given a
computer which had live scoring on it. That is all very well if,
in the heat of the moment, you do not suddenly lose that live
scoring. Just before I received my cue to go on air for my first
live piece for *Sport on Five*, my screen went blank, the
computer lead having been pulled out in best 'Count of No
Account' fashion. And, as usual, just when you need clear
vision, the view of the manual scoreboard was blocked by
numerous bodies. People were hitting the deck as if there were
an air-raid after I bellowed, '*Excuse me!*' I had just about
regrouped in time for, 'It's the Portuguese Open and Norman
Dabell can tell us who is leading on the Algarve . . .'

Among several names I have been called over the years on tour,
is the 'Imelda Marcos of golf writing'. It is true that I have had
cupboards made especially at home to house copious pairs of
shoes. I'm a sucker for them and when we visited Lyon for the

French Open, I couldn't resist the wonderfully comfortable pair of powder-blue suedes I found in the factory outlet across the road from the hotel. When I phoned Sharon on Wednesday night, I was a little coy about telling her I'd bought yet another pair of shoes. I decided I'd break the news gently and produce them when I got home. After our conversation I put my mobile phone in my pocket and sat back to watch the Champions League footie on the hotel bar television, along with about 30 players, press and caddies. It was quite an exciting match and I must confess to jumping about a bit.

At the end of the game, as I finished off my carafe of red, I was aware of a distant tinny voice calling me. I looked around the lounge area and saw no one. Then I realised the voice was coming from my pocket. I whipped out my mobile phone. The tinny voice became a fully-fledged female bark. 'Norman, for goodness sake. I've been trying to get you on and off for over an hour. Your mobile's been switched on. I know all about your new powder-blue shoes, by the way. I heard you ask at least four people what they thought of them. And I can tell you exactly how the football match finished!'

I had somehow pressed the transmit button on the phone while it was in my pocket, probably when someone scored. 'Er, what else did you hear?' said I, frantically trying to think what might have passed between myself and the lads during the past hour.

'Well, apparently one of the waitresses has a gorgeous pair of pins and another has, whorrr, ginormous knockers.'

While José Maria Olazábal carried off the major spoils in France, it was a complete newcomer who took the Benson and Hedges title the following week at The Belfry – Henrik Stenson of Sweden. Henrik led from start to finish, and what a finish! As he sank the putt to round off the tournament, the heavens opened and The Belfry was awash. He did it just in time, otherwise we would have been back Monday because there was no way the tournament could have been finished on Sunday in that deluge. Just as Henrik ended his winner's press conference, there was a shuddering flash and an enormous clap of thunder. When I went back to my laptop it was flashing, hit for six by the lightning strike. For the next hour it did very strange things indeed and I found later that my landline modem lead was unserviceable. I managed to file my copy, but my troubles were by no means over. I had left the sunroof open on my Frontera, it being a lovely sunny day when I arrived in the morning. The car was awash, the seats absolutely drenched. I baled out as much as I could from the well of the car and squeegied as much as I could off the cloth seats, all the while getting soaked, half in and half out of the car. All I could do was place a waterproof jacket over the driver's seat and switch the heater on full blast, turning the inside of the car into a sauna. It was all grossly futile and I had the most uncomfortable journey of my life. When I arrived home, I limped in the house like someone who had just undergone two hip replacements, soaked to the skin and miserable. It took a fortnight before the car fully dried out.

Tiger Woods had a touch of the Dabells the following week in Heidelberg, but losing his head didn't stop him coming from miles behind Michael Campbell after two rounds to win the tour's longest title, the Deutsche Bank-SAP Open, Tournament Players Championship of Europe. Woods' driver head detached itself in practice on Saturday night, and we had one of those nice little stories that pep up a tournament week. A new shaft was brought by courier and attached to the errant head, but the glue didn't dry properly. So the world number one had to borrow a driver off young Adam Scott, an Australian who shared the same coach as him. Then Tiger won the tournament with his borrowed driver.

There was a little incident that brightened up my week, too. On the Wednesday night I went into my hotel restaurant for dinner at about 8.30 p.m. and the head waiter threw up his hands in horror. Apparently he wouldn't have a table free until 11 p.m. I was aghast and marched to reception to try to get something sorted out. They could do nothing for me, but they suggested I try the sports club just down the road. It had an Italian restaurant. And, yes, they took credit cards. I couldn't believe my luck. I found the place and absorbed a carafe of good red and ate a small penne al arrabiatta and a calzone, of course. I asked for the bill and, when it came, placed my credit card on the dish. They didn't take credit or debit cards. I only had 10 marks on me, about four pounds. I broke out in a sweat. Already I could envisage a sink full of pots and my sleeves rolled up. Incredibly, the restaurant manager, a Slav who spoke pretty good English, told me not to worry. I could pay them tomorrow when I'd got cash. Pay them I did, and left a sizeable tip. My faith in human nature was high and I responded by eating there all week.

I did much the same all the next week, but this time it was English food, all beef, steak and kidney, cod, Stilton, and loads and loads of vegetables. The Europeans are not strong on vegetables, but they certainly are in the north-east of England. My only problem was getting across the A68 to the pub opposite my motel. It was all right crossing in the daylight, but you had to have your wits about you at twilight after a good bottle of Chilean. It was an exciting week, with the newly-styled Great North Open tournament won by Andrew Coltart augmented by Slaley Hall's Ryder Cup bid. Our already compact press room was, thus, packed all week and telephone lines were at a premium. My abiding memory of the media centre was the constant bickering by Brian Creighton and Bernie McGuire, fellow freelances, while a certain Japanese photographer kept his head below the parapets at all times. They each had a phone and modem connection, but there was only one line out, which they also had to share with the photographer. It was bedlam in their corner of the room. 'Who the fuck has cut me off? That you, Bernie?' 'When the fuck are you going to finish, Brian? I've only got five minutes to deadline.' 'Will that fucking photographer ever get off the line?' How they managed to get through the week without drawing blood, I'll never know. It made for a lively tournament.

Two weeks in Ireland after that were sheer bliss. Monty was in top form and led the Irish Open at Fota Island in Cork from start to finish, making it a very easy story to write. We enjoyed a couple of fine restaurants during the week, particularly the one on Cobh Quay, near to the spot where the Irish immigrants boarded the *Titanic*. Mark Garrod took his life in his hands by agreeing to drive me across Ireland to Kildare for the following week's tournament at the K Club, via Mount Juliet in Thomastown and the breathtakingly beautiful new 'Old Head' links at Kinsale. On our way we passed through Abbeyleix. We were through the town before I remembered why it had a special place in my heart, and it was unfortunate we didn't have time to turn back. In the early '80s, we provincial golf writers used to be invited over to play and subsequently write golfing travel features about Irish courses. We once stopped off at this wonderful, typical Irish bar called Morrissey's in Abbeyleix. It was run by Patrick J. Mulhall (M.I.A.V.I.) and his lovely daughters. Patrick wore many hats. As well as being a licensed vintner and family grocer at his pub, he also found time to be a commissioner for oaths, building society manager, auctioneer, estate agent, travel agent, insurance agent, newsagent – and funeral director. We were on one of our frantic coach journeys across Ireland and had stopped off early Sunday evening. Having all piled into Morrissey's we were given a marvellous greeting by Patrick but he announced, dolefully, 'I'm sorry boys but there's still half an hour before I can open the bar legally.' The bar looked great and one or two of the stags in the group were definitely taken with a couple of the daughters, so we decided to see out the half-hour. Patrick disappeared out the back but reappeared within a few minutes and said, 'Jaysus, you might as well have a drink while you're waiting.'

Bizarrely, when Mark and I got to the K Club, one of the preview tales concerned the European Tour's starter, Ivor Robson. He got it in the neck for omitting to announce Retief Goosen as the US Open champion during the pro-am when he did his usual job of calling out each player's name and background on the tee. Some say Ivor's got a doddle of a job, just standing there all day calling out players' names. He does, though, have to make sure there's a handy loo.

It was a hectic week for me covering the European Open before Darren Clarke sparked off a mass celebration, as only the Irish know how, when he became the first Irish winner on home soil for 19 years. On the Thursday I awoke in one hotel and slept in another, and, counting the clubhouse lunch, I sat in six restaurants in one day. I had to check out of my hotel after breakfast in the morning because of a wedding taking up all the rooms, and move to another a few miles away that evening. Fellow guest Charlie Mulqueen and I went to our new hotel restaurant but it was clear they would be too busy to serve us for ages, so we went into the town of Naas for sustenance. We found a decent looking place and we were shown to a table. The menu prices were ridiculous, however, so we crept out. At our next restaurant we soon tired of people colliding with us at our table, the place was so packed, so we repaired again. This time we found a quiet and admirable little fish bistro, where I finally enjoyed the piece of cod which passeth all understanding. The next morning I had to change hotels again, because my new one was fully booked.

Open Championships can be heaven and hell all in one week, and the 2001 Open was no exception. I broke my vow of never again staying in rented accommodation and that provided me with an occasionally harrowing week. When I arrived at the flat I was supposed to be sharing with fellow Reuters scribes Mitch Phillips and Mark Lamport-Stokes, to my chagrin I found there were only two bedrooms. My two colleagues had arrived the day before and, of course, had commandeered the bedrooms. The owner offered to put a bed in the lounge, which, with no other accommodation available in the area, I had to accept. It was comfortable enough, but my first morning gave me quite a start. Fortunately, I had my boxer shorts on when I swished open the curtains at 6 a.m. I hadn't taken in just how much I was living in a goldfish bowl and I found myself staring straight out at about a dozen amused people in a bus queue. Another hazard of being a lounge lizard is that you are forced to watch television, even if you are in bed, until your colleagues are ready to turn in.

The Open at Royal Lytham and St Annes could have been rather mundane, although that wasn't really the fault of the winner, David Duval. He is a very introvert person and, even though his win was achieved with great determination, it was hardly with panache. No, it was more the blunder by Ian Woosnam, or his caddie Myles Byrne, if you share the belief that the bagman is responsible for counting the clubs, than Duval's victory that made the 2001 Open one that will be forever etched in my memory. I'd known Myles since he was a kid and he used to caddie for his fellow Irishman John McHenry. Myles was always pestering me for the *Daily Telegraph* crossword, at which he was an expert. I felt for Woosie, but I also understood Myles' misery. There but for the grace of God . . . accidentally leaving an extra club in the bag is just the sort of mishap that would have befallen me if I'd been a caddie.

I'd stood patiently waiting for Duval's caddie to be available after the presentation of the Auld Claret Jug, because I was desperate for him to talk to me for my final chapter of *Winning the Open*, but it was a non-starter. He turned me down flat. However, the real caddie story at Lytham was the one that Myles could tell. Woosnam had decided to keep him on despite the 15-clubs incident, so I knew it might be touch-and-go whether he'd talk. Tentatively, through his brother Brian, who, as one of the notable Byrne caddie brothers from Bray, was also a long-time acquaintance, I tried to arrange an interview with Myles for my final book chapter. Myles was in great demand, even, I understand, going on an American television chat-show. I just hoped he'd find time for me. At the Scandinavian Masters I came across him in the clubhouse and he said he'd think about it, but I'd have to give him time. Unfortunately, time was running out for both of us. On the Sunday morning Myles failed to turn up for duty. Woosie even had to force open his locker door to get out his golf shoes because Myles had the key. It was curtains for Myles and it meant I had to do some frantic ducking and diving for my chapter. The Irishman was going to need more time now than I could really spare.

Myles was not the only caddie to miss a tee-off time that week in Malmo. Keith Nelson, known as 'The Seagull' amongst his fraternity, went to sleep on the back seat of the bus that takes players, caddies and press to the course from the hotel. Nobody woke him up when the bus arrived and, unnoticed by the driver, Nelson slept on as the bus returned to the hotel. His master, Marc Farry of France, had to get someone else on the bag until the sheepish caddie returned to the fold. Farry realised that Nelson had not intentionally dodged the column, though, and didn't sack him.

Having brought my telephone wire-entangled laptop crashing down onto the deck of my radio booth at Celtic Manor, trying to broadcast on Five Live while also commentating for RTE on Paul McGinley's dramatic play-off win in the Wales Open, I was hoping that was mishap of the week out of the way. Not a bit of it. It had been a miserable early August week anyway, lashing down with rain for the most part, turning the tournament into a bit of a shambles. Sharon

231

and I had enjoyed the opulence of the Celtic Manor hotel, of course, but we were getting a little stir-crazy. So, instead of driving back home and arriving late on Sunday night, having done nothing but sit in a press room and watch stair-rods, I booked us into a little country hotel in the back of beyond, somewhere between Newport and Gloucester. The landlord had told me there was hardly anybody else staying there. It would be a romantic night. Well, that was the plan. There was obviously terrible congestion on the roads to Liverpool, following the Charity Shield football final. About 30 Liverpool fans, fed up with the traffic jam, had headed off the beaten track in a convoy, it seemed – and come across our hotel. The little bar and the small restaurant in our bijou inn were heaving all night. Instead of having a quiet candlelit dinner, we were hemmed in by tables full of noisy Scousers arguing about who had been their best striker in the last 20 years. By the time we'd got there, they'd had all the best dishes. Nearly everything was off by the time we got our menu and it took an hour before we even got our apéritif.

Ryder Cup fever had, as usual, gripped the European Tour, and as the summer reached its nadir, Europe's team was finalised in Munich. John Daly had no interest in the match, but showed plenty of interest in winning the BMW International. It was good to see that the 'Wild Thing' appeared to have beaten his demons. I remember him once telling us about how he had actually 'died' for a few seconds through being in an alcohol-induced stupor. Then after the press conference he picked up his travelling guitar at the pro-am party – and gave us a rendition of 'Knock, Knock, Knocking on Heaven's Door'.

Munich provided a memorable week for us England football fans, even if rain delays meant there was no chance of watching the match live down in the city on Saturday night, even though there were tickets to be had. I was the last British journalist working and had to suffer the deafening cheers and hoots from the local press watching the match in the media centre when Germany scored the opening goal. As soon as my work was finished I nipped next door to the VIP lounge, where the rest of my colleagues were watching the match. It was good to be among friends when England equalised. Our hotel was 30 minutes away, so four of us decided to forego the last 10 minutes of the first half and the first 10 minutes of the second in order to get back to watch the denouement. Of course we missed two goals and we could hardly believe it when we ran into our hotel television room to find England were 3–1 up. The other four British press men did better than us, though. They set off, then, unable to stand the suspense any longer, asked their driver to pull over in a lay-by so they could watch the on-board television, which only operated when their people-carrier was stationary. They saw England's second and third goals and made it back to the hotel to see the other two. Our car didn't have on-board television. But we revelled in the famous win and there were great celebrations that night, with accompanying hangovers the next day. I was glad I was not doing any radio work that Sunday.

There are always two tournaments for the press to consider during the most spectacular week of the year on the European Tour when we sit 6,000 ft up in the Alps at Crans-sur-Sierre. To some wannabe pros, the main event takes place on Saturday at the little nine-hole Jack Nicklaus course, just over the road from the tournament. That is when the media can flex their muscles in the annual European Masters Press Challenge. There has often been some serious head-wagging as curious winners have come to the fore when Hugo Steinegger, who runs the press centre for Swiss concerns with wife Gabi, makes the announcements. The European Masters Press Challenge of 2001 would have been one of those instances, but for a sharp-eyed Graham Otway of the *Daily Mail*. Graham is definitely a wannabe pro and is on the ball when these kind of events take place. He spotted one of our Chinese media colleagues, who was in Crans for a Hong Kong Open announcement by the sponsors, taking at least one 'Mulligan'. That is, having another go when the first shot sends your ball into oblivion, as it can on the Jack Nicklaus course. Graham, apparently, also saw this Chinaman playing another wrong 'un, so he was exasperated when he heard the gent had scored an unlikely high amount of points, indeed could even be the winner. His Chinese playing-partner looked like running second. Graham filed a protest. There was a huge huddle but, at first, the result stood. An international incident looked on the cards. Then Hugo and his aides decided to take action. The winner was disqualified. Satisfaction was gained by Mr Otway and friends. The next day the East was not on speaking terms with the West.

Personally, I had had an altogether miserable bid for the trophy. While playing the fifth I got a call on my mobile from press officer Roddy Williams. Thomas Bjorn, who was due to be playing in the Ryder Cup in less than three weeks, had pulled out of the tournament injured. I had to down tools and race back to the press room. It was a hazardous business. I was struck twice by golf balls, despite making my way back well wide of the fairways, once very hard, fortunately on the back of my shoe where it caused little pain. I got back just in time to record an interview with Thomas for the BBC, which went straight on air. In the end it didn't matter whether Thomas was fit or not. The 2001 Ryder Cup never took place, of course, eventually postponed for a year after the horror of 11 September.

When John Huggan and I stood at the Ibis Hotel reception on the Wednesday night of the Lancôme Trophy, there was no fear of a wrong booking. Huggan had booked himself in this time and I had treble-checked my dates. Almost as if in celebration Huggan and I, along with Claire McDonnell of the BBC, and Andy Farrell of *The Independent*, formed a foursome for karaoke at the journalists' favourite restaurant/bar near the Versailles hotel. We were all well relaxed after copious carafes of wine that seemed to materialise every quarter of an hour in the adjacent restaurant, and launched into a rendition of 'Hotel California' that would have made the Eagles' eyes water. There was not much hilarity during the week, though. Many of the European Tour players had been out in America when the atrocities took place and there was a sombre mood before Sergio Garcia won the tournament with a thrilling finish, going past a stumbling Retief Goosen.

I had thought there was just a hint of mint about my luggage when it arrived on the carousel at Cologne airport. When I opened my large clothing bag at my hotel where I was to stay for the German Masters week, I found out what was causing the curious fragrance. My plastic bottle of mouthwash had split, soaking all my boxer shorts and socks. I don't know what the chambermaid thought to a row of peppermint-smelling knicks and socks drying out on the top of the window frame in my room. Bet she thought 'We've got a right pervert here'. I was conscious all week of colleagues and players I was interviewing sniffing occasionally and looking down towards my feet. If only hotel laundry bills weren't so steep, I wouldn't have had a problem.

I felt pretty miserable as I telephoned to offer to record my evening sports desk piece for Five Live on the Saturday evening of the German Masters. I was sure the Greeks had thwarted our attempt to get through automatically to the football World Cup finals. I had been kept up to date on the match by the Beeb and Reuters, and I was sure England had lost. Just outside, the triumphant car horns of celebrating German golf spectators, who were equally sure they were through automatically, exacerbated my gloom.

'Hi, this is Norman in Cologne. Can you take my . . .'

'Hold on, Norm. Yesss, yesss, yesss! He's done it. We've scored. Beckham's scored. I can't believe it. Yesss!'

'Hell's tits, I thought the match had finished.'

'It has now. It's over. We've got a draw in injury time.'

'Fantastic. I'll call you back later.

'Everybody. England drew 2–2. We're through. We're through!' I looked around the press room. All I saw in my first moments of joy were Bernie McGuire, an Australian, who didn't give a stuff whether England had won or not, and the press officer, Gordon Simpson, a Scot, who just raised his eyes to the heavens, cursing the Sassenachs under his breath. Then I was aware of being given the hard stare by the German press still present. Outside, the car horns still bellowed in celebration.

'You can go out and tell them they can stop bloody hooting now!'

The impromptu Cannes Open, laid on at the last minute, was, as David Feherty would have said, an accident waiting to happen for Dabell. Our press room was a garage for golf buggies and offered plenty of scope for careless drivers to collide with scampering reporters. A sudden revving alongside, when I was broadcasting, might leave the listeners a little perplexed, too. The fumes from the buggies were sure to set off a coughing fit as soon as I launched into a piece on air. But no, none of those accidents befell me. My only mishap came on Sunday night, sure enough, right on deadline. Suddenly eight adjacent keys on my laptop keyboard just stopped functioning. They were fairly crucial ones, too, the '8', the '9', the 'I', the 'O', the 'K', the 'L', the comma and full-stop. I had to write a 500-word story for Reuters, along with a 400-word special sidebar for Argentina, on Jorge Berendt's victory, without eight vital ingredients. My story came out most peculiarly. Well, even more peculiar than usual, as my colleagues reminded me. 'Argentna's Jrge Berendt sht a fur-under-par 6 n the fna rund f the Cannes pen n Sunday t wn hs frst Eurpean Tur tte,' was my initial attempt at an introduction. And I can tell you it got far worse after that. I had to plough on without the prodigal keys and then call Reuters and fill in the gaps. It was a debacle. Thank goodness the 'E' didn't fail me as well.

I always seem to have trouble with transport at airports. For instance, I always seem to be the last person dropped off at the last stop for the airport car park on a Sunday night after an exhausting journey, no matter whether I've parked in A, F, K, R or Z parking zones. It's uncanny how it works out. Once, when I used the local taxi driver from my village for private hire, he lost his car at the airport. He couldn't find his car after being moved on by the police and told to use the airport car park. He was sure he'd left it here, he said, showing me the scrap of paper on which he'd jotted down the bay number. We wandered around aimlessly for nearly an hour. He decided he would have to report it stolen. As he slumped off to find security, I had a thought. Many years before I'd come out of Sainsbury's in Swindon, gone to the bay number where my car should have been and found it missing. I, too, was on the brink of calling the police but rang my wife first to warn her. It was her company car. She enquired whether I realised there were two car parks, one either side of the supermarket. They were mirror images of themselves, as were the exit doors. I located our car. So I suggested this scenario to my man. Sure enough, the taxi was on the other side.

This time at Luton, following a trip to watch Retief Goosen clinch the Madrid Open and become European number one, I scrambled onto the car park bus just as it was about to pull away. That would save me a good half-hour's delay, thought I. That was until we sailed past our long-stay car park and drove on and on, about another two miles to the pre-booked car park. I was on the wrong bus. My slog back to my car, with heavy luggage in tow, took me 40 minutes. But my luck with buses and taxis was to take on a whole new turn.

It was bad enough having to be picked up at 2 a.m. by the private hire car and then stand in a Heathrow queue at just after 4 a.m. for a 6 a.m. flight to Milan, then on to Cagliari in Sardinia for the Italian Open. But far worse was to come. As I waited for the check-in desk to open I decided to get my passport and ticket ready. My passport was missing from its usual place in its wallet. It couldn't be. I never forget tickets or passport. I scrabbled around, dumping documents all over the floor. It was nowhere to be found. With my brain scrambling, I thought back to the last time I'd seen it, the previous Sunday night at Luton when I returned from Madrid. It was still in the trousers I had travelled home in from Spain, ones from which I had changed at the last minute that morning. I rang my private hire driver. Could he pick up my passport when he got back to Lincolnshire and bring it down to me? He was off to collect passengers at Gatwick and then he'd call for it at home. He would be about four hours, though. Obviously I would miss my flight. When the Alitalia ticket desk opened they were sympathetic but couldn't rearrange a flight until I had my passport. I not only missed my 6 a.m. flight but further flights at 8 a.m., 9.30 a.m., 10 a.m. and 11 a.m. for connections at Milan and Rome. My driver finally returned at 11 a.m. after picking up my passport from where Sharon had left it under the doormat, then suffering several traffic jams. I rushed to the desk but was told the best they could do was put me on stand-by for a 1 p.m. flight to Milan. That would just allow me to connect for the last flight of the day to Cagliari. Having been found a seat, when I got to Milan I not only had to do some sweet talking to get another stand-by to Cagliari but phone up the Italian Open press officer, Roddy Williams, for information so I could do preview stories. I filed two stories and then made my way to the departure lounge to try my luck on stand-by. It was a cattle market. The departure area was a thronging mass and there were at least 20 fellow stand-by passengers, doing what Italians do in moments of crisis, waving their arms and shouting the odds. I just stood at the back of this cacophony, beaten to submission, sure now that I would be spending the night in Milan and flying the next day, thus well behind the eight-ball for the tournament. I was jolted from my lethargy by a check-in man waving for me to come forward. Apparently he had had enough of being bullied and he gave the first of only five stand-by tickets to me – because I was the only one queuing in a dignified manner. When I arrived at Is Molas, the venue for the tournament, the press lads and tour staff were having a nightcap at the bar. A great cheer went up and there was much back slapping but I had a hard time that week living down my misadventure.

The tournament and the season ended in typical style. There was a mad dash for a plane, and a mislaid story that was finally filed on a mobile phone sitting alongside the driver who had collected my passport for me earlier on in the week.

After Sharon and I had a wonderful wedding in St Lucia, there was just time for one more golf trip. It was to the Desert Springs course near Almeria in Spain, one of the first places I had visited as a freelance operator, to see how the remarkable spot in 'Spaghetti Western' country was progressing. As I disembarked from the plane at Almeria, I was accosted by a person pulling my shirt from behind.

'Here, don't I know you?' challenged my assailant.

'Good Lord. You're my window cleaner.'

'Yes, mate. And you owe me eight quid.'

# FIFTEEN

# FLUSHED

MY 2002 SEASON began painfully. Having finally undergone extensive knee surgery, much of the first few weeks were spent hobbling around and trying to find comfortable positions on planes. I'd needed the surgery to correct both kneecap positions. The left one was out of kilter through a goal-keeping injury that dated back some 30 years and the right one, need I go into the details, was way out due to my accident at Duquesa in 1992.

I had fully expected to be fit by the time I boarded my flight to the Madeira Island Open in March, but no such luck. Both my knees, which at one time looked like a pair of rugby balls, were still heavily swollen and I really should not have gone to the tournament. The Lisbon flight was full and I was badly cramped up. I resorted to limping up and down the aisle, dodging the drinks trolley and any sudden outstretched leg that would exacerbate my misery. I found that liberal dosages of Portuguese wine to go with painkillers helped and was lucky enough to get all three back seats to myself for the trip from Lisbon to Madeira.

While everyone was extremely sympathetic, the weather wasn't. When it became too foggy, play was suspended and the damp had really got into the old knee joints by Saturday night when we had our press dinner. I continually had to stand up to relieve the nagging ache in my knees, so the speaker from the Portuguese Golf Federation could be forgiven for thinking I was anxious to respond to his welcome to Madeira. A little flustered at the idea, but already thinking on my feet, I was about to hold forth when, out of the corner of my eye I saw that Mel Webb had surreptitiously, and with some relief, slid an official thank-you speech back into his jacket pocket. The *Times* man wasn't getting away with it that easily. And, anyway, having again relied on my double doses of anaesthetic, pills and wine, I'm sure my speech wouldn't have been anywhere near as lucid as Mel's.

While we press pack were enjoying dinner at a lovely beach restaurant at Vale do Lobo during the Algarve Portuguese Open the following week, my mobile phone rang. The chilling words, enunciated in a doom-laden monotone by the electrician who installed it, said: 'Burglar alarm going off at the Mill, Crowland.' Just as I'd been in no position to do much about it when I lay on my hospital bed a few weeks before, having hardly come round from my knees operation when the mobile had rung and announced the same mournful message, there wasn't much I was going to be able to do in Portugal when the possible burglary was taking place in Lincolnshire. I rang Sharon frantically. A croaky, sleepy, voice said: 'Oh is it going off? Bollocks!' She'd turned in early because of a crack-of-dawn trip the next day, and had unwittingly set off the alarm in a sort of sleepwalk. I couldn't stop the damned thing calling me up even after Sharon had reset the alarm, causing groans and moans every time it rang during the meal. The boys had already been disturbed earlier when my credit-card company phoned to check up on a largish purchase I'd made at the airport on the way out. Against my better judgement (worried about other emergencies, like lost copy back in London), I turned off the mobile. When I turned it back on the next morning, my voicemail announced: 'You have 35 messages'. I only listened to the first one: 'Burglar alarm going off at the Mill, Crowland'. I had a pretty shrewd idea what the other 34 might say.

Strong winds howling away on the cliff-tops turned the Portuguese event into chaos, with only two fragmented rounds possible. On the Saturday we all placed bets on Press Association man Phil Casey's bookmaker's account. As a non-punter who selects with either a pin or some fateful connotation, I couldn't resist going for 'Blowing Wind' on account of the misery we had been enduring for three days. It didn't win, of course.

On Sunday it tipped down and the title was eventually decided, after an eternity, between David Gilford and the winner Carl Pettersson at the only playable hole. Everyone stood around for hours before a playoff was deemed necessary, the more mischievous ones slyly trying to wake up the rattlesnake in the glass case guarding the $350,000 diamond tee-peg which was an unclaimed hole-in-one prize.

The Seve Trophy team event meant a return to Druids Glen in County Wicklow. Our hotel in Bray was lively, full of Northern Irish wrinklies on a cheap break. They sang 'Danny Boy' at least 12 times most nights and throughout the week demanded the hapless piano player hit the ivories until all hours – right underneath my room.

My bathroom was a liability. The toilet-roll holders were fitted on the wall directly behind the toilet. On my first morning I hadn't noticed that fact and hadn't torn off the appropriate amount of sheets before taking my seat. Only Houdini-like twists and frantic snatches gained the required few torn leaves. The occasionally forgetful Jock MacVicar of the *Express* nearly put his back out on the Thursday morning on his fifth attempt at trying to gain a scrabbled fingerhold on the loo roll. My toilet seat was just as hazardous. It was one of those female seats that refuses to stay up when a bloke wants to do number ones. You either have to be a deadeye dick into the bowl with the seat down, or hold up the seat while doing your business one-handed. The latter regime, though, demands an astute juggling feat at the end, involving your fly-hole, and is nearly always unsuccessful. It invariably means a lost handhold and the seat succumbing to gravity, causing you a fair whack in a sensitive area if you're not a pretty nifty dancer. Judging by the curses and crashes coming through the rather thin walls, all the toilets were mantraps. Mornings in Bray were a little bit like listening to a 21-gun salute. The toilet really was a minefield. The flush was low down to the bottom right of the cistern and as I stooped to press the handle one morning, my mobile squirted out of my shirt top pocket. I was thankful of being quite an accomplished slip-fielder in my cricketing days.

I thought back to one Italian Open when I hadn't been quite

so nimble as my press badge detached itself from its lapel and fell in the locker-room loo. There was no way I was going to retrieve it. Only trouble was, the security guard, who had nodded to me for four days on numerous entries and exits to the media-centre and offered a polite '*bon giorno*' each time, wouldn't let me in without a badge. I had to get a message to the press officer to come out and re-accredit me. They are a strange breed, media-centre security guards. I swear I once spent a couple of minutes passing the time of day and weather with one guard as I left the centre, nipped round the corner to the loo, then, when I returned, was asked, sternly, to identify myself as a pressman (my badge had reversed itself in the wind) by the same bloke I'd chatted to no more than two minutes earlier.

The Seve Trophy made it three weeks out of three with pretty awful weather but Seve Ballesteros himself gave us all a little bit of sunshine by again beating Colin Montgomerie, despite being so bad he sent the gallery scurrying with one drive only a few yards from the tee. Jock MacVicar did not have a happy week altogether. When he tried to get his hire-car out of the press car park on the first day, it was stuck inextricably in oozing mud. It stayed there all week and they had to get a pick-up with a winch to haul it out on the Sunday, so he could return it at the airport. Of course, as his hopeful passenger for the week, I got the old 'It's your fault Dibble; you're a bloody menace', just because I'd suggested where we should park.

My Sunday night coach trip to the airport was another memorable journey from Druids Glen. I'd finished fairly early for once and had time for a couple or three glasses of white wine before boarding the bus. As the journey progressed, with relief I spotted that the coach had its own loo. It was very compact, with little room for manoeuvre. You had to stoop and jam yourself in. With the driver intent on getting to the airport post-haste, his negotiation of a roundabout, on two wheels it appeared to me in my frenetically swaying cubicle, caused several angry muffled shouts which kept the boys amused, outside on the back seat. Another sudden turn, though, caused the toilet door, on which I had had to lean out of necessity, to give up the unequal struggle holding off my 14-st frame. It burst open, leaving me staggering backwards, desperately trying to cover up. The mirth of my colleagues, fortunately male colleagues, was unrestrained.

I really fell on my feet the following week when we made a return to Gran Canaria. My long-time friend and Spanish Open press officer Maria Acacia Lopez-Bachiller had negotiated a splendid rate at a five-star hotel. The hotel food was exceptional but the restaurant experience was not without the sort of incidents that befall me frequently. On my first morning another complete breakfast was swept away while I was only momentarily away from my place. Somehow, once again, a lightning-fast waiter had darted in and cleared up in a flash. It's just part of their course, I suppose. 'Today we will learn how to avoid eye-contact with diners at all times, fanny around with cups and saucers or cutlery, or talk to colleagues while keeping our eyes riveted on anything but a hotel guest. This will be followed by learning how to totally ignore plaintive calls of "excuse me". The afternoon will be devoted to learning how to pounce on a full breakfast table, the second a diner leaves it, using the cover of pot-plants, pillars or other means of camouflage. Crawling on all fours with a tray, commando-style, is recommended in extreme emergencies. Finally we will learn how to jangle diners' nerves and enhance hangovers by rattling knives, forks and cups loudly right alongside them, shouting to colleagues in as loud a voice as possible about the chances of Valencia losing to Real Madrid, while we re-lay tables that aren't going to be used until the next morning.'

If that was a tad frustrating then it was nothing compared to that night. It was a buffet, so I fixed myself a salad and ordered a bottle of Vina Esmeralda. I drank a glassful of wine with the salad and then headed for the main course. When I returned to my table it had been cleared. New knives and forks were out, the bottle had disappeared. Never did it occur to me that someone would consider that three-quarters of a bottle of wine was leftovers, so, rather stupidly, I hadn't kept a close eye on my table. Attempts to recover my lost bottle came to naught and a fresh one was brought by an apologetic wine waiter. I expected this one to be gratis after such a debacle but when I checked out I found I had been charged for two bottles. I subsequently missed my transport to the golf course while arguing and trying to get one of them removed from the bill.

It was a rather untidy week all round. The computer company that does the scoring had all its computers stolen the night before the tournament started and when a whole new batch was installed, found them all crashed because of a power-surge during the night. Dark glances came my way. As I was one of those who had been operating an ill-fated computer, using its live scoring for my broadcasts, the Dabell jinx was blamed.

The hosting El Cortijo club was so new that there was just a huge hangar that housed everything, locker room et al. I made a point of talking about the lack of a clubhouse when asked by one *Five Live* presenter what the venue was like, then ran through the scoreboard:

'Sergio Garcia holds a one-shot lead on the course but the leader in the clubhouse is England's Greg Owen.'

'Er, I thought you said there was no clubhouse, Norman?'

With facilities unfinished it was hardly surprising that the telephone system in the media centre was unpredictable. Your incoming calls could pop up anywhere, a little awkward for live broadcasting, at times. And at one point when my phone rang it also rang at three other desks concurrently. I'd gone from 'No-bell Dabell' to 'Four-bell Dabell'.

As construction work continued under our noses, dust, black lava rock dust, was all-pervading. When Garcia came in for the press conference he refused to sit on the interview room chair because it was so mucky. It had got a full valet by the time he'd won on the Sunday.

At the British Masters at Woburn, Justin Rose proved he really had made the transformation from toiling young hopeful to accomplished professional. There were no embarrassments this time for the press officer Roddy Williams. The year before he could have really blotted his copybook in a style perfected by his dad. As he drove back to the press room on a buggy, Williams came to the 17th green and stopped dutifully, with players about to putt. A startled Williams then jumped like a gazelle as a loud hooter went off. Surely there wasn't lightning about? The players looked over angrily and Williams looked about him, wondering who on earth was making such a racket. He stared all around him, leaning out of the buggy. That seemed to stop the miscreant making the din. After the players putted out, he drove on but had to stop at the 18th tee to await other players teeing off. Incredibly, the maniac who was hooting began a fresh discourse, stopping those on the tee in their tracks. As Williams again glanced all around him, prepared to show his authority as a European Tour official, the hooting bleated even louder. Play stopped altogether, not only on the tee but further down on the fairway as people wondered if they should come off for lightning. Then the penny dropped for Williams. He was leaning on the buggy hooter, set so inconspicuously he had not noticed it. Admirably hiding his embarrassment, Williams jumped off the buggy and went through a charade of trying to discover where the hooting was coming from. Naturally not discovering a transgressor, he remounted the buggy and quietly waited for the players to tee off, then set course for the press room with butter giving no sign at all of melting in his mouth.

When the tour circus moved across country to Forest of Arden for the English Open, there was a shock for Sky presenter Bruce Critchley. Taking a quick decaff break, I settled down in the small lounge in the media centre and watched a little of the play on television. Ewen Murray said: 'Well, I'm supposed to be handing you over to Bruce now but the Colonel [Murray's nickname for Critchley] must really be enjoying his lunch.' Suddenly the pink tent on the sofa opposite me that was Critchley avidly studying his stocks and shares in the *FT* exploded with a 'Good Lord, is that the time?' as he shot off for the TV compound.

There was cause for great media-centre celebration about that time due to David Beckham's brilliant penalty-kick against Argentina in the World Cup. Only a few days before I'd spotted a signed Beckham England shirt in a Peterborough shop window and snapped it up at a daft price after spending about an hour walking up and down outside the shop before I decided to take the plunge. I reckon his spot-kick quadrupled its price, so I needn't have procrastinated. Doesn't matter what it's worth. It's priceless as far as I'm concerned and occupies pride of place on our mill wall.

I wasn't too happy with my pal Scott Crockett (a

professional Scot who couldn't wait to see the Sassenachs suffer) at the Great North Open when England went out of the World Cup a little bit later, running around the press centre doing high-fives with himself when Brazil scored.

Late June saw me on the Emerald Isle again, this time for a two-week stay, first revisiting Cork and the beautiful Fota Island for the Irish Open, again staying in Limerick with my old friend Charlie Mulqueen, then moving down to Kildare for the European Open at the K Club. The first week was really interesting because we stayed at Cobh, where Irish emigrants to America used to board the liners to cross the Atlantic, the most famous embarkation, of course, being when the unfortunate souls joined the *Titanic*. It proved an interesting news week when Seve disqualified himself after hitting into the lake so many times at the 18th he miscounted his score, and Monty left on Sunday night warning he might miss the Open Championship because of a bad back. In the event, the hapless Seve did cause a sensation by withdrawing from the Open but Monty's back rallied so well that he could even play the following week, never mind in the Open. He accused us all of exaggerating! The subsequent Seve and Monty stories that were flying around in between the two Irish events meant there was no time for golf for me, though. I was particularly disappointed to miss out on a second foray over Lahinch, spending the time I should have been playing those wonderful links chasing up stories and filing in the clubhouse. Several pints of the black liquid that produces perfect prose helped me get over my woe at missing the golf. Apparently it was quite hazardous out on the links. It was the day of the South West of Ireland Priests Championship and the Fathers perhaps relied too heavily on heavenly intervention when launching their drives. Building-site hard-hats were more de rigueur than golf visors.

Even Charlie was perplexed by some of the road signs we spotted while driving from Limerick to our hotel in Kill (honest, that's the village's name). You see a sign that warns: '11 deaths in the past two years'. But the 11 has been lightly crossed out and a figure 9 put next to it, signifying that the sign has been brought up to date. Now, how on earth can they reduce it? And it wasn't in just one instance. We saw several examples: '21 deaths 1999–2002' with the 21 replaced by 18. Is somebody miscounting? Or has there been a glut of resurrections?

On arriving at the K Club media centre, I heard a brilliant story. Dai Davies, the likeable but blunt doyen of *The Guardian*, definitely does not suffer fools gladly. But he was forced to admit to a Dabellism. To get to Dublin from Doonbeg, where he had been playing Greg Norman's new course, Dai had to take the train from Limerick. As the train pulled in to Dublin, he decided he had perhaps better answer a call of nature for comfort's sake for the next part of his journey. So he quickly set his luggage and clubs down on the platform and dived back into the train loo. Halfway through his tiddle, to his chagrin he felt the train start to move. Hastily zipping up he flung open the loo door – just in time to wave his now orphaned luggage goodbye as his train gathered speed. A cry of help to the platform fell on deaf ears – the only person on it, a cyclist who had disembarked from the train with his bike, was more interested in getting his chain back on. With mounting panic, Dai thought he was headed back to Limerick and was on the point of pulling the communication chord and damn the expense when the train slowed and pulled into a siding about half a mile away. He was saved a hazardous walk back along the lines when a guard informed him the train would be returning to the platform. After a hiatus, a relieved prodigal owner was reunited with his luggage. Dai will no doubt wait for a ruling before taking relief that way again.

The summer wore on, Ernie Els finally won the Open he had craved, the weather relented and by the time we arrived in Stockholm it was sweltering. So there was the perfect excuse to visit the famous Ice Bar, formed completely of ice. Even the glasses were made of ice. It was a bizarre way to spend half an hour: don a huge insulated coat with hood and mitts; drink a cocktail (I went for a 'Blue': vodka, champagne, Blue Curacao and a squeeze of lemon. Fellow freelancer Bernie McGuire understandably went for a 'Brainraise': vodka, Pisang Ambon, whatever that was, and a squeeze of orange, while photographer Stuart Franklin couldn't resist a 'Northern Light': vodka, champagne and strawberry liqueur), then stand around looking at each other in a small room after entering through a sort of space-station chamber. A very kind lady from Oklahoma took our pictures, got them developed back in America and then sent each of us a montage of our really weird night out.

It was the Irish Bar, rather than the Ice Bar, at the Scandinavian Masters that did the roaring trade, though, so it was appropriate we had ourselves an Irish winner in young Graeme McDowell, who had only just turned pro.

Flying home, a cross between Mr Fussy and Mr Angry stopped us boarding as he insisted on taking a pushchair on the plane instead of allowing it to go in the hold. No way was he going to board without it, he said, blocking the gangway. Eventually the captain came out and warned him that he and his family would be taken off the flight if there was much more. Mr Fussy/Angry resorted to whining, but to no avail. The pushchair went into the hold. Then he wasn't satisfied with his seating arrangements when he finally did get on board. We took off at least 45 minutes late. I was lumbered with a seat across the aisle from him, his wife and child. The bloody kid whimpered loudly for the first half-hour, raised its tempo to a full-belted wail for an hour, and punctuated the approach and landing with screeches that would have left an Andean Condor sticking its chest out. It takes a lot to put me off a wind-down drink after a tournament has finished on a Sunday night, but the kid did it. As we got up to disembark, the wretch still grizzling, I looked over at the family and said to the father: 'Takes after his dad, doesn't he?'

It must be obvious that I don't like disturbance when either drinking or eating. Therefore the male voice choir that was trotted out at the Wales Open at the Celtic Manor Hotel was, to me, something of an imposition when the singing became so loud you couldn't hear a word your bar-mate was saying. Press officer Gordon Simpson and I were contemplating a bar meal in the hotel but the choir, led in effusive style with pumping arms by Celtic Manor owner Sir Terry Matthews OBE, were, quite frankly, a put-off. We adjourned to the main restaurant to get out of their way but, just as we were ordering, in came the male voice choir, again led by Sir Terry. They launched into song, fairly rattling glasses and cups. Sir Terry came over to us and said: 'What do you think to the boys; great, aren't they?'

Do you want the sycophantic answer or do you want my genuine opinion?' replied I.

'Pardon?'

'Well, if I decide on room service, promise me you won't send the buggers upstairs.'

An unprecedented fourth week in Ireland took us to the breathtaking links of Ballyliffin in County Donegal. I knew it would be a tough week for the pros when I played in the pro-am with my old mate Roger Winchester. There was no hole-in-one this time. In fact most of the time, in stair-rod rain and high winds, I was pleased to get a hole-in-five. As the winds grew stronger, a rather ambiguous message appeared on the locker-room noticeboard: 'Third round suspended because players' balls moving on the greens.'

Saturday was all stop–start, with the players coming home in the dark. I stayed in a really friendly hotel with a peculiar system for Sky Sport, chosen on a first–come–first–served basis. Apparently they could only get one channel at a time and that was at the behest of whoever requested it first. I had to look hard into my orange juice the next morning as fellow guests moaned at breakfast about their sporting fare: 'Who the divil asked for feckin' Leicester versus Stoke on Sky Sport Extra?'

A good old Scotch mist enveloped Gleneagles for part of the Scottish PGA Championship, before young Adam Scott ran away with the title. There was a fog in my hotel bathroom when my mobile phone went off. It was Radio Scotland, who were a good half-hour early. 'Ah, Norman; sorry to bother you, but can you do that live piece in a couple of minutes, just a little run–down on how the tournament's going and how the Scots are doing?'

'But you've just got me out of the shower.'

'Don't worry. It's not television.'

Thank God. Dabell, lying on his bed in the middle of a muddle of scores and notes, talking on his bedside phone – starkers! Calendar Girls eat your hearts out.

Sharon's second trip to Crans sur Sierre began sedately, in direct contrast to her first in 1993, but then nearly hit the rails. On arrival in Geneva I purchased two return train tickets from Geneva to Sierre. Satisfyingly, the man on the ticket desk understood my French perfectly: *'Deux billets attorne Sierre, s'ils vous plais; premiere classe.'* I was proud I didn't have to crassly resort to asking: 'Do you speak English?' We settled down to a tuna-melt panini and dry white in a particularly sumptuous station restaurant. Sated, we were thinking about taking a steady walk to the platform.

'Sure everything's OK with the tickets, darling?'

'Of course.' (But I thought I'd better just do a double-check.)

'What do you think "Aton" means sweetheart?' Dabell pushing evidence under wife's nose.

'Sure that's not the restaurant bill?'

'Of course it's not the bloody restaurant bill. It's our sodding tickets. We look as though we're heading from Geneva to somewhere that means bloody tuna fish. I can't see Sierre anywhere on the flaming ticket. What's the bloody moron given us?'

'Hate to worry you but the Sierre train's leaving in ten minutes.'

'Hell's tits; come on.'

Grabbing wife and bursting out of the restaurant with our heavily laden luggage-trolley, cornering on one wheel and scattering diners like the parting of Lake Geneva, we hurtled out into the station causeway. Sharon's job was to collect anything that fell off as I broke the Swiss all-comers 200m record for athletes/luggage-trolleys, heading for the ticket office. In a welter of burning rubber (trainers and trolley wheels), I screamed to a halt, glaring malevolently at five startled people queuing up for tickets. Wrong approach. We only had seven minutes left now to departure for Sierre. It was going to have to be softly, softly and nicely, nicely.

'*S'ils vous plais. Mes billets est mals. Je requirez a change.* Oh bugger it. Can I go in front? I've been given wrong tickets.'

I didn't wait for acquiescence and dived at the booth, just vacated, where the man who had sold me the suspect tickets was looking quizzically from his window.

'Do you speak English?'

'But of course, sir,' in a perfect public school accent.

'We've got five minutes to catch the train to Sierre, for where I thought I'd bought my tickets [best to use good grammar with this cove, even if I'm nearly off the head with panic]. Can you please give me the correct tickets?'

'Oh, but you said you wanted to go to Aton.'

'No, I said "*attorne, attorne*," that's French for return isn't it? Attorne to Sierre, two, rapidement.'

As I glanced in anguish at my watch – four minutes to go now – feeling ten sets of unsympathetic eyes boring into the back of my head, the ticket man offered me my new tickets.

'The journey to Aton is more expensive than Sierre, so you must receive the balance.'

'Put it in the bloody retired station staff fund.'

As we swept onto the platform, the guard was just blowing his whistle and the doors were about to close when the Dabells, superhumanly hurling their luggage before them, landed in the nearest carriage like a rugby scrum unravelling.

'Promise me this is not going to be one of those weeks,' said Sharon.

I don't think it turned out too badly, even with me suddenly suffering from a new malady to enter my lexicon for hypochondriacs. It came on at an alleged dinner, a further couple of thousand feet higher up the mountain, to celebrate the opening of Montana's new casino. Well I say 'dinner'. It proved to be another of those wretched raclette evenings, nothing but cheesy potato. After one portion we gagged at the thought of more. By the time the casino manager, sitting alongside us, droned into his second hour telling us how the region was going to benefit from his slot machines, we were ready to leave the party. I had a splitting headache and felt queasy from what I was told later was altitude sickness. But the bus was not due to depart for two more hours. The casino cove's speech was just starting, a reprise of what he had imparted to us already. We were saved by a German photographer. Like us, he was prepared to forego his free casino entry pass and he also detested cheese. Heinz (what we would have given for beans on toast at that stage) dropped us off at a pizzeria, while he went in search of a McDonald's. My altitude sickness had disappeared by the time I was tucking into a calzone.

When the media dinner, this time with all the trimmings and not a raclette in sight, took place on the Saturday night, Sharon and I arrived a little late at the venue, which, rather bizarrely, was in a room that had a small zoo at its entrance. We were late because the minibus that picked us up dropped us off at the hotel hosting the tournament gala dinner. I smelt a rat when I spotted Cindy Crawford just in front of us as we were being asked our names at the foyer, in order for them to be announced in grand style by an usher. Wrong dinner.

Come to think of it, though, I also smelt a rat after Sharon and I got the only seats left at the press dinner, near the entrance and the zoo. Or was it a coypu?

Talking of Cindy Crawford, my larger than life photographer friend Norbert was noticeable by his absence this year. The 24-st German, I was told, had finally retired, having never really got his shooting arm back in shape after Miss Crawford smashed her drive into him some years before, when he was taking pictures of the model during the pro-am at Crans sur Sierre. La Crawford seemed quite smitten by the Omega European Masters winner Robert Karlsson's film-star build and blond good looks when she presented the tall Swede with the trophy on Sunday night.

It had taken six 'dummy runs' to finally pin down Ernie Els's caddie Ricci Roberts, to interview him for his account of Ernie's Open Championship win, for the latest paperback edition of my book *Winning the Open*. To make sure I'd fully snared Ricci in Cologne during the German Masters, I'd accompanied him and Ernie for a couple of drinks, endured watching his favourite football team Leeds on the television at the Irish pub, then escorted him to a pizzeria. Finally, I could get my tape recorder out while we tucked in. Ricci got into full flow, showing how convivial he was feeling by topping up my half-full glass of dry white with red wine – 'not to worry; rosé is always nice anyway, Ricci'. I had enough on him to write his autobiography after about 90 minutes. He pressed on, alternating wildly enthusiastic accounts of Muirfield with occasional lapses of memory that enabled me to dart in and fill glasses with the correct colour wines. Nervous glances at the tape showed me we were getting to the end of the second side of it. 'Click' went the ominous and terminal sound, just as Ricci was explaining in vivid detail how the playoff unfolded. I had lent my other tape out the day before, fully expecting the two hours' worth I had on this one, to be enough. It was another three weeks before we finished the interview, when Ricci returned to Leeds from his latest trip. In all, that final chapter took ten weeks to nail down.

I was into recording again a couple of weeks later at the golf event of the year, the Ryder Cup at The Belfry. Europe's win under Sam Torrance was thrilling but then the whole week was. I was lucky enough to be invited to the Ryder Cup gala dinner, exciting enough in itself, but when the cabaret star turned out to be Ronan Keating, I really regretted the invitation had not included wives. Sharon is mad on Ronan and when he launched into our 2001 wedding song: 'When you say nothing at all' (well, marriage is all about give and take isn't it?), I just had to phone her. I couldn't get a signal so cadged European Tour public relations director Mitchell Platts' mobile. Mitchell, although used to my eccentricities, looked a little quizzical when the manic Dabell swayed up by the stage, waving the mobile in the air so that Sharon could get her own little cabaret.

There wasn't going to be much that could top that week in 2002. The season came to a close in a spectacular venue, though, with the Italian Open in Rome. My hotel was a typical old Italian hostelry that would have been very comfortable in the '60s (1860s), equipped with wooden-veneered walls that rather camouflaged the doors. This was very disorientating and I could have caused a real incident one night if the passageway outside my room had not been deserted. Needing to pay a nocturnal visit I groped for the bathroom door, opened it and found myself lurching into said passageway. I always sleep nude.

The lift seemed dodgy right from the off, groaning into life and then taking an age to go up and down, ending its journey with an almighty bone-jarring thud. As there was no dining room in the hotel, we press boys staying there had earmarked a nice restaurant down the road and arranged to meet in the small hotel bar. Having spruced up, I entered the lift at my fourth floor and pressed the button to stop at reception. Down creaked the lift, steadfastly refusing to stop at reception. Its journey ended, with the familiar jolt, at lower basement level. The door opened. Nobody there. I angrily pressed the button for reception. The door closed. The lift stayed where it was. I pressed for reception again. Nothing. I hit more buttons, lit up the whole vertical row from floor five to basement, but budge the doors would not. I pressed the 'open doors' button frantically about a dozen times. Nothing. I started shouting and banging on the doors. No response. Mobile – no signal. After five minutes of GBH on my surrounds, the doors suddenly opened. I was confronted by a worried duty manager and, for reasons never explained, by an alarmed-looking chambermaid who offered me a bowl and a large towel. The boys had kindly waited for me, perplexed at noises coming from the basement but not in the least surprised when a sweating Dabell (the bowl and towel?) emerged from the emergency stairs.

Thunderstorms were so bad on the Friday that play was wiped out altogether and that gave us a rare chance of an afternoon's sightseeing in the Eternal City. We did the full bit: Colosseum, Spanish Steps, Trevi Fountain. It surprised me just how far you had to hurl your coin over your shoulder and over a milling mass of people, for it to actually land in the Trevi waters. This is to ensure you will return to Rome someday, and have a wonderful Italian-style love-life to boot, like Frank Sinatra. Of course it became a point of honour between the press pack let loose in Rome. With hundreds of people lining the steps down to the fountain and not much room to manoeuvre from roadside, it was hardly surprising that not all our coins found their true destiny, or, indeed, destination. Bernie McGuire swears I fetched a bloke a real good one in the back of his neck but I'd suggest it was sour grapes after his coin landed in a woman's duffle bag.

'That's in rather bad taste isn't it?'

'Why? Thought it was fairly appropriate for a Gulf stringer.'

After it was deduced that I was covering sport not war, we were in business. There was a good story on the Friday night, albeit a late one, right on deadline. Seve had fallen foul of a referee and been given a time warning for taking too long to play. After furious finger-wagging in the car park between him and the tournament director and furious finger-jabbing on my chest to hammer home his side of the story, Seve stormed off, sure the incident had cost him qualification for the weekend. On the Saturday morning I was working out when Seve, who was staying at the same hotel, stuck his head inside the gym. He was holding mask and flippers, ready for a swim, and you'd never believe the affable charmer who playfully tweaked my biceps and asked if I was going in for 'Mr Universe', was the same raging bull of the night before. When I got to the course, I found the weather had changed, the scores from the incomplete second round had billowed up, and Seve's aggregate was good enough to get him into the final two rounds after all.

Seve hogged the headlines that week, just as he had when he startled us all by showing us his new tattoo of his famous 1984 Open Championship winning pose the year before. A few weeks later at the Italian Open near Verona, he was at it again. Sharon was with me at beautiful Lake Garda, and on Saturday morning, well before the leaders were due out and with no great reason to be on duty too early, we went shopping with Bernie McGuire and his fiancée Ana. Ana needed to buy a new dress for the gala dinner that night and was in the fitting-room when my mobile went off. It was press officer Scott Crockett, warning me that Seve, one of the first to play that morning, had just been disqualified for what amounted to refusing to accept a slow-play penalty shot. We were only a couple of miles from the Garda golf course, but I needed to file a piece right away, so I got the gist of what had happened from Scott while Bernie grabbed Sharon and Ana in the fitting-room. We all piled into Bernie's hire car and I began ad-libbing a dozen paragraphs to the office, apologising for filing by telephone instead of laptop, explaining, accurately but deviously, that I was temporarily away from the media centre. I was just formulating my last paragraph, with the office unaware I was making a mad dash to the course, when an ambulance went screaming past us, its siren going off full-belt.

'Oh, has someone been taken ill on the course, Norman?'

I was certainly in time to follow up the Seve story, expanded by him coming in and throwing around accusations that were going to get him into a lot of hot water. Seve suddenly shouted 'Mafia', a comparison he was making to those he insisted were victimising him. That caused nervous glances around the interview room. One of the Italians actually ducked.

Swede Mathias Gronberg carried off the title in Italy, along with it his body weight in Parmesan cheese, a bizarre bonus, and we carried off an expensive bottle of Italian wine after a really entertaining wine-tasting on the Sunday. The tasting was conducted by a chap who was wasted on just talking about various vintages and regions, as he had his audience in stitches with his Monty Python-type approach. And that included Bernie McGuire and I – who didn't have a clue what he was talking about.

Queuing to go through the security screening at the airport, I incurred the wrath of a security guard when I moved slightly forward to allow a fellow passenger in front of me room to manipulate her large bag through the X-ray machine. Whether this bloke with a frizzy mane and unruly moustache was having a bad hair day or not, I don't know, but he leapt at me, pushed me hard in the chest and snarled something in guttural Italian. Fazed by this unexpected, and totally unwarranted, attack, I snarled back at him in equally guttural English, whereupon he re-snarled: 'Fickin' Limey'. I suppose I should have just accepted this accolade but regrettably gave as good as I'd got on the insult front. As the queue was building behind me (Sharon had tiptoed away), something had to give. Grabbing my laptop bag, he marched it over to a lady security officer, shouting to her something like: 'Give this bastard the works.' Everything came out of the bag but I was confident there was nothing to worry about. The guard had the last laugh, though as his female accomplice eventually found the lovely ornate corkscrew, with which I had been presented to open that bottle of Italy's best. I'd forgotten I'd put it in my laptop bag after the wine-tasting. It was ceremoniously, and with an extravagant, triumphant flourish, acknowledged satisfyingly across the floor by the guard and confiscated as a dangerous weapon.

A couple of weeks later Seve was reprimanded and fined for his outburst when the tour arrived at the Volvo PGA Championship. We all stood around the tour headquarters waiting to talk to him but he left by the back door and didn't even play in the tournament, claiming a bout of flu had laid him low. As a golfing hero of mine, it was heartbreaking enough writing about the demise of his game. But going through all the unsavoury aspects of the last few weeks was just about the bottom of the golf-writing barrel for me.

As spring turned into summer we returned for the Wales Open. I didn't have to dodge the male voice choir because I didn't stay at Celtic Manor this time. There was purgatory to be endured, though. Phillip Price's singles win over Phil Mickelson in the Ryder Cup the previous year was a magnificent achievement, and counted in no small way to Europe claiming back the trophy. But it's easy to get fed up with the feat when it's on the media centre television monitor about 20 times a day – all week. Phillip himself was highly embarrassed by Celtic Manor's new version of Groundhog Day, although the likeable Welshman made a good fist of trying to win before Ian Poulter claimed the honours.

The tour's most oddly named event of the year was the Aa St Omer Open. The prefix represents the area, named after the French river along which the golf course lies, about 40 miles from Calais, as opposed to the roadside emergency service. Remarkably, given my records, I didn't need any assistance, as press officer Roddy Williams (I know, it really was tempting fate) kindly drove me to the event, via the Channel Tunnel.

'This is nice and relaxed, isn't it?'

'Yes, you don't need to travel first class when it's like this. Is there first class, by the way?'

'Yes, you get out of your Honda when you get on board and they sit you in a Rolls Royce until you get to Calais.'

My Auchterarder digs during the Diagio Championship at Gleneagles in June, provided me with another chapter in my tour breakfast saga. I seated myself at a small dining-room table at my hotel on the first morning at 7.25 a.m. and was immediately chastised by a daunting Scotswoman who came crashing through swing-doors like an avenging gunslinger. I should have waited to be seated, it seemed, although I was the only one in the room. As she appeared with two curlers still in, I assumed I'd caught her a little off guard. With a sniff, I was escorted to another table, identical in size to the one at which I'd installed myself. Telling me neither the cooker nor the cook were operational yet, the female Rob Roy disappeared. I sat for a couple of minutes, became bored and so shuffled over to investigate the cereal table. 'PLEASE [barked loudly and insincerely] don't touch anything until 7.30 when breakfast starts OFFICIALLY,' came the command from behind the swing-doors. Perhaps she was watching on CCTV. I dropped the cornflakes ladle and scuttled back to my table, where I sat in stony silence, staring hopefully at my watch. Two minutes later, right on the button, muzak suddenly boomed deafeningly around the room. Louis Armstrong rendered: 'All the time in the world'. With that, appearing magically like bleary-eyed rabbits pulled out of a hat, 12 fellow guests invaded the room, easily outstripping me in gaining the cereal counter. All the streetwise dozen, a Scots golf society, had quickly ordered full breakfasts from a transformed, beaming waitress before I got my turn.

When we returned to France for the French Open, Versailles once again dumbfounded me. The hotel at the National course had, some years before, had a system I thought was peculiar to it alone: you could get red wine at the bar but not white, and white wine in the restaurant but not red. This time there was no white wine at all in my hotel.

'No bloody white wine? But this is France!'

It didn't end there. We tried three restaurants and it was the same – in the middle of Versailles! Something to do with the deliverymen striking, apparently. I had to settle for warm rosé with ice. Bernie McGuire pointed out it wasn't quite as bad as a pub with no beer.

July meant Ireland, although this time the Smurfit European Open at the K Club and the Irish Open at glorious Portmarnock were not back-to-back and came at the start and the end of the month. This meant I didn't have my usual little interlude at Charlie Mulqueen's home in Limerick and again couldn't enjoy Lahinch. I hoped the Brothers enjoyed their annual tournament and nobody got brained. Charlie and I stayed at our usual hotel in Kill. I made enquiries about a stop-off we had to make on our way to a European Tour function, to pick up a colleague.

'How far is it to the Swallow Hotel please?'

'Two miles as the crow flies.'

'But we aren't in a crow, it's a Renault.'

'Well I'd say about 15 minutes then; it's the second roundabout on the dual-carriageway.'

The European Open proved to be rather embarrassing through no fault of my own. Legendary Irish striker Niall Quinn caddied for Philip Walton that week and, predictably, commanded as much attention as the golfers. I was asked to bring him into my portable studio for a chat on radio but all he did was sit around in soaking trouser bottoms and wait for an eternity to go on air. Then they decided not to run the interview. After that he was collared by about 100 fans for autographs as he left the press centre, when all he wanted was a nice pint of stout.

Bernhard Langer was a happy man the following week as he was named Europe's Ryder Cup captain at the Irish Open in Portmarnock. Tommy Bjorn had let the Open Championship slip through his fingers at Royal St George's, but he pulled himself together magnificently and only just lost out in a playoff to Michael Campbell.

It was not an enlightening week for me, though. I was given the last room in a rather seedy hotel in Malahide. I had to remember to duck to avoid whacking my head on the sloping ceiling. It desperately needed redecorating and there was no shaver socket in the bathroom. By Friday morning my rechargeable shaver had spluttered out its life, giving me a mighty painful nip on the jaw as it did so, with only half my face shaven. With time running out before I was picked up to go to the course I scoured the bedroom for a socket so that I might then be able to borrow an adapter from reception to complete my shave. The only socket I could find was for the bedside lamp, which I managed to drag off its table while tracking it under the bed. Whether it was my confession to one broken lampshade or not, I got no joy on the adapter front from reception. I don't think my courtesy car driver twigged I was half-shaven, probably because I kept my hand across my face in the style of *The Thinker* for the whole journey. I was able to complete my shave by jamming my razor lead into a plug in the press room, but not before coming in for the usual derision.

My experience in the hotel was to get worse, despite being moved from the pit on Saturday. True, though not sumptuous, the new room was a little more comfortable. Trouble was, when I got back late in the evening, not one light would work in it. Every bulb appeared to have blown. With the receptionist now doubling as barman and the hotel bar and disco full to bursting, the chance of a few replacement bulbs was highly remote. So here the furtive Dabell swung into action. I knew the door of my old room was dodgy. The only way I'd been able to close it was by giving it a hard shouldering, the resultant wall-shuddering bang going down well with still-sleeping guests first thing in the morning. No matter how I'd tried, though, it had never locked properly. I crept out of my new room and, as stealthily as I could, forced the old room door open, praying no new unfortunate had taken up residence. With some relief at finding it empty, I nipped around like a demented cat burglar looking for booty he could sell on quickly. I whipped out every light bulb, transferred them to my new room and then refitted the dud ones in the old room. You had to think fate had got it in for me, though, when there was a loud 'pop' and one of my ill-gotten gains also gave up the ghost a little later, plunging me in darkness in the loo in the middle of a pee. I'd hardly had a chance to memorise the toilet's geography either.

After the Scandinavian Masters in Malmo, I went straight on to Copenhagen, via the bridge between the two countries, for the inaugural Nordic Open. The Simon's club in Denmark, where Ian Poulter chalked up his second win of the year and Colin Montgomerie lost his best chance of winning in 2003, was a new experience. My first task was to get a visa from the Russian embassy while I was in Copenhagen for a trip to Moscow the following week. I had the embassy address and was relieved when my bus driver, speaking perfect English, said I was on the correct route. Recognising a nervous passenger, he assured me he would let me know when my stop came up. As we drove into the centre of Copenhagen we seemed to stop an inordinate number of times, often where I could see no immediate evidence of a bus-stop. Each time I looked over at him expectantly but just saw a puzzled look on his face as he glanced up and down the bus, which was fairly packed. By the time he at last informed me I was on the right block and just had to cross the road and walk up the opposite street about 50 yards, he seemed a broken man. I suddenly realised I might be his persecutor. To steady myself, and to make sure I kept him in sight in his cab in case he might have forgotten his promise, my shoulder had, periodically, been leaning on one of the 'request stop' buttons.

I'd never been to Russia, so my trip to Moscow for the Russian Open in August was another first for me on the European Tour. It got off to a bad start when the Wednesday pro-am was washed out and the course got waterlogged. It didn't stop a Russian oompah band from going through its paces in pouring rain to celebrate the tournament's opening, nor the bus-load of journalists wanting to be accredited and pick up their 'bung', a free gift of a golf shirt. As our press tent was only the size of a single garage, there was quite a squeeze on as beleaguered press officer Mike Gibbons did his best to give personal treatment to about 50 media people who must have come from local newspapers from Siberia to Moscow. With preview stories filed early, we had the chance to see such sights as Red Square, Lenin's Tomb, the Bolshoi Ballet and, of particular interest to me as a former Foreign Office man, KGB headquarters. When I arrived back at Le Meridien, the course hotel, a wildly inaccurate story had already circulated that Norman Dabell had been arrested and thrown in a Moscow gaol. Apparently one of the official tour sightseeing party of golf pros and Sky television crew had ignored a sign and vaulted over a barrier to a part of Red Square that was closed to the public and got his collar felt. Wasn't me this time.

Despite the rain, the tournament squelched on to the weekend when we were invaded by Moscow society's elite, few of whom had any idea about golf, judging by the amount of provocative miniskirts and stilettos on show. There was another invasion of 'journalists', 50 or so again, this time to pick up the free lunch tickets. When press officer Mike Gibbons and I went to get a spot of lunch in the public restaurant tent, there was a huge queue. This black leather-jacketed bloke, though, went straight to the front and ensconced his two lady escorts (Prada and Jimmy Choo) at a table that was already being used by a clearly intimidated couple. As the two cuckoos spread out, the couple gave in and vacated the table. I wasn't having black jacket muscling in. I shouted from my place about 12 spots from the front of the queue: 'We're not standing here for the good of our health.' Black jacket gave me a stare that intimated I wouldn't have any good health if I carried on. People in the queue ahead of me looked worried. A bloke a couple of places up, said: 'Leave alone. It for the best.' Black jacket was served by nervous-looking staff and the incident was over. Apparently black jacket was one of the feared Russian 'Mafia' who had obviously taken a day off from nefarious activities down in the city to see what this golf game was all about. Probably be a good idea not to stray too far away from the hotel tonight and lock the door.

When I returned to the press tent, I found one of the Russian journalists, few of whom had shown any visible signs of communication with their offices all week, using my computer to collect his e-mails. I decided to let him finish off to assist diplomatic relations. And it did cross my mind that he looked as though he might be black jacket's brother.

An interesting week ended in chaos. Due to work commitments the following week, I was the only press man leaving on Sunday night. A coach for pros and officials had been laid on to get to Moscow airport and, despite a few more grey hairs following one of those protracted playoffs, I finished work in time to catch it. When I got to the hotel from the press tent, I found, to my dismay, that the bus departure time had been brought forward an hour and nobody had thought to inform the media. So the hotel, after 45 minutes, during which I tore out all the new grey hair I'd gained, found me a car and a driver to take me to the airport. The car was rather old and the driver, wearing overalls as if he'd just been dragged away from toilet-cleaning duties, was given commands in Russian which I took to mean: 'Airport, and as quick as Christ'll let you'. He looked a mean man, hawk-faced, like all the Soviet secret servicemen you've ever seen in James Bond films, and without any English at all. I tried to break the ice but, without any Russian, was treated to stony silence, face straight ahead and hands gripped to the steering wheel. By the time we had somehow crossed one of the busiest dual-carriageways I've seen in my life and then wended our way through a series of lanes next to shabby, hapless-looking, country apartment blocks, we'd gone no more than five miles in thirty minutes. Panic set in and I urged my man to get a move on by way of forward-flailing arms which I then turned into flapping Boeing 737 wings. With a growl he hit the throttle and we took off. With our car at full revs, we careered up the road, overtaking on inside and outside, narrowly avoiding at least five accidents. We joined a second dual-carriageway with equally frenzied dodgem cars on it. By now my driver, reminding me of Jack Nicholson in *The Shining*, had the bit between his teeth. Suddenly, though, there was burning rubber as we came down the speedometer in a series of frantic jerks on rounding a bend, where two policemen were monitoring traffic with radar-guns. We were stopped and documents produced, my driver now turning to jelly. I feared his certificate as a leading toilet cleaner was going to cut no ice. Another ten minutes were lost while my man either got off the hook or was warned a ticket would be in the post, then off we went, heading for the airport road. It was bumper-to-bumper but nothing compared to the scene that greeted us when we turned into the airport itself. Domodedovo International airport has its car park directly in front of departures and arrivals. It was gridlocked. My man tried to con his way into the taxi queue that would at least free us of a jam of cars pointing in every direction on the compass and going nowhere, but he was refused entry. Even though my departure area was a good par-five away, I had to make a run for it. My driver leapt out, causing an instant cacophony of hooters from drivers who were stuck so fast it would have taken the AA, RAC, Direct Line and a New York traffic cop a week to untangle them. As I'd now made my driver a candidate for Moscow's Most Wanted files and probably got him a speeding ticket, I gave him every rouble I'd got on me. He looked at me incredulously and began weeping. I found out afterwards that I'd given him a big enough tip to start up his own toilet-cleaning business. With immigration to negotiate as well as check-in, and only 20 minutes to take-off, I feared the worst. But my flight had been delayed by two hours.

After drinking in spectacular views of Crans sur Sierre for a 15th year, the tour moved on to the Lancôme Trophy at the St Nom la Breteche club in Versailles. It looked like being the event's swansong so I was going to make sure I didn't miss out on one of the treats of the year – the club's renowned crème brulée. I was just in the process of consuming my 59th career club caramel when I suffered my seventh career chair collapse. This one evolved in near slow motion and looked almost graceful, according to my dining-room colleagues, befitting at such an elite club. I heard the chair emit a mortal sigh and one of its four legs gave up the ghost. I somehow had the presence of mind to lob my crème brulée on to the table, even avoiding a carafe of wine. In those split seconds I mentally congratulated myself for refusing to succumb to instinct and clutch desperately at the table cloth. I might be lying in a heap but it was a clean heap. As I rose resignedly to my feet I waited for my marks out of ten for artistic merit and degree of difficulty. The French press rather generously awarded me 5.9; a German photographer uncharitably decided on only 5.5; but, and I knew I could rely on getting a good 'homer' mark, the British media put me in a gold medal position by giving me the maximum 6.0.

South Africans Ernie Els and Retief Goosen, and a Korean, K.J. Choi, occupied the winner's enclosure during this busy period, but Lee Westwood then won again to show he really had reached the end of a very dark tunnel. He'd lost his way a little since a heady 2000 when he became European number one and my mum, one of his greatest fans, was a happy lady.

The season was winding down but in Hilversum for the Dutch Open I did a little winding up. I'd asked for a quiet room when I booked my hotel. I was placed right on the hotel front, within a few yards of the busiest junction in the town, Hilversum's Hyde Park Corner. My room was directly under the stairs, a few feet away from the reception desk, the small bar and the breakfast room. The incessant traffic noise kept me awake until I dozed off, fitfully, around 2 a.m. when it subsided. Then I would be awoken from nightmares by furious hammering, accompanied by curses. This was coming from guests who had mislaid the little slip we were given with the front door security code numbers on it. The stairs were in use until all hours, either by dirty stop–outs or late hotel bar users. At around 5 a.m. the players with early starts staying at my hotel would descend in diving boots, followed by caddies dragging clubs down in a series of hangover-induced thumps at each stair. Peace descended then for only about half an hour before the early-morning shift waiter started clanging cutlery sadistically in the nearby dining room like a novice xylophone player trying to master 'Tubular Bells'. I don't mind admitting, by Friday I was shagged out. 'If that's a quiet room, mate, I dread to think what one of your noisy jobs must be like,' said I to an unsympathetic receptionist.

On the Friday night I enjoyed some fine hospitality from the tournament officials at a Chinese restaurant. Strict instructions to only serve me dishes that didn't contain any Chinese food, because of my allergy, baffled the waiters enough, but sniffing each plateful extravagantly like an addict to Superglue, stopped all conversation around the tables.

On Saturday morning I finally got a room change. This one was next to a pair of swing-doors on the first floor that actually shook the walls whenever they were used, which was frequently.

Fancying a quiet meal on my own, I opted for Mexican on Saturday night, checking the sign on the door saying the house took about six different kinds of credit card, including my two. The meal was a bit unsatisfactory but it took a turn for the worse when a nervous waiter told me the sign on the door was out of date. They only took cash. I'd run out of euros and had just a £20 note. I entered into an hour-long argument that was finally only resolved when the manager was called in from a barbecue in Amsterdam and accepted my 20–spot. As I walked home sullenly, I spotted two of the caddies who I was sure had attempted to break down my hotel door on Thursday night when they'd forgotten the numbers to key in. They were hovering around a building with the name 'Havana' above its door, obviously in the mood for some late-night entertainment and anticipating Hispanic and Caribbean hostesses. However, from their slurred conversation, they hadn't got any response from this door either.

'You need to knock four times to get in,' I offered from

across the road in concealing shadows, even though I'd never seen the place before in my life. I watched the chosen knocker of the two giving exaggerated and expectant raps on what could have been a Dutch tobacconist's door for all I knew.

'Was that four?'

'Well, obviously not you pillock, or someone would have answered the door. Let me try.'

'That was three, you prat. You're too pissed to count properly.'

Revenge was sweet as I enjoyed their consternation before breaking cover at speed, hoping I'd not been recognised, and desperately trying to remember the hotel security code.

It was tough on Sharon when she took her second 'sunshine' break of the year with me during the Majorca Classic at Pula. It rained very hard that week. Our hotel was full of Germans accompanied by 2.4 children. It was amusing to see the families sitting transfixed in rows in the huge bar, being given what sounded like quite a stern lecture by an imposing woman with an easel and pointer. Perhaps she was explaining the battle plan to secure all the sun-beds before breakfast. We thought it was an odd way to be entertained on a rainy day but the Germans were lapping it up.

Work-wise it was a strange old week. I went out to watch Lee Westwood ping his first two drives of the week over the cart path into an orchard fence and subsequently lose all chance of winning (much to mum's disgust). Then José Maria Olazábal, who was about to start work re-designing the course after the tournament, hit out of town at the penultimate hole on Sunday to hand victory to Miguel Angel Jimenez. I bet the 17th was the first to get dug up when Ollie got to work.

The Madrid Open the following week was my season's finale. David Beckham was in the Real Madrid side on Wednesday night to play Partizan Belgrade at the Bernabéu Stadium. Against all odds, I managed to buy a couple of tickets for Press Association man Mark Garrod and I. Touts were asking about £50 a ticket but I was delighted to pay less than £20 at the gate, even though the tickets were like gold dust. I soon found out why they were so cheap. We were right at the very top of the towering stadium, with a wonderful view looking down on the intricacies of Beckham, Zidane, Ronaldo and Raúl. Directly above us, though, were the huge stadium heaters, which were so hot they could keep the linesmen warm. We were absolutely roasted. By half-time I was virtually down to my underwear and Mark and I left the stadium with our singed hair still smouldering.

There was chance for one final breakfast debacle. I didn't have time for desayuno until the Sunday, the last morning. With a tired toaster not even glowing and merely crisping the stale bread even harder, the scrambled eggs resembling wallpaper paste and the orange juice an indefinable watery yellow, I wished on this occasion the waitress had taken it away while I was getting my decaff. I was just going to start again with a cheese roll when a youngster in front of me sneezed all over the cheese. When the sleepy-eyed girl, no doubt discoing only an hour before in downtown Madrid, asked me for my room number so that the meal could go on the bill, I refused to give it on the premise I hadn't eaten any.

That was it. Even Luton Airport was welcome. Another season over.

When I checked my e-mail on arrival at home at the Mill, there was a message from one of the Volvo Masters organisers which began: '*Dead* AGW member . . .'

Rumours of my demise had been somewhat exaggerated. But it had been a damn close call a few times.